Exploring Education Policy World: Concepts, Contexts,

C000044447

Series Editors

Eryong Xue, Faculty of Education, Beijing Normal University, Beijing, China

Simon Marginson, University of Oxford, Oxford, UK

Jian Li, Faculty of Education, Beijing Normal University, Beijing, China

This book series explores education policy on Pre-K, K-12, post-secondary education, and vocational education, informing multiple experts from academia to practitioner, and specifically pays focuses on new frontiers and cutting-edge knowledge that transforms future education policy development. It has been initiated by a global group of education policy research centers and institutions, whose faculty and staff includes internationally recognized researchers in comparative education policy studies. The series' mission is to advance the modernization of the education and social construction.

This series provides policymakers and researchers with an in-depth understanding of international education policy from diverse perspectives. Topics include cutting-edge and multidisciplinary studies on identifying, analyzing and uncovering education policy reform and practice among the fields in education policy and pedagogy. It addresses how education policy shapes the development of education systems in different regions and seeks to explain how specific education policies concentrate on accelerating the development of quality education and social progress. More importantly, this book series offers policymakers and educational stakeholders, government, and private sectors a comprehensive lens to investigate the trends, rationales of education policy development internationally.

More information about this series at http://www.springer.com/series/16621

Jian Li · Eryong Xue

Education Policy in Chinese High Schools

Concept and Practice

 Springer

Jian Li
Faculty of Education
Beijing Normal University
Beijing, China

Eryong Xue
Faculty of Education
Beijing Normal University
Beijing, China

Eryong Xue and Jian Li share the co-first authorship and contribute equally in this book.

ISSN 2730-6356   ISSN 2730-6364   (electronic)
Exploring Education Policy in a Globalized World: Concepts, Contexts, and Practices
ISBN 978-981-16-2360-8   ISBN 978-981-16-2358-5   (eBook)
https://doi.org/10.1007/978-981-16-2358-5

This Springer imprint is published by the registered company Springer Nature Singapore Pte Ltd.
The registered company address is: 152 Beach Road, #21-01/04 Gateway East, Singapore 189721,
Singapore

Preface

This book investigates the education policy in Chinese high schools from both concept and practice perspectives. It offers a specific lens to explore Chinese higher school education since the reform and opening up, the teacher policy in Chinese high schools, the curriculum and textbook policy in Chinese high school, the school layout policy of Chinese high school education, the enrollment policy of college entrance examination and the diversified development of high school education in China. All those dimensions related to exploring the education policy in Chinese high schools offer an understanding of the modernization of high school education in contemporary China since 1949. This chapter provides multiple perspective to investigate the systematic landscape of high school education, contextually.

Chapter 1 concentrates on the policy analysis of Chinese higher school education since the reform and opening up. High school education is the hub of communication between compulsory education and higher education, which has profound significance for personal growth, social development and national progress. This research in the field of high school education since the reform and opening up in China, on the basis of the focus of the policy to comb the evolution process of the college entrance examination policy in China is divided into "restore the university entrance exam stage (1977–1985)," "education reform and perfecting the policy (1985–1993)," "education popularization and deepening reform stage (1993–1999)" and "comprehensively promote quality education stage (1999–present)". China's high school education policy not only has its distinctive features in structure, but also has accumulated profound achievements in curriculum construction, school layout and motivation mechanism. The reform and evolution of China's high school education policy reflects the nature and will of the country politically, reflects the economic situation, economic policy, financial policy and economic globalization comprehensively in the economy, and is closely related to the social transformation and development, and reflects the cultural changes of modern and contemporary China. This study believes that China's high school education still has many problems in its own positioning, educational goals and ideas, policy discourse, curriculum design, system structure and talent training, and puts forward some policy Suggestions for further deepening the reform of the system in high school education.

Chapter 2 involves the policy analysis of the teacher policy in Chinese high schools. Teachers are the foundation of education. Since the reform and opening up, the state has deeply recognized the importance of the construction of teachers and insisted that teachers should be the first to make the country stronger. Therefore, many teacher policies have been formulated to fundamentally ensure the quality of education. In a series of educational processes, the high school education plays an important role as a bridge between compulsory education and higher education. Teachers are shouldering the historical mission of spreading knowledge, ideas and truth, and the important task of shaping the soul, life and people. They are the first resource for the development of education and the important cornerstone for the prosperity and prosperity of the country, the revitalization of the nation and the happiness of the people. Through the interpretation of these teacher policies, the core characteristics of China's high school education teacher policies can be seen through the following three points that, the requirements for teachers' professional quality are getting higher and higher; gradually improve the treatment of teachers; the teacher policy leans toward the countryside. This paper will analyze the above three characteristics from four aspects: politics, economy, society and culture.

Chapter 3 focuses on an analysis of the curriculum and textbook policy in Chinese high school. In particular, the analysis of curriculum and textbook policy in Chinese high school education, the analysis on the causes of curriculum and teaching material system in senior high schools in China, the current situation of high school textbooks and curriculum, and questions and suggestions on high school curriculum and textbooks have been offered in this chapter to explore the rationale of the curriculum and textbook policy in Chinese high schools.

Chapter 4 concentrates on an analysis of the school layout policy of Chinese high school education. High school education is an important part of basic education. The state has also issued many relevant policies on the layout of high school. Here, we will enumerate and analyze the current policies. This paper will analyze the logic behind the current school layout policy from political, economic, cultural and social perspectives. Then, starting with the cities and counties, the author will analyze the current situation of the layout of high schools, find the deficiencies of the current layout and put forward some opinions and suggestions on the existing problem.

Chapter 5 involves an analysis of the enrollment policy of college entrance examination. Specifically, the question on what the admission policy of the general college examination in China is has been explored to understand the rationale of enrollment policy. Both the questions and suggestions on the enrollment policy of general college examination have also been offered. In addition, the suggestions on enrollment reform are also been examined.

Chapter 6 concentrates on an analysis of the diversified development of high school education in China. In particular, this study aims to understand what is the policy change of diversification in Chinese high schools and why this policy. In addition, the issues and suggestions on diversification development policies of senior high schools, the problems in the diversification of high schools and suggestions on the diversified development of high schools have been provided to examine the landscape of the diversified development of higher school education in contemporary China.

Beijing, China   Jian Li
Eryong Xue

Acknowledgments In the realization of this book, our contributors have been supportive and willing to share their opinions and perspective on how to explore the overall Chinese education policy landscape from a concept-added policy chain perspective. We are really grateful for the generosity and positive spirit of collegiality.

Contents

About the Authors

Jian Li is the Assistant Professor in China Institute of Education Policy, Faculty of Education, Beijing Normal University. She received her Ph.D. degree in Educational Leadership and Policy Studies (ELPS), School of Education, Indiana University Bloomington. Her research interests focus on Education policy studies, Globalization and Internationalization of Higher Education. She has published over 60 articles and books in regard to China's education policy and comparative higher education studies. Dr. Li currently also serves as think tanker at China Institute of Education and Social Development, Beijing Normal University. China Institute of Education and Social Development (CIESD) was co-founded by China Association for Promoting Democracy and Beijing Normal University. It was founded on the base of China Institute of Education Policy and China Academy of Social Management of Beijing Normal University. Dr. Li general area of scholarship is on the assessment of education policy within education institutions comparatively. Within this general area, she has pursued four themes: the education policy studies, globalization of higher education, higher education policy and management, undergraduate students' global learning performance assessment, faculty academic innovation perspective within higher education and comparative higher education development as a framework for institutional research. Dr. Li has published over 30 articles, monographs and book chapters and delivered over 20 workshops and seminars and offered more than 20 keynote, peer-reviewed and invited presentations throughout the USA and in Europe, Africa, and Asia.

Eryong Xue is the Professor in China Institute of Education Policy, Faculty of Education, Beijing Normal University. Changjiang scholars (young scholars) awarded by the Ministry of Education in China. He is also a research fellow of the center for science and technology and education development strategy in Tsinghua University. He is also a postdoctoral fellow in the public administration of Tsinghua University. He has published more than 100 Chinese and English papers in the field of educational research. He has produced more than 100 CSSCI articles. He has won the seventh award for outstanding achievements in scientific research in institutions of higher learning, the fifth national award for outstanding achievements in educational scientific research, and the award for outstanding achievements in political participation and discussion by the central committee for the advancement of the people for more than 40 times. More than 40 independent or co-authored consulting reports were adopted by decision-making departments or approved by leaders.

Chapter 1
Policy Analysis of Chinese High School Education Since the Reform and Opening Up

This chapter concentrates on the policy analysis of Chinese higher school education since the reform and opening up. High school education is the hub of communication between compulsory education and higher education, which has profound significance for personal growth, social development and national progress. This research in the field of high school education since the reform and opening up in China is on the basis of the focus of the policy to comb the evolution process of the college entrance examination policy in China. It is divided into "restore the university entrance exam stage (1977–1985)", "education reform and perfecting the policy (1985–1993)", "education popularization and deepening reform stage (1993–1999)" and "comprehensively promote quality education stage (1999–present)". China's high school education policy not only has its distinctive features in structure, but also has accumulated profound achievements in curriculum construction, school layout and motivation mechanism. The reform and evolution of China's high school education policy reflects the nature and will of the country politically, reflects the economic situation, economic policy, financial policy and economic globalization comprehensively in the economy, and is closely related to the social transformation and development, and reflects the cultural changes of modern and contemporary China. This study believes that China's high school education still has many problems in its own positioning, educational goals and ideas, policy discourse, curriculum design, system structure and talent training, and puts forward some policy Suggestions for further deepening the reform of the system in high school education.

1.1 The Stage Division of Policy Evolution

According to important documents, the author divides the policy change of high school education since the reform and opening up into the following stages.

J. Li and E. Xue, *Education Policy in Chinese High Schools*, Exploring Education Policy in a Globalized World: Concepts, Contexts, and Practices, https://doi.org/10.1007/978-981-16-2358-5_1

1.1.1 The College Entrance Examination (1977–1985)

In 1978, the Third Plenary Session of the Eleventh Central Committee of the Communist Party of China (CPC) decided to implement the policy of internal reform and opening up to the outside world, marking the beginning of reform and opening up. On October 6, 1977, the Ministry of Education issued *Opinions on 1977 College Enrollment work* (hereinafter referred to as "*Opinions*"), after the State Council approved the transfer, formally effective, "Opinions" stipulated the new college enrollment policy, namely the abolition of the recommendation system, the restoration of cultural examination, the admission of the best. This decision, as an effective measure to encourage students to study hard and improve the quality of education, was welcomed by the broad masses, and China's college entrance examination system was officially restored. By the end of 1977, about 5.7 million young people across the country had taken the entrance examination for colleges and universities, and 273,000 students were admitted from the best universities and colleges, greatly improving the quality of freshmen (Li, 2020; Li & Li, 2019; Li et al., 2020; Wang & Liu, 2009; Zhu & Li, 2018).

1.1.2 Stage of Educational Reform and Policy Improvement (1985–1993)

After the resumption of the college entrance examination system, China's education gradually exposed some problems. In response to the exposed problems, the government decided to use more perfect policies to ensure the fairness of education, better play the role of education. On May 27, 1985, the Ministry of Education issued *the Decision of the Central Committee of the Communist Party of China on the Reform of the Education System* (hereinafter referred to as "decision"). The "decision" pointed out that the fundamental purpose of the reform of the education system is to improve the quality of the nation, more talent, talent. In view of the high school education reform mainly adjust the education structure, due to the time of the vocational and technical education is very weak, and socialist modernization construction need millions of educated vocational and technical education of middle and junior technical personnel, management personnel, technicians and other well vocational training of urban and rural laborer, therefore, vigorously developing vocational and technical education is the secondary education reform is an important measure. "Decision" indicated that, according to the requirements of vigorously developing vocational and technical education, the majority of teenagers in China should generally start from the middle school phase of diversion: a part of junior middle school graduates into the general high school, a part of the high school vocational and technical education; Some high school graduates go on to ordinary universities and some receive higher vocational and technical education. Those who have received the vocational and technical education of junior middle school stage after primary school graduation can obtain employment or go to higher schools. The student that general did not rise to average high school, average university and vocational technical school, can pass short-term vocational technical training, obtain employment next.

For the high school to ascend the way of university, this "decision" pointed out that we need to change high school to press national plan to unify recruit students entirely. On February 2, 1992, the Ministry of Education issued *the Interim Provisions on the Administration and Punishment of the National Unified Examination of College Enrollment*, which clearly defined the punishment for the students who cheated or were suspected of cheating in the college entrance examination, making the college entrance examination more fair and more reflective of the real level of the students (Li, 2020; Li & Li, 2019; Li et al., 2020; Wang & Liu, 2009; Zhu & Li, 2018).

1.1.3 Stage of Education Popularization and Deepening Reform (1993–1999)

On February 13, 1993, the CPC Central Committee and the State Council issued the *Outline of China's Educational Reform and Development* (hereinafter referred to as the outline), which pointed out the situation and tasks facing China's education. We establish a socialist market economy, accelerate reform, opening up and modernization, further liberate and develop the productive forces, and bring the overall quality of the national economy and overall national strength to a new level. This is not only a rare opportunity for education, but also a new task and requirements. Under the new situation, the task of education work is: follow the spirit, *the Party's fourteenth Construction* has the Chinese characteristic socialism theory as a guide, adhere to the Party's basic line, fully implement the education policy, face the modernization, facing the world, future-oriented, speeding up the reform of education and the development, further improve the quality of the laborers, the cultivation of talent, establish to adapt to the socialist market economic system and education system, the reform of politics, science and technology system to better serve the socialist modernization construction.

By the end of the twentieth century, the general goal of China's education development is: the education level of the whole people has significantly improved; The pre-service and post-service education of urban and rural workers has developed greatly; The possession of various kinds of specialized talents basically meets the needs of modernization; To form the basic framework of the socialist education system with Chinese characteristics and oriented to the twenty-first century. After several decades of efforts, we need to establish a relatively mature and perfect socialist education system and realize the modernization of education. The direction of education system reform is to change the pattern of government-run schools, and gradually establish a system in which government-run schools are the main body and all sectors of society run schools together. At present, the basic education should be run mainly by local government. Higher education should gradually form a new pattern in which the central government, the provincial government (autonomous region, municipality directly under the central government) and the government at the two levels play the leading role in running schools and the society from all walks of life participate in running schools. Vocational and technical education and adult education mainly rely on the industry, enterprises, institutions and social aspects of the joint education. We put forward to fully implement the educational policy, comprehensively improve the quality of education, the construction of teachers, increase education funds (Li, 2020; Li & Li, 2019; Li et al., 2020; Wang & Liu, 2009; Zhu & Li, 2018).

On July 3, 1994, the State Council issued *the Opinions on the Implementation of the Chinese Education Reform and Development Compendium.* This opinion used the data, which clearly points out the specific goals of education reform in China during this period. By 2000 the national basic nine-year compulsory education (including vocational education) of the junior middle school stage, that is 85% of total area of the nine-year compulsory education. The enrollment rate in junior middle schools is about 85%, and the national primary school enrollment rate is more than 99%. On the basis of the popularization of nine-year compulsory education, high school education (including regular high school and vocational education in high school) should be actively popularized in the urban areas of big cities and coastal areas with a higher degree of economic development. Ordinary high schools can be developed according to the needs of different places and the right amount. By the year 2000 there will be about 8.5 million students in regular high schools. Each county should focus on one or two secondary schools for the whole county. The national focus on the construction of about 1,000 experimental and demonstration high schools. We carry out in a planned way a three-tier system of post-primary, post-middle and post-high schools, vigorously develop vocational education, and gradually form a series of education programs in which primary, secondary, and higher vocational education and general education develop together, link up with each other, and have a reasonable proportion. Among them, most of the regions are mainly divided into secondary vocational education, vigorously developing secondary vocational education, and gradually achieving 50–70% of middle school graduates to enter secondary vocational schools or vocational training centers. By 2000, the proportion of the annual enrollment and the number of students in all kinds of secondary vocational schools in the number of senior high school students remained at about 60% on average nationwide. Cities with universal high school education could achieve 70%. It can be seen that in the late twentieth century, compared with the general high school education, the country placed more emphasis on the development of secondary vocational education, hoping that more people could receive vocational education. The inseparable from the focus of efforts to develop productivity, which requires more skilled labor force; Moreover, from the perspective of Chinese society, influenced by the ancient mainstream ideology, the whole society does not have a high degree of recognition for secondary vocational education, and the development of secondary vocational education is far less smooth than that of ordinary high school education. Therefore, it is necessary to use policies to support the development of vocational education (Li, 2020; Li & Li, 2019; Li et al., 2020; Wang & Liu, 2009; Zhu & Li, 2018).

On April 10, 1996, the Ministry of Education issued *the Ninth Five-year Plan for National Education and the Development Plan for 2010* (hereinafter referred to as the plan), which mentioned that since the implementation of the program for China's education reform and development. China's education has further developed and made remarkable achievements. In 1995, the number of students in all kinds of ordinary secondary vocational schools (referring to secondary vocational schools, technical schools and vocational high schools) reached 9.393 million, an increase of 55.3% over 1990, representing an annual growth rate of 9.2%. There were 7.132 million students in regular high schools, 41,000 fewer than in 1990. Students from various vocational schools accounted for 56.8% of the total high school students, up from 45.7% in 1990, an increase of 11.1% points. Secondary vocational education has been further developed, and the excessively single educational structure in senior high schools has been significantly improved. "Planning", points out that, in the period of the overall goal of the education development in our country is: earnestly implement and full implementation of "Chinese education reform and development compendium", put forward of the fifth plenary session of the fourteenth of the reform and development goals, task to popularize nine-year compulsory education and eliminating illiteracy among young and middle-aged adults, vigorously develop vocational education and adult education, moderately developing higher education, optimize the structure of education, efforts to improve education quality and benefit, form with Chinese characteristics, oriented toward the twenty-first century, the basic framework of the system of socialist education. High school students of all kinds reached 21.25 million nationwide, an annual growth rate of 5.2%. Large cities and economically developed coastal areas are striving to popularize high school education. With the expansion of the scale of higher education, the average high school reached about 8.5 million, 138,000 more than in 1995, with an annual growth rate of 3.6%. Vocational education focuses on the post-junior high school, and it is divided into three levels after primary school, junior high school and senior high school. About 12.75 million students are enrolled in various vocational schools in senior high schools, an increase of 3.357 million over 1995, representing an annual growth rate of 6.3%. The proportion of high school students in vocational schools in China has been raised to about 60%.

1.1.4 Comprehensive Promotion of Quality-Oriented Education (1999–Present)

On December 24, 1998, the Ministry of Education issued *the Action Plan for the Revitalization of Education for the twenty-first century (hereinafter referred to as the plan)*. The main objectives of the action plan are as follows: We need to improve the system of vocational education, training and continuing education, so that new workers and on-the-job workers in urban and rural areas can receive education and training at all levels and in all forms. We actively and steadily developed higher education, with an enrollment rate of about 11%. Aiming at the goal of national innovation system, train and train a group of high-level talents with innovation ability; To strengthen scientific research and make the high-tech industry in colleges and universities contribute to foster new growth points of economic development; We need to deepen reform, establish the basic framework for a new educational system, and take the initiative to adapt to economic and social development. By 2010, on the basis of fully realizing the "two bases" goal, the senior high school education will be gradually popularized in urban and economically developed areas, and the length of schooling of the population in China will reach the advanced level of developing countries. The scale of higher education has been greatly expanded, with an enrollment rate of nearly 15%, and several universities and a number of key disciplines entering or approaching world-class levels. We basically establish a lifelong learning system and provide sufficient talent support and knowledge contribution to the national knowledge innovation system and the modernization drive. The plan points out that the implementation of the "cross-century quality-oriented education project", the overall promotion of quality-oriented education, comprehensive improvement of the national quality and national innovation ability. The reform of curriculum system and evaluation system, the initial formation of modern basic education curriculum framework and curriculum standards in 2000, the reform of educational content and teaching methods, the introduction of a new evaluation system, the development of teacher training, the launch of new curriculum experiments. After about 10 years of experiments, we will try to implement the twenty-first century basic education curriculum and textbook system throughout the country (Li, 2020; Li & Li, 2019; Li et al., 2020; Wang & Liu, 2009; Zhu & Li, 2018).

On June 13, 1999, the Central Committee of the Communist Party of China, the State Council issued *Deepening Education Reform to Comprehensively Promote Quality Education Decision* (hereinafter referred to as "decision (2)"). "The decision (2)" pointed out that facing the new situation, such as subjective and objective reasons, our education concept, education system, education structure, training mode, education contents and teaching methods relative lag, affect the adolescents' all-round development, cannot meet the need of improving national quality. We must be from the cause of socialism in our country the whole party and the whole society to flourish and the overall situation of the great rejuvenation of the Chinese nation, guided by the Deng Xiaoping theory, fully implement the party's 15 big spirit, deepen education reform, comprehensively promote quality education, to build a vibrant socialist education system with Chinese characteristics, for implementation of the strategy relying on science and education to lay the solid foundation for talent and knowledge. On May 29, 2001, the State Council issued *the Decision on the Reform and Development of Basic Education* (hereinafter referred to as the decision). The goal of basically making nine-year compulsory education universal and basically eliminating illiteracy among young and middle-aged people has been preliminarily achieved, and quality-oriented education has been comprehensively promoted. However, the overall level of basic education in China is not high, the development is not balanced, some places do not pay enough attention to basic education. In the new century, basic education is facing new challenges, and the task of reform and development is still arduous. The "decision" mentioned that we should vigorously develop high school education and promote the coordinated development of high school education. We need to maintain a reasonable proportion of regular high schools and secondary vocational schools and promote their coordinated development. Encourage the development of communication between general education and vocational education in senior high schools. We shall support the development of high school education in rural areas in the central and western regions where nine-year compulsory education has become universal. During the tenth five-year plan period, local people's governments at all levels should make the popularization of nine-year compulsory education and the elimination of illiteracy among young and middle-aged people the "top priorities" in their educational work, and further expand the coverage of the nine-year compulsory education population. The enrollment rate of junior middle schools should reach over 90%, and the non-illiteracy rate of young and middle-aged people should remain above 95%. The enrollment rate in senior high schools reached about 60%, and preschool education was further developed (Li, 2020; Li & Li, 2019; Li et al., 2020; Wang & Liu, 2009; Zhu & Li, 2018).

On July 29, 2010, the Ministry of Education issued *the National Medium and Long-term Education Reform and Development Plan Outline (2010–2020)* (hereinafter referred to as the outline (2), the outline (2)" pointed out that in the next 10 years, to speed up the popularization high school education and by 2020, popularizing high school education, meet the demand of the junior high school graduates to accept high school education. According to the needs of economic and social development, we should reasonably determine the enrollment ratio of ordinary high schools and secondary vocational schools and keep the enrollment scale of ordinary high schools and secondary vocational schools roughly the same in the future. We will increase support for high school education in poor areas in the central and western regions. We will comprehensively improve the comprehensive quality of students in ordinary high schools and promote the diversified development of ordinary high schools. We vigorously develop vocational education, mobilize the enthusiasm of industrial enterprises, accelerate the development of vocational education in rural areas, and make vocational education more attractive (Li, 2020; Li & Li, 2019; Li et al., 2020; Wang & Liu, 2009; Zhu & Li, 2018).

1.2 The Changing Characteristics of Chinese High School Education Policy

Since the reform and opening up, it is not difficult to see the main trend of policy changes in the following aspects from a general view of the policy texts of great significance in the field of high school education in China.

1.2.1 The Type Relationship: From One Side to the Other to the Parallel Development

High school education in our country includes two major aspects: the general education and the vocational education. In different historical periods since the reform and opening up, the number of schools of these two different types of education varies greatly and the relationship is not the same.

In the early days of reform and opening up, the development of ordinary senior high school education and vocational senior high school education presented a state of "one goes down and the other goes up". Between 1978 and 1992, the number of ordinary high schools in China gradually decreased from 49,215 to 14,850, and the enrollment of ordinary high schools also gradually decreased from 6.922 million to 2.347 million. However, between 1980 and 1992, the number of vocational secondary schools in China gradually increased from 3,314 to 9,860, and the enrollment of vocational secondary schools increased sharply from 307,000 to 1,521,000.

Although from 1978 to 1992, Chinese ordinary high school have absolute advantage relative to the vocational high school, but ordinary high school in the school and the decline on the enrollment is very intuitive, and at the same time vocational high schools and enrollment showed a steady growth. This apparent trend in quantity reflects in essence the structural view of the relationship between general education and vocational education in China. For a long time, we have neglected the role of vocational and technical education in socialist construction and have not given it its due place. The teaching plan, curriculum and teaching materials of ordinary high schools are basically for the purpose of promoting universities and cultivating a small number of senior professionals. The requirement of cultivating labor reserve force in the dual task of secondary education is not well reflected. If this situation is not reformed, not only does not conform to the reality of most middle school students, more serious is not to adapt to the four-modernization construction of talent in many aspects, will affect the end of the century industrial and agricultural annual output value quadruple the realization of the strategic goal. Of course, China needs high-level talents, but more importantly, it needs a large number of skilled primary and intermediate technical and managerial talents. At this stage, the state emphasizes "adjusting the structure of secondary education and vigorously developing vocational and technical education" and identifies vocational and technical education as "the weakest link in the whole educational cause of our country at present" and develops it. Accordingly, "the majority of teenagers in our country should start from the middle school stage: one part of the middle school graduates to the general high school, the other part to receive high school vocational and technical education; Some high school graduates go to ordinary universities and some receive higher vocational and technical education (Li, 2020; Li & Li, 2019; Li et al., 2020; Wang & Liu, 2009; Zhu & Li, 2018).

With the continuous development of our country's social economy, the relationship and development mode between ordinary high school education and vocational high school education have changed quietly. Since 1993, the number of ordinary high schools in China has been at least 13,240 in 2015, and at most 16,153 in 2006. In the past 25 years, the number has been basically maintained at 14,400 per year. The number of vocational secondary schools in China was at least 4,856 in 2011, and at most 10,147 in 1995 (data is missing after 2012). In the past 25 years, the number of vocational secondary schools has basically maintained at 7,800 per year. On the other hand, the enrollment of ordinary high schools and vocational middle schools also reflects different characteristics from the previous: the enrollment of ordinary high schools in China has been continuously increasing since 1993, reaching a maximum of 8.77 million in 2005, and then steadily decreasing to about 8.2 million students per year. China's vocational secondary school enrollment has been stable for many years, basically stable at 2.3 million students per year, and there is no significant change.

The parallel development of general and vocational education reflects the change in our understanding of them. The popularization and development of basic education, the more pertinent and comprehensive understanding of high school education, the promotion of high school education status, and the integration of general education and vocational education. A series of factors make China's high school education policy pay more attention to the balance between the two and the common prosperity.

1.2.2 Curriculum Construction: From Flat Single to Three-Dimensional Multiple

The construction of curriculum itself is closely related to the development of economy and society. As China's economic and social situation becomes more and more complex, the high school education must respond to the important aspects of the former in a timely manner. In addition, to improve the quality of education, the people's satisfaction of education, has always been a fundamental aspect of education in China. All these elements are embodied in the construction of the curriculum system.

In the early stage of reform and opening up when China's high school education recovered and developed, the educational objectives of the curriculum tended to be single, and the curriculum construction was also in the early stage on the whole. In 1981, we think the high school education is the foundation education, should be "to cultivate a worker with socialist consciousness of culture, for high qualified primary school freshman, cultivate good labor reserve force for the society", the cultivation of student's ability and quality are the basic focus on "patriotism" and "communist morality", "proletarian world outlook and outlook on life", "cultural science basic knowledge and basic skills" such as category, also basic on the regulation of specific subjects, with an eye to the tradition such as Chinese, math, foreign language and political subjects, For elective courses, only "single elective" and "selective" division, and explain the above two arrangements of elective courses, by the choice of each place. There is a preparation process for these two kinds of elective arrangements.

"besides, there is no substantive provision for elective courses. It can be seen that during this period, the high school education was in the early stage of the discussion of the educational goals and contents, and the measurement, evaluation and supervision of education were just beginning to explore.

In the progress of curriculum construction in our country is fast, thanks to the reform and opening up China's socialist economic, political, cultural, and social and so on various aspects of in-depth development, direct synchronization in cultivating the excellent talents, functional categories of conform to the trend of The Times and improve the level and quality of education for the purpose of a happy life. In 2001 and 2003, the ordinary high school education is clearly defined as "the education for the mass, in the advanced stage of basic education, further improve the national quality and lay a foundation for the lifelong development of students". The 2001 documents centrally reflected the achievements on course construction: in education, not only to "to make the students have the spirit of patriotism, collectivism, love socialism, inherit and carry forward the fine tradition of the Chinese nation and the revolutionary tradition", and to make students "has the preliminary innovation spirit and practice ability, and environmental science cultivated manners and humanities cultivated manners; Have the basic knowledge, basic skills and methods to adapt to lifelong learning; Have a strong body and good psychological quality, develop a healthy aesthetic taste and lifestyle, become a new generation with ideals, morality, culture and discipline"; In the curriculum setting, we should not only pay attention to the foundation and historical tradition of the subject division, but also promote the enrichment and indi- viduation of the curriculum system through various comprehensive practices such as "information technology education, research learning, community service and social practice, and labor and technology education". In addition, the document makes a detailed description in the aspects of curriculum standards, teaching process, text- book development and management, curriculum evaluation, curriculum management and teacher cultivation and training, etc., and initially constructs a multi-dimensional curriculum system in the basic education stage, which is of profound significance to the development of ordinary high school education. The importance of research- based learning, the importance of promoting comprehensive quality evaluation. The curriculum changes in the field of vocational education have a similar trend, which will not be repeated here. All these are enough for us to see the historic achievements of curriculum construction in China's high school education system (Li, 2020; Li & Li, 2019; Li et al., 2020; Wang & Liu, 2009; Zhu & Li, 2018).

1.2.3 School Layout: From City Priority to Overall Consideration

In the historical development of high school education in China, the interrelationship between the two concepts of "efficiency" and "fairness" has always been a core contradiction, and its embodiment is the spatial distribution and quality distribution of all kinds of high schools in China.

The early reform and opening up, "ChongDianJiao" and "scheme" is the key of the construction of high school, the people's governments at various levels shall be "on the manpower and material resources, financial resources offer a great support to key middle school", which is in considering our country "was a large population, a meager, unbalanced development, teachers, and limited funds, equipment… It is impossible for all secondary schools to advance their education level in parallel, and it is not in line with the objective law of the development of things. With the vigorous progress of all aspects of China's economy and society, on the one hand, the development of national education has more capital, larger scale and higher quality, on the other hand, the broad masses of the people are more and more attention to the unfair problem in the field of education, this problem has indeed produced a lot of bad effects in the society. In this context, the development of high school education increasingly puts "equity" in a prominent position. On the one hand, as far as ordinary high school education is concerned, educational equity is becoming an increasingly important concept. In the program of China's educational reform and development, it is clearly pointed out that policy preference should be given to education in ethnic minority areas, and vocational high school education should be developed in rural areas with difficult conditions to promote the progress of ordinary high school education. The 2016 policy text explicitly calls for "universal high school education," rather than treating regular high school education as an elite privilege. On the other hand, with the development of vocational education in China and its close connection with economic and social progress, the policy of vocational high school education also pays more and more attention to the issue of educational equity. Expand the scale of school, increase the number of students, mobilize social forces to establish vocational training institutions… The inclusive development of vocational education at all levels is in itself the best response to promoting equity in education (Li, 2020; Li & Li, 2019; Li et al., 2020; Wang & Liu, 2009; Zhu & Li, 2018).

1.2.4 Dynamic Mechanism: From Government Domination to Social Participation

The convening of the Third Plenary Session of the Eleventh Central Committee restored the once chaotic educational order and re-established the educational administrative management pattern of "unified leadership and hierarchical management". Not only by the central government to lead of macroscopic direction of education, and in many of the rules and regulations of the specific level, there are quite a voice, this state of "different" in "about to organize a group of key implementation of primary and secondary schools", "full-time sixth-form key middle school teaching plan to try out the draft of the" and five-year high school full-time teaching plans to test a draft revision opinions such as policy has very distinct reflected in the text.

The development of early vocational education should also be strictly subordinated to the center of the national economic construction, so as to escort the reform of the socialist market economy.

In the context of the continuous improvement of the government's governance capacity and the optimization of the governance system, a broader "society" is also rising, and many private forces have begun to play their roles, sometimes emitting their light and heat in places beyond the reach of the government. Under the background of streamlining administration and delegating power and multi-party cooperation, profound changes have taken place in the relations between the central and local governments, governments and society. On the one hand, the central government began to devolve power in education, 1985, "decision on reform of the education system" made clear that "the government responsibility is limited to major policy formulation and macro planning, basic education development of the specific operation of power and responsibility", the local government on the development of the education of subjectivity is more significance. On the other hand, civil power has increasingly become an important foundation for educational reform and development. In1993, *Chinese Education Reform and Development Compendium* explicitly proposed to "build the government as the main body of running a school and the social from all walks of life common school system", 1998 "education facing the twenty-first century revitalization action plan" is pointed out that "the next 3-5 years, the basic form of government education as the main body, the social from all walks of life to participate, public schools and private schools' common development of the school system". The "private education promotion law of the People's Republic of China, has put forward" the state shall implement a non-government education actively encourage, support, correct guidance, in accordance with the management policy of, The public has increasingly become an important factor affecting the development of education.

1.3   The Dynamics of the Change of Chinese High School Education Policy

This part attempts to examine the changing dynamics of China's high school education policy from the perspectives of politics, economy, society and culture.

1.3.1   The Political Impetus for the Change of High School Education Policy

The political system is the fundamental point that determines the direction of all public policies in a country, the embodiment of the will of the ruling class in a country, and the product of the game and compromise between different interest groups. The saying "education serves politics" is true in all countries, because education, as the position of cultivating the next generation, is bound to be held by political power subjects, and the policies made must serve politics. In any country, education policy is bound to be shaped by the political system. High school education policies should serve the interests of the country as a whole and the interests of political parties (Li, 2020; Li & Li, 2019; Li et al., 2020; Wang & Liu, 2009; Zhu & Li, 2018).

In the new era, the report to the nineteenth National Congress of the Communist Party of China (CPC) made a new comprehensive plan on "giving priority to the development of education", stating clearly that "to build China into a strong educational country is the foundation project for the great rejuvenation of the Chinese nation. This provides direction and guidance for the reform of high school education policy. In the new era, senior high school education should focus on the following four tasks: cultivating and practicing the core socialist values, carrying out in-depth reform of the talent training system, promoting the reform of the examination and enrollment system, and popularizing senior high school education, so as to promote the scientific development of the entire educational cause. China is a socialist country under the leadership of the communist party of China, which determines that our education must take the training of socialist builders and successors as the fundamental task, and train generation after generation of useful talents who support the leadership of the communist party of China and the socialist system of China and are determined to fight for socialism with Chinese characteristics. This is the fundamental task of education and the direction and goal of education modernization. Similarly, the high school education policy also reflects our national ideology. As an important part of the communist youth league under the leadership of the communist party, the communist youth league played an important role in the ideological and political education of high school students. According to the guidelines of the party, the examination selection in senior high school is also under constant reform. The Report on the 19th National Congress of the Communist Party of China states that, we must fully implement the party's educational policy, carry out the fundamental task of cultivating people with morality, develop quality-oriented education, promote equity in education, and train socialist builders and successors who are well developed morally, intellectually, physically, and aesthetically."

In September 2014, the State Council issued *the Implementation Opinions on Deepening the Reform of the Examination and Enrollment System and* made plans to thoroughly implement the requirements of the Third Plenary Session of the eighteenth CPC Central Committee on Promoting the Reform of the Examination and Enrollment System. The Ministry of Education determines the "how to" promote the path and choose Shanghai, Zhejiang to "two basis, a reference to" comprehensive reform examination recruitment model as the core, publish academic level examination reform, the overall quality appraisal reform, the college entrance examination policy adjustment, reform of university independent recruitment of students test method and four supporting documents promote reform, while requiring the provinces respectively formulate reform implementation details. From the central to the local level, college entrance examination reform is advancing systematically and prudently. The role of the government at the present stage has an important impact on high school education policy. In the current period, the government has been continuously streamlining administration and delegating power, transforming from micro-management to macro-management, and from direct management to indirect management. It has been continuously expanding the scope of authority of local management education and giving local governments more autonomy in education. It aims to ensure that local governments at all levels to earnestly implement the policy of the central and organization, the central government also stressed several times in the file through the evaluation of national policy and evaluation mechanism, to monitor the local government and different levels of the organization's operations. This redefines the state as a guarantor of quality and equity rather than a direct provider (Li, 2020; Li & Li, 2019; Li et al., 2020; Wang & Liu, 2009; Zhu & Li, 2018).

1.3.2 Economic Impetus for the Change of High School Education Policy

The development of education needs a certain material basis, so the economic development has a significant impact on China's high school education policy. In terms of the overall level of the economy, after the reform and opening up, China's economic aggregate in the world economy has been climbing, from the eighth place in 1970 to the second place in 2010. In the 1970s and 1980s, China's GDP was on a par with Canada's. In 2000, China's GDP surpassed Italy's to become the world's sixth-largest economy. In 2005, China's economy overtook the UK's to become the world's fourth largest after the us, Japan and Germany. In 2007, China's GDP grew by 13%, overtaking Germany to become the world's third-largest economy. Just three years later, in 2010, China's GDP surpassed Japan's to become the world's second largest. Since then, China has maintained its position as the world's second largest GDP. The all-round development of the economy urges the Chinese government to expand school education on a large scale and cultivate talents needed by the market economy. High school, as an important stage to provide reserve talents and new labor force for colleges and universities, plays an important role in the national economy. In order to meet the needs of the socialist modernization drive, the 1991 decision and the 1993 program clearly stated that "we should give priority to improving the quality of workers and cultivating junior and senior talents" and "develop high school education in an appropriate amount according to the needs and possibilities of various regions." In 2001, the State Council issued *the Decision on the Reform and Development of Basic Education* (Guo fa [2001] no. 21), further established the strategy of adhering to the priority development of basic education, proposed to further deepen the reform of education and teaching, vigorously strengthen the construction of middle school teachers, and promote quality education (Li, 2020; Li & Li, 2019; Li et al., 2020; Wang & Liu, 2009; Zhu & Li, 2018).

At the same time, in order to promote the development of socialist modernization, the secondary vocational education is also developing. The National Conference on Education held in 1978. In 1980, the Ministry of Education and State Labor Administration jointly issued *Reform of the Secondary Education Structure Report*. The report looks at the changing structure of secondary education is too single, secondary education and the development of national economy the phenomenon of the disconnect, requires not only will add professional (technology) in ordinary high school education, is also part of the change of average high school do to secondary vocational schools, and to encourage all walks of life to hold vocational (a mechanic) school. In 1983, the Ministry of Education jointly issued *the reform of the Secondary Education Structure and Opinions of the Development of Vocational and Technical Education* (hereinafter referred to as "opinions"). It clearly put forward that the various types of vocational and technical school in 1990, to the proportion of students and ordinary high school students. After more than 30 years, Chinese medium basic education policy is to vigorously develop vocational education as a strategic focus of education work, to expand the scale of recruit students of secondary vocational education is an important goal, strive to ordinary high schools and secondary vocational schools in the recruitment of students scale to realize "the same", to promote the high school stage of education to coordinate the healthy and continuous development.

With the rapid development of science and technology, the Internet access rate of schools at all levels has increased from more than 20% six years ago to 90% now. In line with the trend of the information age, the Ministry of Education has put forward the action of deepening the coverage of online learning space, promoted the implementation of the guidelines of the ministry of education on strengthening the construction and application of online learning space and the guidance on the construction and application of online learning space, and accelerated the popularization and application of online learning space in various regions. In 2019, the annual national network learning space application popularization activities, relying on the national digital education resources public service system, organization opened real-name network learning space between teachers and students, the number of 10 million new, in basic education, vocational education, higher education and continuing education within the scope of selected 40 network learning space applications show the excellent area and 200 excellent schools, promotion, gradually realize the "one person one room, everyone in space". Online education platforms are also emerging. Platforms such as wisdom tree have created new forms of high school education and enhanced the vitality of education.

After the reform and opening up, China's economy transformed from planned economy to market economy. The influence of marketization on China's high school education policy is mainly reflected in the diversification of educational investment and school-running system. In 1993, the program clearly stated that "we should accelerate the reform of the school-running system, further change the state of government-run schools, and form a new system that combines government-run schools with the participation of all sectors of society". Around the "decision" in 1999 pointed out that "will encourage policies and preferential measures, accelerate the reform of school-running system and various social forces to support a variety of forms for ordinary high school, and in ensuring that existing state don't reduce the number of average high school under the premise of building a batch of" state-owned private "and" help "of the people of the public ordinary high school, according to the voluntary school running mode, promote the development of diversified school-running system". In 2002, the law of the People's Republic of China on the promotion of private education stipulated: "private education is a public welfare enterprise and a component part of socialist education. The state shall actively encourage, strongly support, correctly guide and administrate privately-run education. People's governments at all levels should incorporate private education into their plans for national economic and social development." In 2004, the plan further stated: "reform and improve the education investment system, establish the education financial system in line with the public financial system, ensure the sustained and steady growth of funds, broaden the channels of financing, and establish an effective incentive mechanism for social investment, investment and donation in running schools... The funds for running schools for non-compulsory education shall be Shared by the government, with the government as the main channel. We will gradually form a stable and sustainable education investment mechanism that is compatible with the socialist market economy and meets the needs of public education. At present, the pattern of diversification of investment subjects and school-running modes in high schools in China has been preliminarily formed, mainly including: government-run high schools; Relying on the public high school to hold "four independent" (independent campus, independent legal person, independent financial and independent management) private high school; Joint education; The state-owned private enterprise; Completely private (Li, 2020; Li & Li, 2019; Li et al., 2020; Wang & Liu, 2009; Zhu & Li, 2018).

It is worth noting that the original intention of the national policy to encourage private education has also undergone a fundamental change. In the early days of reform and opening up, the state encouraged private educational undertakings to absorb more social forces in order to solve the shortage of educational funds and overcome the shortage of government investment in education. Now, it is more to further promote the formation of the diversification of school-running modes by promoting the diversification of school-running subjects, innovating the educational mode and stimulating the educational vitality. Despite the remarkable achievements China has made since its reform and opening up, modern China is now the world's second largest economy. However, there are still great differences in economic levels between regions, such as urban–rural differences, east–west differences and so on.

The government realized that the huge regional economic differences led to the uneven distribution of educational resources, so it increased investment in education equity to promote the rational allocation of educational resources. The government took measures to recruit a large number of rural teachers and develop rural education. The government-funded normal university student policy requires normal university students to return to their provinces to teach in primary and secondary schools after graduation and commit to work in primary and secondary education for more than six years. At the same time, those who work in urban schools at public expense should work in rural compulsory education schools for at least one year. This measure has effectively balanced the education gap between urban and rural areas and promoted rural development. On the universal education, the party's eighteen big first proposed the basic popularization high school education, the fifth plenary session of the eighteenth further to make a strategic decision of popularizing high school education, the timely released in April 2017 the high school stage of education popularization crucial plan (2017–2020), in October 2017, "popularizing high school education" to the party's 19 report. This indicates that the popularization of high school education will become a major national strategy after the full popularization of nine-year compulsory education in 2011.

In the early days of reform and opening up, the country was in urgent need of developing economy and increasing GDP, and it was in urgent need of "quick talents". At the same time, educational resources are limited. Therefore, in the actual development process of high school education, the principle of efficiency first is more followed. This "efficiency first" development idea, the prominent performance for the key high school system to promote and implement. In January 1978, subject to approval by the State Council, the Ministry of Education issued "about to organize a group of key implementation of primary and secondary schools, further put forward" earnestly do a good job in a number of key primary and secondary schools, to improve the quality of primary and secondary schools, and demanding in terms of funds, teacher, hardware, students to the key school tilt, formed from the state to the provincial, city and county "layers of key" small "pyramid" type of development pattern. In October 1980, the decision of the ministry of education on the success of key middle schools in stages and batches required people's governments at all levels to "give strong support to key middle schools in terms of manpower, material resources and financial resources".

In the 1990s, the economic policy was adjusted to some extent. Correspondingly, the development policy of key high schools was also adjusted, and the formulation of "key high schools" was replaced by "model high schools". In 1994, the opinions of the state council on the implementation of the program of China's educational reform and development put forward that "each county should establish one or two key secondary schools for the whole county. The country will focus on building around 1,000 experimental and demonstration high schools." In the following year, the state education commission issued a notice on the evaluation and acceptance of about 1,000 demonstration ordinary senior high schools (hereinafter referred to as the notice), which required the construction and evaluation of about 1,000 demonstration ordinary senior high schools by stages and in batches before the year 2000. Ideally, the transition from a key high school to a model high school means that the value orientation of China's high school education policy starts to shift from efficiency to fairness.

At present, the economic strength enters the new stage, the economic policy. The development of senior high school education in China has changed from merely focusing on the expansion of quantity to focusing on the improvement of quality, from emphasizing that "some people get rich first" and paying attention to the development of senior high school education in urban and developed areas to emphasizing the development of senior high school education in rural areas and promoting the coordinated development of urban and rural areas. The funds of public schools are basically all from the government financial allocation. Fiscal departments at all levels adhere to the strategy of giving priority to the development of education and continuously increase input in education. From 2013 to 2018, the national general public budget teaches (Li, 2020; Li & Li, 2019; Li et al., 2020; Wang & Liu, 2009; Zhu & Li, 2018).

1.3.3 Social Impetus for the Change of High School Education Policy

According to the stage characteristics of the development of high school education and the promulgation time of the important policies of high school education, the evolution of China's high school education policies since the reform and opening up can be roughly divided into three periods: 1978–1992 is the slow development stage, 1993–2009 is the exploratory development stage, and 2010–present is the golden development stage.

The slow development stage (1978–1992). In December 1978, the reform and opening up that changed the destiny of China's education officially began. The whole society entered the warm state of opening up and exploration, and China began the transformation from planned economy to market economy. The all-round development of the economy urges the Chinese government to expand school education on a large scale and cultivate talents needed by the market economy. On October 6, 1977, the ministry of education issued the opinions on college enrollment in 1977, and China"s college entrance examination system was officially restored. In 1985, the central committee of the communist party of China and the state council issued the "decision on the reform of the education system", which emphasized the adjustment of the structure of high school education and the development of vocational education. Since then, the central government has issued a series of policies, laws and regulations to reform the basic and high school education system, investment in funds, teacher development and curriculum teaching.

During this period, the reform of high school education was hindered by the national conditions and could only grope forward within a certain scope. In 1980, the central in the about group to organize key middle school, point, because China's large population, weak economic foundation, uneven development between regions, as well as the education resources are limited, the average development all school difficult to achieve, therefore this stage issued policy from planning objectives, tasks, and more complete ChongDianJiao specific aspects such as construction, "key, demonstration school" priority development, development is relatively slow.

At the same time, it can be seen that the value orientation of the high school education policy is mainly based on the society. First, it is based on the social reality, affirming the social needs and social values, according to the needs of the society to implement the education reform, determine the talent training model; Second, it pays attention to the social purpose of education, emphasizes the service function of education to the society on the basis of the overall interests of the society, and requires the cultivation of excellent talents through education to promote social development. The value orientation of social standard is to take the social demand as the mold, to train talents according to the needs, it focuses on the cultivation of people's knowledge, professional skills and other external attributes, through improving the external attributes of people to achieve development. Investigate its reason, after the introduction of "reform and opening up" big decisions, main focus on national economic development, increasing demand for a variety of professional technical personnel, the requirement for the education system in our country, the structure of the education reform, education method to change the talent training mode, so as to socialist construction continuously conveying labor, and high school is a critical period of cultivating young talents, able to produce on a large scale to meet the needs of economic development and has received a good education of labor and technical personnel.

The exploration and development stage (1993–2009). At the end of the twentieth century, the nine-year compulsory education gradually completed the popularization of the task, middle school graduates have a greater demand for high school education, the sustained and rapid economic growth also needs more technical personnel and professional talents. Therefore, the general high school education and vocational education began to be valued and developed rapidly. In 1985, the central committee of the communist party of China and the state council issued the "decision on the reform of the education system", which emphasized the adjustment of the structure of high school education and the development of vocational education. Since then, the central government has issued a series of policies, laws and regulations to reform the basic and high school education system, investment in funds, teacher development and curriculum teaching. In 1997, the fifteenth national congress of the communist party of China made it clear that the strategy of "rejuvenating the country through science and education" should be earnestly implemented, and hundreds of millions of high-quality workers and tens of millions of specialized talents should be trained to meet the requirements of modernization, so as to give full play to China's huge advantages in human resources. In accordance with this spirit, in October 1998, the ministry of education formulated the action plan for the revitalization of education in the twenty-first century, proposing to deepen the reform, vigorously promote quality-oriented education, and establish the basic framework of the new education system that takes the initiative to adapt to the economic and social development (Li, 2020; Li & Li, 2019; Li et al., 2020; Wang & Liu, 2009; Zhu & Li, 2018).

From the perspective of policy, firstly, the nature of ordinary high school education is clear. Later, in the education policy, the general high school education began to have its own independent status. In the two policy texts of 2001 and 2003, it was defined as "a mass-oriented education, at an advanced stage of basic education, to further improve the national quality and lay a foundation for the lifelong development of students". Secondly, with the change and development of economic policies and values, ordinary rural high schools have been attached great importance in order to accelerate the development of rural education, deepen the reform of rural education and promote the coordinated development of rural economy and society and urban and rural areas. At this stage, the values of China's general high school education policy changed from "development according to needs" to "pay attention to the development of high school education in urban and economically developed areas" to "attach importance to high school education in rural areas". Finally, the curriculum reform began to get attention. After 2010, the high school education policy began to focus on the promotion of curriculum reform.

In general, with the rapid change of social economy and the exchange and collision between Chinese and western education systems, high school education developed rapidly during this period.

Gold development stage (2010–present). Since 2010, China has been at a critical stage of reform and development. The increasing pressure on population, resources and the environment, as well as the rapidly changing economic development pattern, all emphasize the importance and urgency of improving people's quality and cultivating innovative talents. The future development of China depends on talents and is based on education. In the period of national economic and social transformation, providing the labor market with talents that meet the needs of the economic sector is a huge challenge for any country, and reforming the formal education system is the natural way. During this period, the development pattern of ordinary high schools has a trend of reversing, and its development characteristics are mainly shown as:

(1) Independence is increasingly prominent, and development is constantly standardized. In the working points of 2012, the goal of "promoting diversified development" was proposed for ordinary high school education, and the nature of high school education was redefined as: "high school education plays a key role in the formation and independent development of students' personality and has special significance for the improvement of talents' quality and the cultivation of innovative talents". This is the first time that the significance of high school education has been made clear in national policy.

(2) Pay attention to the comprehensive development of students. With the popularization of high school education, its development goal has changed from the past elite education to the mass education and the education of basic civic quality and spirit. For students in ordinary senior high school education, education policy attaches importance to moral, intellectual, physical, aesthetic, labor and mental health. Among them, from the curriculum form to the student mental health education carried on the stipulation. At the same time, in the second half of 2017, primary and secondary school teacher qualification examination also added "mental health education" subject.

(3) Education in poor areas should be strengthened and high school education should be made universal. After 2010, in order to achieve the goal of universal high school education by 2020, several education attacks plans have been issued to pay more attention to the development of ordinary high school education in poor areas. For example, the key education plan for senior high schools (2017–2020) released in 2017 focused on the access to education in areas with weak educational foundation and special groups.

The change process and content of high school education policy in China, according to the development of high school education in China has experienced a pay attention to the expansion of the amount to pay attention to quality, by emphasizing "part of the people become prosperous first", pay attention to the high school education development of cities and developed areas to pay attention to develop the rural high school education, promote the coordinated development of urban and rural areas of twists and turns.

In general, the reform of high school education carried out in China in the past four decades is mainly in response to the general demand for improving the quality of education, strengthening accountability and meeting the needs of the socialist market economy in the process of accelerating the development of high school education. The reform has gone through a tortuous process from focusing on quantity expansion and unbalanced development to focusing on quality improvement and balanced development. The focus of the reform is to vigorously develop high school education, effectively transform government functions, and gradually form a diversified pattern of investment subjects and school-running modes in high school education (Li, 2020; Li & Li, 2019; Li et al., 2020; Wang & Liu, 2009; Zhu & Li, 2018).

Theorize and summarize the effect of social changes on the policy changes of high school education. The reflection of social conflict in all fields of social activities, reflected in the field of education is education conflict, this principle is also applicable in the stage of high school education. Educational conflict is a manifestation that education does not adapt to the rapidly changing society. The faster society changes, the more educational conflicts are likely to arise. Since the reform and opening up in 1978, China has been in a long period of social transformation. The reform will inevitably lead to the friction between the old and new systems, and the opening up will inevitably lead to the collision between eastern and western cultures. On the one hand, social transformation promotes the transformation of social political, economic, cultural and scientific and technological systems, and then causes changes in people's values, life attitudes, thinking and behavior. On the other hand, education is difficult to adapt to the rapid social transformation and the reform is imminent, which is also related to the characteristics of education itself.

This kind of social transformation is a kind of benign development, which plays an important role of ideological liberation in the adjustment of high school education policy. The social transformation promotes people to observe and analyze the change of the perspective of things and causes the conflict of educational ideas. The social transformation liberates people's thoughts, and people begin to pursue a rich and colorful future life, which leads to the conflict of educational self-target. The social transformation has aroused the new demand for talents of various levels, types and forms of education, thus causing the conflict of educational structure. Social transformation accelerates the reform of social management system and causes the conflict of education system. The social transformation has caused the change of people's thinking mode from "focus on the present" to "focus on the future", as well as the thinking on "what kind of people should be trained" and "what knowledge should be imparting" in education, thus causing the conflict on the choice of educational content.

The social modernization is closely related to the modernization of high school education. The 12th national congress of the communist party of China (CPC) in 1982 identified education as one of the strategic priorities of the socialist modernization drive. In 2001, the state council issued the decision on the reform and development of basic education (No. 21 document of the state council [2001]), which further established the strategic position of basic education in the socialist modernization drive. Social modernization is a process of comprehensive development, and its most fundamental feature is the modernization of human beings. In order to ensure the smooth realization of China's socialist modernization, our requirements for human modernization must also have the characteristics of socialist nature and modern knowledge and consciousness. To establish the modern education in China, we should reform the traditional exam-oriented education thought and educational content of high school education, vigorously develop quality-oriented education and general education, and realize the modernization of educational concept, educational content and educational method. This direction has also been reflected in the education reform and policy adjustment in the later high school education stage.

The social education and education socialization in senior high school have evolved mutually. "Social education" refers to the process of expanding the educational function to all aspects of society by building an education network with school education as the main body, so as to meet the needs of social members and promote the integration of social education. "Social education" is embodied in the following aspects: the society consciously provides resources and oriented services for school education; To exert educational influence on its members in a purposeful and planned way; The society and the school jointly promote the progress of social culture, science and technology, and improve the quality of citizens. After entering the twenty-first century, the theory of social education has a remarkable development in the stage of high school education.

On the other hand, school education, as the main branch system of modern education, with the opening up of the whole society and its extensive participation in education, has been moving from closed to open and continuously expanding its social functions, which is the trend of "education socialization". Education socialization is the common trend of school education reform in the world and the inevitable trend of the development of high school education in China. The emergence of this trend is conducive to the formation of a development education path suitable for China's national conditions, the further deepening of China's school education reform, and the full use and development of social material resources and intellectual resources.

At the same time, we should also note that China is currently in the period of social transformation, many reforms are still in the exploratory stage, and the further development of the socialization trend of high school education will inevitably encounter various difficulties and resistance. First, the traditional concept of exam-oriented education hinders people's correct understanding of the meaning of education; Second, the lagging educational system reform restricts the rapid process of high school education socialization; Third, the national resource allocation policy is still encouraging the dependence of some ordinary high schools; Fourth, the narrow-minded mentality exacerbates the indifference and prejudice of the whole society towards vocational education. Social education and educational socialization are mutually evolving and transforming. The positive interaction between them is of great significance to the formation of a learning-oriented society. Since the reform and opening up, these two trends have developed rapidly and become a prominent feature of high school education in the twenty-first century.

1.3.4 Cultural Impetus for the Change of High School Education Policy

Slow development stage (1978–1992). Before the reform and opening up, China's senior high school education was dominated by ordinary senior high school education with a single structure. In 1975, there were 39,120 high schools in China, while 2,213 secondary technical schools and secondary normal schools accounted for 5.7% of the total. Of the 11.637 million people living in ordinary high schools, only 6.1% are in secondary professional schools. In 1977, the former state education commission decided to resume the national college entrance examination to solve the talent gap caused by the decade-long cultural revolution and the unsustainable problems of the country and society. This is not only a reform of the education system, but also marked a shift in the ideological structure of the society. It has changed the "reading useless theory" of learning concept, so that the whole society quickly formed an unprecedented scale of large review, big learning upsurge, inspired the students' learning enthusiasm and learning enthusiasm, promoted the development of high school education.

Exploration and development stage (1993–2009). During this period, there were special education policies for senior high schools, and even special education policies for ordinary senior high schools or secondary vocational schools. Most of them were the further modification, supplement and improvement of general education policies and original relevant policy documents. The policy text not only covers many fields: focusing on rural education, strengthening secondary vocational education, supporting minority students and promoting the development of special education, but also forms a complete reform and development system on the basis of relevant policies of the previous period.

The development of quality-oriented education and the realization of the all-round development of human beings is obviously the theme of the education policy of senior high school in China at this time. The government actively promotes the reform of senior high school education in all aspects in various forms, which reflects the obvious trend of populism. Since 1993, China has promulgated a large number of policy texts to implement the "popularization" of high school education. In 1999, "popularization" and "improvement" were integrated together, and "improvement" of education quality was emphasized simultaneously on the basis of "popularization" of education. This is the main essence of "populism"—both quantitatively and quantitatively.

Gold development stage (2010–present). The rapid arrival of the information age makes all kinds of thoughts and cultures bloom and blend with each other, changing the growing environment of student's day by day. Students' thoughts are more independent, and their personalities are more distinct, which increases certain difficulties for the cause of high school education in China. It seems that the educational policy of "comprehensive development" cannot solve the problem of The Times. Therefore, the party and the country have put forward a series of educational policies focusing on "personality development". The national medium and long-term education reform and development plan outline (2010–2020) "(hereinafter referred to as" program for education in 2010) to "education" as a basic requirement of education work, and for the first time in the national policy independent education meaning for high school education, to make clear the property of the high school education, think high school is one of the most important for the student individuality development period, the requirements shall be in this period, students' independent ability, independent learning ability and social adaptation ability. The outline of the education plan in 2010 shows the new requirements of high school education in the new era for training talents, which is undoubtedly another important turning point in the development history of high school education in China.

Although China's senior high schools continued to carry out quality-oriented education on the whole during this period, a lot of contents conforming to students' development characteristics were added in the policy, which provided a practical and operable way for the cultivation of specific qualities and abilities. We should carry out the reform of quality-oriented education and emphasize students' learning experience and feelings in school teaching. In terms of curriculum setting, we should strengthen the construction of textbooks for senior high schools, develop characteristic courses, implement research learning, social practice and create a variety of elective courses, so as to promote the comprehensive and personalized development of students. Special attention should be paid to improving the evaluation system of senior high school and increasing the comprehensive quality evaluation. Also added some content about mental health education and safety education.

In a word, the series of educational policies issued and implemented by the state during this period took "educating people as the foundation" as the purpose, and cultivated students' various qualities, so that each student could receive education in line with physical and mental development and closely related to individual characteristics. "Education for this" reflects the nature of education, because it is a value of "people" care, adhere to the "people" for this, adhere to the development of the "people", adhere to "people" lifelong development for this, but this kind of "human" development needs by "education", it comes to "what education should cultivate people", "education should be how to cultivate people" problem. The educational concept of "educating people" regards people as the main body and the root, thinks about "educating" from the perspective of "people", and really pays attention to the internal attributes of "people", which reflects the people-oriented value orientation.

In the past 40 years of reform and opening up, the high school education policy has gone through a tortuous process from emphasizing external value and then deepening to internal value, from emphasizing the parallel development of unilateral quality and quantity, to giving consideration to both quality and quantity, and then returning to individual characteristics. This process profoundly reflects the characteristics of the change and development of The Times, and responds to the general demand of the society for meeting the needs of the socialist market economy, promoting educational equity, improving educational quality and respecting and caring for each individual in the process of accelerating the development of high school education. With the gradual formation of people-oriented education policies in senior high schools, it is still necessary to steadily promote long-term education policies in senior high schools on how to carry out courses that can not only arouse students' resonance but also achieve their personalized development, and how to ensure a reasonable, fair and effective evaluation method (Li, 2020; Li & Li, 2019; Li et al., 2020; Wang & Liu, 2009; Zhu & Li, 2018).

The cultural change influences the change direction of educational reform. On the one hand, the backwardness of culture leads to the backwardness of high school education reform. China's "cultural revolution" can be classified as a typical "backward" cultural change. The political despotism, ideological imprison and cultural ignorance during the "cultural revolution" led to the "retrograde" reconstruction of Chinese education. Such as the arbitrary shortening of the school system, the non-specialization of the school authority, the loss of the dignity of teachers, the devaluation of the value of systematic scientific and cultural knowledge, the abolition of the college entrance examination system and the simplification of the secondary education structure.

On the other hand, advanced culture has affected the progress of high school education reform. In terms of culture, school education mainly imparts the long historical culture or advanced existing culture to students through ideology such as political view, moral concept, belief, art, etc., and enables students to understand and adapt to the development of society through the dissemination of culture. In the modern society with developed science and technology, entering the era of knowledge economy, the cultural form is advanced, which determines the educational content to be diversified. The high school education reform has improved the degree of knowledge enrichment, deepened the depth of knowledge, paid attention to the innovation of the way of thinking of knowledge dissemination, the carrier of knowledge dissemination from hand to mouth to written books to scientific and technological network.

The logical trend of high school education reform under cultural changes. Anthropologists believe that cultural change is based on two basic processes, one is cultural transmission, the other is cultural creation. The process of cultural transmission tends to spread from one group to another, while the process of cultural creation focuses on the generation of new cultural factors. Education reform has the closest impact on cultural change. Education can not only promote the continuous dissemination of culture, but also promote the re-creation of culture. In the process of cultural communication, education selectively integrates the value orientation of the whole society to feedback, modify and inherit the cultural communication content. At the same time, education promotes cultural creation. In the process of transmitting and disseminating culture, education has never simply copied culture. It may give new meaning to the existing culture due to social changes, different physical and mental conditions of educates and differences in educators' own values. Or due to the integration of local culture and foreign culture, so that the nature, function and other aspects of the original culture changes, derived new cultural elements. These new cultural meanings or cultural elements often become the germination of cultural creation and innovation.

In the process of transmitting and disseminating culture, education generates new cultural elements and cultivates creative talents. School education is to use the slow accumulation of human knowledge and experience to cultivate people's creative spirit, thereby accelerating the realization of cultural re-change. With the rapid development of science and technology, cultural changes have a profound impact on the diversification and globalization of educational contents, which requires the educational reform to face the open world and increase international cooperation and exchanges in education. Cultural modernization has improved the breadth and depth of knowledge, requiring the content of educational reform to pay attention to the cultivation of innovative spirit and creative thinking. In addition, the rapidly updated mode of cultural communication also emphasizes that the educational reform should make good use of the Internet resources, and intensify the development of distance education, online quality courses, "micro-courses". Only through the continuous reform of high school education, can it positively cope with the challenge brought by the cultural change.

1.4 Problems and Suggestions on China's High School Education Policy

1.4.1 Problems Faced by China's High School Education Policy

High school is an important period for a person to become an adult. This period is an important foundation for developing a strong constitution and healthy personality, for laying an important foundation for knowledge and skills, for maintaining a correct attitude towards the world, values and outlook on life, and for cultivating and creating top innovative talents. As a link between compulsory education and higher education, ordinary high school education not only needs to provide excellent students in institutions of higher education, but also needs to directly train a large number of qualified workers for the society. Therefore, high school education plays the role of a bridge linking the past and the future in the national education system, which is of unique importance.

According to the previous summary of the overall interests, it can be found that the current high school education reform and development in the process of the following problems:

1. **The positioning of high school education is not clear**. High school education is at the node of the connection between compulsory education and higher education. In different stages of development in China, it focuses on different development goals, and at the same time, it should deal with different promotion modes. However, there is a lack of academic consensus and broad recognition on its essence, nature and task. To clarify the philosophical origin of high school education is the key to determine the policy starting point and the direction of policy practice. In the existing policy documents of our country, there is a description of the positioning nature of high school education as follows: In 1981, the ministry of education issued the teaching plan of full-time six-year key middle school (trial draft), which proposed that "middle school education is basic education". In 1996, the state education commission issued the curriculum plan for full-time regular senior middle school (experimental and revised draft), which clearly states that regular senior high school education is the basic education of the first level connected with nine-year compulsory education. In 2003, the ministry of education issued the curriculum plan (experiment) for ordinary senior high schools, which also conveyed the view that "ordinary senior high school education is the basic education for the public to further improve the national quality on the basis of nine-year compulsory education". But in the new era of development of high school positioning in a wide range of discussion after the lack of consensus recognition. High school education as the basis of high-level education and bound in the "basic education" piecemeal or accompanied it, how to show it with the similarities and differences of compulsory education in the era of the new stage of development, how to properly join the compulsory education and higher education, how to realize the ordinary high school and coordinated development of secondary vocational education and so on, all need to answer after clear positioning.

2. **The concept of efficiency first runs through the development process of high school**. In 1954, the CPC Central Committee first put forward the policy of running "key" middle schools. In 1977, Deng Xiaoping put forward the construction of key primary and secondary schools and key universities. In 1980, the ministry of education requested people's governments at all levels to give strong support to key middle schools in terms of manpower, material and financial resources. China has gradually formed a "little pyramid" pattern of development at the national, provincial, municipal and county levels, which provides funds, teachers, hardware and students for key middle schools, so as to effectively respond to the strong demand for "quick talent" in national construction. Although "model high school" gradually replaced "key high school" in the 1990s, there was little value tendency of changing from efficiency to equity, and "model high school" was inevitably branded as "key school" in practice. After blindly pursuing the coverage rate and the gross enrolment rate, the gross enrolment rate of high school education is expected to reach 90% by 2020. How to adjust the value orientation of policy to promote the mutual adjustment of fairness and efficiency becomes a problem that cannot be ignored. In the present stage of the basic popularization of nine-year compulsory education

and the rapid growth of the scale of higher education, if the high school education cannot guarantee enough quantity and quality, it will have a great impact on the overall development of China's education and the national training and modernization of national education.

3. **The policy is dominated by economic discourse, and the discourse culture rules are simple**. In our statistical educational policy documents, the vast majority of policies focus on economic discourse, emphasizing that education ADAPTS to the economy, education reacts to the economy and promotes its development, or focus on education investment and education finance, and pay attention to the investment and management of education. However, this single cultural rule of discourse makes the practice process ignore the role of education in other aspects, such as from the perspective of sociology, paying more attention to education to promote social harmony and stability, and from the perspective of ethics, education helps to regulate and promote the development of moral behavior. The single economic discourse in the policy will give incomplete direction guidance to the specific practice link, making it unable to exert the maximum effect.

4. **Talent training mode and training objectives in senior high school**. For many years, China's high school education has been taking a consistent approach in the way and goal of talent training, especially in the ordinary high school talent training mode, is almost completely consistent. The biggest drawback of this model is that students have no independent choice, development and possibility, and it is difficult for them to stand out in the selection of innovative talents. However, there is no diversification of talent training model and training objectives, there is no real sense of educational equity. Because "no kind of education" is just formal fairness, but "teaching according to aptitude" is a higher level of education fairness.

5. **The structure of high school education**. For a long time, we have divided high school education into regular high schools and vocational high schools, and we have never tried to integrate them. With the acceleration of social change, people's living standard and life style will be more diversified in the future. People need to face more uncertainty on important issues such as career planning and life goal selection. Only when students have comprehensive knowledge structure and ability, constantly learn to adapt to the new environment, and constantly seek to adapt to their own life choices, can they better cope with the future challenges. In our country, the traditional way of running a school that is either popular or vocational has seriously restricted the overall independent development of students, and it is unable to meet the needs of the development.

6. **The reform of the college entrance examination system**. The reform of college entrance examination system is not only a heavy topic, but also an important issue related to the future development of the country. The shortcomings of the existing college entrance examination and enrollment system must be solved. However, the reform of college entrance examination is neither an independent problem, nor a problem that can be completely solved within the

education system. The reform of college entrance examination system should be combined with the reform of national personnel management, professional title promotion, school evaluation, entrance examination and talent selection system.

7. **Curriculum reform**. At present, there are still many problems in our curriculum reform. For example, to solve the problem of too many subjects and too much weight in the middle school curriculum, scientifically define which compulsory courses should be learned in high school and how many compulsory courses should be learned? Correspondingly, the new curriculum standard must consider some basic problems of the curriculum, such as defining the scope of the curriculum, the basic allocation of hours, etc. Educational reform should continue to be classroom-centric, and our classrooms should never be deviated from, because education will not change until the classroom changes. The national reform of new curriculum should not only be guided by policies, but also be provided with special funds. Only in this way, the new curriculum reform can be truly effective. In my opinion, we should organize special financial and human resources to carry out experimental research on "school-based national curriculum".

8. **Development and application of educational technology in the information age**. The rapid development of information and network has brought about the innovation of educational technology. Today, more and more high schools are introducing high-end technology as a classroom aid. On the one hand, in developed areas, the application of advanced educational technology has greatly improved the teaching efficiency and the utilization rate of teaching resources. On the other hand, the proper application of educational technology can also promote education in weak areas, make them share teaching resources and improve teaching level. But the application of technology and equipment also poses a challenge, then the double-edged sword of science and technology features, more critical applications in the field of education, how to make advanced education technology and equipment for the maximum utility and as far as possible to eliminate its negative influence, is the field of education in the high speed information network developed today have to face the problem.

9. **Question of the rights and duties of the principal**. For a long time, school management has been regarded as the internal affairs of the school in our country, and the community and parents of students have no need to intervene, nor have the right to intervene, and students are the passive recipients of school management. In this case, on the one hand, the school will lose the attention, support and supervision of the society, leading to the school closed door, separated from the society; On the other hand, some of the responsibilities that the government and the society should take on have been transferred partly or completely to the headmaster. For example, departments of safety, hygiene and epidemic prevention can reach the principal without too much detail. As the legal representative of the school, the principal undertook many tasks that he could not undertake by himself. Their powers are limited, but their responsibilities are unlimited, so they are often treading on thin ice. The principal cannot

concentrate on the core work such as school development planning, education training guidance, curriculum reform and teacher professional development, which will seriously restrict the development of the school.

10. **Difficulties in the education development of ordinary senior high schools in poor areas in central and western China**. The education development of ordinary high schools in the poor areas in the central and western regions is confronted with many difficulties, which are caused by resources, economic and social development, as well as institutional and institutional factors, social and cultural factors, and targeted poverty alleviation through education. Due to the constraints of the natural ecological environment and social and historical factors in the central and western regions, compared with the developed regions, the ordinary high schools in the poor areas in the central and western regions of China are at a congenital disadvantage in terms of resources, school conditions and other aspects. Economy is the material foundation of educational development, and educational activities themselves are the result of material production development to a certain stage. As an important part of social development, educational development must be based on economic development. Due to the backward economic development and a large number of poor people in the central and western regions of China, the overall investment in ordinary high school education is insufficient, which seriously restricts the sustainable development of ordinary high school education in the poor central and western regions. In addition, some special groups, such as students from poor families, disabled students, children of migrant workers in cities and other groups, their education also needs to be guaranteed. The dilemma caused by this has hindered the development of ordinary high schools in poor areas in central and western China.

11. **Coordinated development of the general population**. Although the number of ordinary high schools and vocational high schools has been developing in parallel with each other recently, it is still an undeniable fact that Pugao is crowded and vocational high schools are empty. For a long time, ordinary high school secondary school in the school, vocational high school employment has become a fixed pattern in people's minds. Statistics from the ministry of education show that secondary vocational schools accounted for 47% of high school education in 2011, 46% in 2012, 43% in 2013, 42.7% in 2014 and 41% in 2015. After the peak of secondary vocational school enrollment in 2009 and 2010, it has been decreasing year by year in the past five years. In the ordinary high school gradually popularized today, how to achieve the coordinated development of the problem is gradually apparent (Li, 2020; Li & Li, 2019; Li et al., 2020; Wang & Liu, 2009; Zhu & Li, 2018).

1.4.2 Policy Suggestions on Deepening the Development of Chinese High School Education

As the "hub" of the national education system, ordinary senior high school education is the core of the entire education system in China, which will have a great impact on the compulsory education, higher education and vocational education. From the perspective of the educational environment of the whole society, it will affect the development of the learning society which is the core of educational management. Because of this special position, the development of ordinary high school education has become an important factor to measure the comprehensive strength and intellectual resources of the country. It has important practical significance and theoretical value for the development and improvement of China's general education policy.

1. **Highlight the independence of high school education, pay attention to the quality improvement and diversified development of high schools**. Legislation may become an effective way to define the orientation and nature of high schools, and to define their educational norms and responsibilities through legal provisions. In vertical construction, high school education forms a good link between basic education and higher education and establishes a good connection with the society horizontally. Pay attention to the development of the school itself, adhere to the development of students, improve the development of school quality. Firstly, regional characteristics can be established according to geographical and cultural characteristics, economic development level and urbanization process. Secondly, a variety of high schools can be set up according to the needs of student groups to meet the development needs of different students. Finally, each school can carry out diversified design of school-based curriculum according to its own development situation, teachers, students' interests and hobbies and ability levels, so as to realize the improvement and diversified development of high school quality from all aspects.

2. **Pay attention to the guidance of cultural rules of policy discourse and listen to public opinions extensively and actively**. The rules of discourse culture in policy have a strong guiding and motivating effect on the implementers of policy. Therefore, it is necessary to pay attention to its left and right sides, to respect and introduce public opinion in the opinion solicitation process, to ensure the main position of students, parents, teachers, educational administrators, researchers, and so on, and to constantly explore a variety of ways to promote the expression of public opinion, which is widely used in education portals, social networks, campus networks, e-mails, letters, etc. At the same time, we should establish appropriate evaluation criteria for policies, conduct scientific analysis and evaluation on the will of the public, fully consider the long-term and direct interests of different groups on the basis of respecting the basic law of education development, rationally absorb opinions and make scientific decisions.

3. **Suggestions on talent training mode and training objectives in senior high school**. Based on the above high school talent training mode and training target, and the current situation and environmental education in our country, to realize

the real according to their aptitude, we should make the following efforts: first, if there is the possibility of the elementary education curriculum reform, we need to improve the school education evaluation mode, to guide school characteristic development and the connotation development, and in the school autonomy, the curriculum, teacher training, capital using the right back to school. Second, while guaranteeing the basic right of citizens to receive education, we should promote, advocate and support elite education and characteristic education, so that students with different talents, talents and aspirations can get adequate and appropriate education, so that students can grasp the choice of their own life development. Third, at the national level, we should establish a system and system for the selection and training of top innovative talents, conduct special education for students with special talents, promote outstanding talents and encourage them to stand out. The national policy should be: there is a bottom line, not the top. Fourth, the career planning course will be introduced into the classroom, so that students learn to choose as soon as possible, learn to grasp their own future life path, so that students dare to be responsible for their choice.

4. **Suggestions on the structure of high school education**. For the above-mentioned high school education structure problem, give the following Suggestions. First, we should abandon the thinking mode of "either general education or vocational education", gradually blur the boundary between general education and vocational education, and actively develop comprehensive high schools integrating general education and vocational education. Second, we should fully integrate and make use of the existing resources in our hands to actively build an interchange bridge between ordinary high schools, comprehensive high schools and vocational high schools. Third, while diluting the boundary between ordinary high schools and vocational high schools, schools should also be encouraged to set up special high schools according to their own reality, such as special high schools that are good at arts, science or other technical and artistic education, so as to provide diversified development resources for students.

References

Li, J. (2020). Compulsory educational policies in Rural China since 1978: A macro perspective. *Beijing International Review of Education, 2*(1), 159–164.

Li, J., & Li, J. (2019). Educational policy development in China in the 21st century: A multi-flows approach. *Beijing International Review of Education, 1*(1), 196–220.

Li, J., Yongzhi, Z., Eryong, X., & Zhou, N. (2020). Faculty ethics in China: From a historical perspective. *Educational Philosophy and Theory, 52*(2), 126–136.

Wang, B. Z., & Liu, C. Y. (2009). Reflections on some basic problems of high school education. *Journal of Chinese Education, 19*(7), 86–87.

Zhu, X., & Li, J. (2018). Conceptualizing the ontology of higher education with Chinese characteristics. *Educational Philosophy and Theory, 50*(12), 1144–1156.

Chapter 2
Policy Analysis of the Teacher Policy in Chinese High Schools

This chapter involves the policy analysis of the teacher policy in Chinese high schools. Teachers are the foundation of education. Since the reform and opening up, the state has deeply recognized the importance of the construction of teachers and insisted that teachers should be the first to make the country stronger. Therefore, many teacher policies have been formulated to fundamentally ensure the quality of education. In a series of educational processes, the high school education plays an important role as a bridge between compulsory education and higher education. Teachers are shouldering the historical mission of spreading knowledge, ideas and truth, and the important task of shaping the soul, life and people. They are the first resource for the development of education and the important cornerstone for the prosperity and prosperity of the country, the revitalization of the nation and the happiness of the people. Through the interpretation of these teacher policies, the core characteristics of China's high school education teacher policies can be seen through the following three points that, the requirements for teachers' professional quality are getting higher and higher; gradually improve the treatment of teachers; the teacher policy leans towards the countryside. This chapter analyzes the above three characteristics from four aspects: politics, economy, society and culture.

2.1 The Teacher Policy of High School Education

Since the reform and development, in order to ensure the quality of education, the professional development of teachers and the high-quality development of the teaching staff, the state has formulated and implemented a number of teacher policies, which are aimed at all aspects of the teacher profession.

2.1.1   The Main Contents of the Teacher Policy

1. Teacher selection and employment policy. To obtain qualifications for a teacher of a senior middle school and a teacher of a secondary vocational school, a technical school, a vocational high school or a professional course, one shall have a bachelor's degree or above from a normal college of higher learning or from another university; The educational qualifications required for students to obtain the qualifications for guidance teachers for internship in secondary vocational schools, technical schools and vocational high schools shall be prescribed by the administrative department of education under the state council. The employment of teachers shall follow the principle of equal status of both parties, and the school and the teacher shall sign the employment contract, which clearly stipulates the rights, obligations and responsibilities of both parties.

2. Rights and duties of teachers. Article 7 of the latest revision of *Teachers Law of the People's Republic of China* stipulates that teachers enjoy the following rights: (1) to conduct educational and teaching activities, carry out educational and teaching reform and experiments; (2) to engage in scientific research and academic exchanges, participate in professional academic organizations and fully express their opinions in academic activities; (3) to guide students' study and development, and to assess their conduct and academic performance; (4) to receive wages and remuneration on time, enjoy welfare benefits as stipulated by the state and paid physical leave for cold and summer holidays; (5) to put forward opinions and Suggestions on school education, teaching, administration and the work of administrative departments of education, and to participate in the democracy and management of schools through the congress of staff and workers or other forms; (6) to take refresher courses or other forms of training. (1) to observe the constitution, laws and professional ethics and to be a teacher; (2) to implement the educational policy of the state, observe the rules and regulations, implement the school's teaching plan, fulfill the teacher's employment contract and complete the tasks of education and teaching; (3) to educate students in the basic principles stipulated in the constitution and in patriotism and national unity, in the legal system, in ideology, morality, culture, science and technology, and to organize and lead students to carry out beneficial social activities; (4) to care for and care for all students, respect students' personality, and promote their all-round development in moral, intellectual and physical aspects; (5) to stop ACTS harmful to students or other ACTS that infringe upon the legitimate rights and interests of students, criticize and resist phenomena harmful to the healthy growth of students; (6) constantly raising ideological and political awareness and raising the level of education and teaching.

3. Teachers' training and learning policies. In *the Opinions of the CPC Central Committee and the State Council on Comprehensively Deepening the Reform of the Construction of Teachers in the new era*, it is mentioned that the quality of primary and secondary school teachers should be comprehensively improved to build a high-quality and professional teaching team. Improve the level and quality of teacher training. We push forward supply-side structural reform of teacher training. We focus on cultivating teachers with comprehensive quality and professional expertise at the undergraduate level in compulsory education schools, and on cultivating teachers with outstanding specialty and profound foundation at the graduate level in high school education schools. We vigorously promote the cultivation of teachers at the postgraduate level and increase the enrollment program for master's degrees in education, with a tilt toward the central and western regions and rural areas. According to the needs of the reform and development of basic education, the curriculum system of teacher education should be optimized based on practice, and training of basic teaching skills and skills such as pen-writing, brush-writing, powder-writing should be strengthened. The educational practice of normal university students should be no less than half a year. We need to strengthen the training of teachers in short and weak subjects, special education and bilingual teachers in ethnic minority areas. We need to train all primary and secondary school teachers to promote lifelong learning and professional development. We should change the training methods, promote the organic integration of information technology and teacher training, and carry out hybrid research and training combining online and offline. We should improve the training content, closely combine the practice of education and teaching, organize high-quality training, make the teachers study the teaching and improve the teaching level. We will carry out independent selection of training courses, implement the management of training credits, establish a bank for training credits, and build an "overpass" linking teacher training and academic education. We should establish and improve local teacher development institutions and professional trainers, gradually promote the construction and reform of county-level teacher development institutions based on existing resources and local conditions, and realize the organic integration of training, teaching and research, audio-visual education and scientific research departments. We try to continue to implement the national education program for teachers. Encourage teachers to study abroad (Li, 2020; Li et al., 2020; Sun & Lin, 2014; Tan and Liu, 2016; Zhao, 2019).

4. Teacher training policies. We implement the action plan for revitalizing teacher education, establish a system of normal education with Chinese characteristics, with normal colleges as the main body and high-level non-normal colleges participating, and promote the coordinated education of local governments, institutions of higher learning, and primary and secondary schools. We study and formulate standards for the construction of normal colleges and universities and the running of normal specialties, focus on building a number of normal education bases, and improve the overall running level of normal colleges and universities. We encourage local governments to raise funding standards for students majoring in normal education in a timely manner in light of their actual conditions and raise the level of guarantee for normal education. To effectively improve the quality of students, in line with the relevant policies and regulations, to adopt on-job refund or public funds training, directional training, etc., to attract outstanding young people to actively apply for normal colleges and normal majors. We will improve the policy on publicly funded education for normal university students directly under the ministry of education and adjust the length of service to six years. We will reform the enrollment system and encourage some teachers' majors in colleges and universities with good conditions and high teaching quality to adopt batch enrollment in advance or secondary selection after admission, so as to select outstanding students who are interested in teaching to enter the teachers' major. We need to strengthen the development of teacher education. The awarding units and authorization points of master and Doctor of Education are inclined to normal universities. We strengthen the construction of the teaching staff in teacher education and give preferential support in professional development, promotion of professional titles and employment of posts. The evaluation of normal colleges should reflect the characteristics of normal education, ensure that normal colleges insist on taking normal education as their main business, and strictly control that normal colleges are renamed as non-normal colleges. To ensure the quality of teacher training, we carry out the certification of teacher training.

5. Strengthen the guarantee of teachers and conditions. "The general office of the state council on the new era to promote the reform of ordinary high school education guidelines": to strengthen the construction of teachers. Local governments should further strengthen the overall planning and deployment of their teaching staff and complete the approval of the staffing of ordinary senior high schools by the end of 2020, so as to meet the needs of selecting courses and moving classes. All provinces (autonomous regions and municipalities directly under the central government) should improve the management method of merit pay for ordinary high schools, give appropriate preference to the total amount of merit pay when determining it, and guide schools to improve the distribution method. We should innovate the way of teacher training and focus on improving teachers' ability of implementing new courses, guiding students' development and teaching management.

"The latest revision of teachers' law of the People's Republic of China": in order to ensure teachers to complete the tasks of education and teaching, people's governments at all levels, educational administrative departments, relevant departments, schools and other educational institutions shall perform the following duties; (1) to provide educational and teaching facilities and equipment in conformity with national security standards; (2) to provide necessary books, materials and other educational and teaching supplies; (3) to encourage and assist teachers in their creative work in education, teaching and scientific research; (4) support teachers in stopping ACTS harmful to students or other ACTS that infringe upon the legitimate rights and interests of students (Li, 2020; Li et al., 2020; Sun & Lin, 2014; Tan & Liu, 2016; Zhao, 2019).

Opinions on comprehensively deepening the reform of the construction of teachers in the new era; We improve the long-term linkage mechanism for the salaries of primary and secondary school teachers, take into account the actual income level of local civil servants when determining the total amount of performance-based pay, and ensure that the average salary level of primary and secondary school teachers is not lower or higher than the average salary level of local civil servants. We conscientiously implement policies such as subsidies for difficult and remote areas; fully implement the policy of providing living allowances to rural teachers in contiguous poverty-stricken areas; make differentiated subsidies to schools based on their level of hardship and remote conditions; and encourage localities where conditions permit to raise their subsidies. We improve the social security mechanism for teachers in privately-run schools where schools, individuals and the government reasonably share the funds. Privately-run schools should sign contracts with teachers in accordance with the law, pay their salaries in full and on time, guarantee their welfare and other legitimate rights and interests, and pay social insurance premiums and housing accumulation funds in full for teachers.

6. Rural teacher policy. The notice of the general office of the state council on printing and distributing *the Support Plan for Rural Teachers (2015–2020)*, which mainly contains the following contents:

(1) Comprehensively improve the ideological and political quality and moral level of rural teachers. We will make unremitting efforts to arm the minds of rural teachers with the theoretical system of socialism with Chinese characteristics, further establish and improve the learning system of rural teachers' political theory, enhance the pertinence and effectiveness of ideological and political work, and constantly improve the theoretical quality and ideological and political quality of teachers. We will effectively strengthen party building among rural teachers, and community-level party organizations should give full play to their role as political cores, pay more attention to the education of rural teachers, and appropriately increase efforts to develop party members. We carry out various forms of teacher ethics education, integrating teachers' professional ideals, professional ethics, education on the rule of law, and education on mental health into the whole process of pre-service training, market access, post-service training and management. We put in place a long-term mechanism for the construction of teachers' ethics that combines education, publicity, assessment, supervision, rewards and punishments.

(2) Expand supplementary channels for rural teachers. People's governments at the provincial level are encouraged to establish a supplementary mechanism for rural teachers to be selected through overall planning and unified selection, so as to continue to send a large number of outstanding college graduates to rural schools. We expand the implementation of the special post scheme for rural teachers, with the focus on supporting rural teachers in poor areas in central and western China, such as old ethnic minority areas, border areas, poor islands, and other areas, and raise salary subsidies for teachers with special posts at an appropriate time. Local governments and normal colleges are encouraged to strengthen localized training in accordance with the actual needs of local rural education and adopt a variety of ways to train "one specialist and many able" rural teachers. Graduates of colleges and universities who obtain teacher qualifications and teach in rural schools for a certain period of time shall, in accordance with the relevant provisions, enjoy the policy of tuition compensation and state student loan repayment. All localities shall take effective measures to encourage retired special-grade and senior teachers in cities and towns to teach and give lectures in rural schools, and the central government shall give appropriate support to the special teacher program of the talent support program for outlying and poverty-stricken areas, border areas inhabited by ethnic minorities, and old revolutionary base areas (Li, 2020; Li et al., 2020; Sun & Lin, 2014; Tan & Liu, 2016; Zhao, 2019).

(3) Improve the living conditions of rural teachers. We fully implement the policy of providing living allowances to rural teachers in contiguous poverty-stricken areas

and apply differentiated subsidies to schools based on their level of hardship and outlying areas. The central government will continue to grant comprehensive awards and subsidies. All localities shall implement the policy on the salary and treatment of rural teachers in accordance with the law and pay the housing accumulation fund and various social insurance premiums for teachers in accordance with the law. Within the current institutional framework, we will do a good job in assisting rural teachers with major diseases. We will accelerate the construction of revolving dormitories for teachers in rural schools in remote and difficult areas. Each district should bring the housing of eligible rural teachers into the scope of local housing security as a whole.

(4) Unified urban and rural teaching staff staffing standards. The establishment of teaching staff in rural primary and secondary schools shall be unified and verified in accordance with urban standards, among which the establishment of village primary schools and teaching sites shall be verified and verified in accordance with the ratio of students to teachers and the ratio of class to teachers. Education departments at the county level shall, within the approved total establishment amount, make overall plans for the allocation of teaching and administrative staff in each school according to the class size and source of students, and shall report to the establishment departments and financial departments at the same level for the record. We will make further efforts to favor sparsely populated teaching centers and village primary schools by adjusting staffing and strengthening personnel allocation, with a focus on ensuring full coverage of teachers, and ensuring that rural schools are fully equipped with the national curriculum. Under the circumstance of having qualified teachers, it is strictly prohibited to "make up without making up" and to use temporary employees for a long time. It is strictly prohibited for any department or unit to occupy or occupy the teaching staff establishment of rural primary and secondary schools for any reason or in any form.

(5) The title (position) evaluation and employment to rural schools. All localities should study and improve the conditions and procedures for the evaluation and employment of rural teachers' professional titles (positions), so as to achieve an overall balance of the proportion of posts in urban and rural schools in counties and give more preference to rural teachers. Rural teachers should not make foreign language achievements (excluding foreign language teachers) and publish papers when they are awarded professional titles (positions). They should adhere to the rigid requirements of education as the foundation and moral education as the priority, and pay attention to teachers' moral quality, educational and teaching performance, educational and teaching methods, and front-line practical experience in education and teaching. Urban primary and secondary school teachers to promote the title of senior teachers (post), should be in rural schools or weak schools teaching more than one year of experience.

(6) Promote the mobility of outstanding teachers from cities and towns to rural schools. We will comprehensively promote the reform of the management system for the recruitment of teachers in compulsory education under the supervision of counties and provide institutional guarantee for organizing urban teachers to teach in rural schools. Various approaches and methods should be adopted to guide outstanding principals and key teachers to rural schools, such as regular exchanges,

cross-school competition and recruitment, integrated management of school districts, school alliances, counterpart support, and teachers' walking and teaching in township and central schools. In the county region, teachers from county schools are mainly promoted to exchange and rotate posts in rural schools, and teachers from central schools in towns and villages are mainly promoted to exchange and rotate posts in village primary schools and teaching sites. Effective measures should be taken to keep excellent teachers in rural areas relatively stable.

(7) Comprehensively improve the ability and quality of rural teachers. By 2020, all rural teachers and principals will receive 360 hours of training. We need to incorporate rural teacher training into the basic public service system, ensure funding, and ensure the time and quality of rural teacher training. The people's governments at the provincial level should make overall plans and support training for all staff, and the people's governments at the municipal and county levels should earnestly fulfill their main responsibilities for implementation. We will integrate high-quality resources from institutions of higher learning, county-level teacher development centers and primary and secondary schools and establish a professional development support service system for rural teacher principals. Teachers' moral education as the primary content of rural teacher training, promote teachers' moral education into teaching materials, into the classroom, into the mind, throughout the training process. We will comprehensively improve the ability of rural teachers to apply information technology, actively use remote teaching, digital courses and other information technology means to solve the problem of insufficient quality teaching resources in rural areas, and establish an incentive mechanism to support schools and teachers to use relevant equipment and provide necessary guarantee funds. We will strengthen the training of teachers in subjects in short supply such as music, sports and beauty in rural schools and bilingual teachers in ethnic minority areas. According to the actual needs of rural teachers, the training methods should be improved, including post replacement, network research and study, sending teachers to the countryside, expert guidance, school-based research and study, so as to enhance the pertinence and effectiveness of the training. Since 2015, the state education plan has focused on supporting the training of rural teachers and principals in central and western regions. Encourage rural teachers to study on the job and improve their educational level (Li, 2020; Li et al., 2020; Sun & Lin, 2014; Zhao, 2019).

(8) Establish the rural teacher honor system. The state shall issue certificates of honor to teachers who have taught in rural schools for more than 30 years in accordance with relevant regulations. Provinces (districts, cities) and counties (cities, districts and banners) shall give encouragement to teachers who have taught in rural schools for more than 20 years and for more than 10 years respectively. The people's governments at the provincial level may, in accordance with the relevant provisions of the state, commend teachers who have been engaged in teaching in rural schools for a long time. We will encourage and guide social forces to set up special funds and give material rewards to outstanding teachers who have taught in rural schools for a long time. In the selection and recognition of the education system advanced collective and advanced individual and other aspects to rural teachers. We will extensively publicize the noble spirit of rural teachers to stick to their posts and make silent

contributions, and vigorously create a strong atmosphere of caring and supporting rural teachers and rural education in the whole society.

2.2   The Characteristics of Teacher Policies in Senior High School Education

2.2.1   The Requirements for Teachers' Professional Quality

Teacher is a special profession, not only to teach students good cultural classes, but also to improve his ability to adapt to the society, improve the quality of life. Especially high school education, this age group of students are in an important period of physical and mental development, the guidance of teachers is particularly important. The main purpose of education is to cultivate innovative individuals and cultivate students' innovative spirit and practical ability. The key lies in the innovation of education and the innovation of teachers, which is the process of teachers' exploration and combination and self-construction and needs teachers' ability to develop and improve themselves continuously. Nowadays, students' horizon is more and more broad and their thirst for knowledge is stronger and stronger, so teachers' reserve of professional knowledge should also be increased. The new curriculum reform also puts forward the requirements for teachers' professional quality.

In recent years, the status of teachers has been constantly improved, and more and more people like the occupation, one of the important reasons is that the salary of teachers is constantly improved. In recent years, the state has continuously issued policies to increase the degree of teachers' commendation and strive to improve teachers' political status, social status and professional status. In 2018, the state has repeatedly proposed that teachers' salaries should not be lower or higher than civil servants' salaries. With the proposal of the implementation plan, the implementation of this policy will be promoted step by step. The free normal university student policy and the special post teacher policy are the national special policies for rural teachers. For rural teachers, in recent years, the state has implemented the policies of living allowance for rural teachers and allowance for teachers in difficult and remote areas and raised the subsidy standard for many times. In addition, in order to narrow the gap between urban and rural education, the provinces have also introduced many policies according to their own specific conditions.

In May 1985, the decision of the central committee of the communist party of China on the reform of the education system was promulgated, which put forward the development of normal education and the training of in-service teachers as strategic measures for the development of education.

In June 1999, the central committee of the communist party of China and the state council promulgated the decision on deepening educational reform and comprehensively promoting quality-oriented education, which proposed to build a "high-quality teaching team".

In September 1999, the ministry of education issued the regulations on continuing education for primary and secondary school teachers in order no. 7, which included ideological and political education and teacher ethics cultivation into the content of continuing education for primary and secondary school teachers.

In 2001, the state council promulgated the decision on the reform and development of basic education.

On August 8, 2001, the ministry of education promulgated the "provisions on the administration of teacher qualification certificates", which stipulated in detail the use methods, management agencies, accreditation agencies, certificate specifications, recovery conditions and numbering methods of teacher qualification certificates. The teacher qualification system was formally and comprehensively implemented.

In February 2002, the ministry of education issued the opinions on the reform and development of teacher education during the tenth five-year plan period, emphasizing that teacher education should develop the innovative spirit and practical ability of teachers.

In 2003, the ministry of education issued the tenth five-year plan for the construction of primary and secondary school teachers, which clearly stated the "specialization" of teachers.

In February 2004, the ministry of education promulgated the action plan for the revitalization of education 2003–2007, requiring "new ideas, new curriculum, new technology and teacher ethics training" as the main content of the training of primary and secondary school teachers.

In September 2004, the ministry of education issued the opinions on accelerating the national teacher education network alliance plan to organize and implement a new round of total training for primary and secondary school teachers and the total training plan for primary and secondary school teachers from 2003 to 2007.

In 2007, the ministry of education issued the opinions on vigorously promoting volunteer teaching practice for normal university students.

In 2011, China began to implement a unified examination system for teacher qualifications. In January, the ministry of education issued the opinions on strengthening the training of primary and secondary school teachers. On October 8, the ministry of education issued the opinions on vigorously promoting the reform of teacher education curriculum and the curriculum standards of teacher education (trial), which divided teacher training into three dimensions: educational belief and responsibility, educational knowledge and ability, and educational practice and experience, and standardized the curriculum of in-service teacher education.

In 2013, the Ministry of Education issued "interim measures for primary and secondary school teachers' qualification examinations" and "interim measures for primary and secondary school teachers' qualification registered on a regular basis", the detailed rules for teachers' qualifications examination way of qualification examination, condition, content, such as requirement of primary and secondary school teachers' qualification in 5 years for a cycle, regular registration, broke the teacher's qualification "for life".

In 2014, from the height of realizing the great rejuvenation of the China, general secretary Xi Jinping put forward the basic requirements for teachers to have ideals and convictions, moral sentiments, solid knowledge and benevolence, and put forward new standards for teacher education.

In 2015, the ministry of education released the rural teacher support plan (2015–2020). In October 2017, the ministry of education issued the measures for the certification of normal majors in ordinary institutions of higher learning (interim). With the basic concept of "student center, output orientation and continuous improvement", the three-level certification of teacher education institutions is implemented.

On January 20, 2018, the CPC central committee and the state council issued the opinions on comprehensively deepening the reform of teacher troop construction in the new era.

In 2004, the ministry of education began to implement the "teacher training program for rural senior high school teachers", in which some outstanding fresh graduates were selected to teach in senior high schools in "key counties of national poverty alleviation and development" in the central and western regions among the universities with the qualification of recommending exam-free postgraduate students.

In 2007, the ministry of education asked six affiliated normal universities to implement a program of "free normal students" (renamed "free normal students" in 2018) to train teachers for rural areas.

In December 2008, the 26th meeting of the academic degrees committee of the state council deliberated and adopted the "program for the establishment of professional degrees of doctor of education" and decided to establish and pilot the professional degrees of Doctor of Education in China (Li, 2020; Li et al., 2020; Sun & Lin, 2014; Tan & Liu, 2016; Zhao, 2019).

2.2.2 The Political Perspective

Since the reform and opening up, China's society is stable and harmonious, the economy is booming, and education has made great progress. At present, the principal contradiction in Chinese society has been transformed into the contradiction between unbalanced and inadequate development and the people's ever-growing needs for a better life. Fair and quality education has become the basic premise for the people to live a better life. High school education is a key link between the national education system and the youth's growth. Therefore, the role of high school teachers in this process is particularly important.

The teacher education policy itself has the distinct political nature. Teacher education policy refers to state organs, political parties and political groups in the specific historical period, the teacher education to achieve development goals and tasks and solve the problems that exist in the teacher education development, on the basis of the basic task of the party and the country in a certain historical period, basic principle and basic policy of teachers on teacher training, teacher induction education, teacher training and development action criterion, reflected on the quality of teachers and teacher selection, appointment, evaluation, training, etc. The provisions of the relevant systems and in salary, job title, also meet the requirements of the rewards and punishments and other welfare benefits. Since the reform and opening up, China's teacher education policy has been developing and improving. At present, the formulation of education policy in China is still the formation of mandatory system under the guidance of the government to some extent, which reflects the initiative and decisive role of decision-makers in the policy process. As an important part of education policy, the decision-making process of teacher education policy is similar to that of education policy. Its future development direction will be to decentralize government power, respect the initiative at the grassroots level, fully protect the rights and basic interests of non-state subjects, especially the masses, to participate in the policy process through the interest expression and integration mechanism, and promote the participation of teachers in the formulation of education policies in the field of education. Teacher education bears the responsibility of training teachers for the country. From the moment of its emergence, it has shown its absolute dependence on social politics. The state firmly controls the development of teacher education, so the teacher education policy is the embodiment of realizing the national will. According to the relevant concepts of the theory of "balance and discontinuity", the changes of teacher education policy in China since the reform and opening up embody four forms of institutional changes, namely, system fine-tuning, system replacement, system and system rupture. Teacher education develops from maintaining its "tool value" to satisfying the parallel direction of "tool value" and "personal value", which provides the possibility for training comprehensive people and the possibility for the sustainable and healthy operation of the society. In the future policy adjustment process, humanism is still and must be the long-term emphasis. From a political perspective, this part will analyze the characteristics of China's teacher education policy, especially the teacher policy in high school education, since the reform and opening up, mainly including three aspects: emphasizing the improvement of teacher quality, the policy favoring rural teachers, and the continuous improvement of teacher status (Li, 2020; Li et al., 2020; Sun & Lin, 2014; Tan & Liu, 2016; Zhao, 2019).

1. Teachers' professional concept. In the course of the "cultural revolution", the cause of teacher education suffered a devastating blow, and the majority of teachers suffered severe persecution, which led to a serious shortage of teachers in China for a long time to come, and the quality of teachers is not optimistic. In 1978, the third plenary session of the eleventh central committee of the communist party of China was held successfully, and normal education has since entered the historical development period of putting order behind order. After the reform and opening up, in order to quickly solve the problem of the shortage of teachers, the teacher education policy at that time focused on expanding the scale of teacher education and increasing the number of teachers, so as to meet the demand of the increasingly developing educational career for the number of teachers. Since the 1990s, the bipolar structure of the international community has disappeared, and the world is moving towards multi-polarity. All countries are facing new opportunities and challenges. With the establishment and development of China's socialist market economy system, Chinese society is undergoing profound changes, and the demand for the quantity and quality of talents is increasing. In the late 1990s, the main contradiction of teacher education in China has been changed to the requirement of teacher quality. Therefore, the requirements of high school teachers in China have been changed from "competent in basic teaching work and educational compensation" to "improving teachers' teaching ability and ethics". At the same time, it also puts forward to improve the teachers' "scientific research ability" and some regions "master degree teachers to reach a certain proportion" and other higher level requirements, pay attention to the teachers' ability to implement quality education and improve the ability of lifelong learning and innovation. And the goal of focusing on the overall quality of teachers and improving the level of academic degree (which is different from the previous compensation for academic degree) has been reflected in the relevant policy documents. Although there will be some changes in the composition of the overall quality of teachers, the main tone has not changed.

In teacher education of China has a policy of text content analysis as an example, the central committee of the communist party of China in June, 1999, promulgated by the State Council on deepening education reform and comprehensively promote quality education decision "put forward the construction of 'high quality of the teachers', published in 2003, the Ministry of Education 'primary and secondary school teachers team construction of' tenth five-year plan 'clearly put forward the teachers' specialization', in 2007 the national education career development of the eleventh five-year plan outline further put forward the 'high-quality, new teachers, even teachers increased to the height of the' national educator". With the strategic deployment of "giving priority to developing education and building a powerful country with human resources" proposed at the 17th National Congress of the Communist Party of China (CPC), *the Outline of the National Medium and Long Term Education Reform and Development Plan (2010–2020)* and *the Opinions of the State Council on Strengthening the Construction of Teachers, the Improvement of Teacher Education Quality* has once again become the focus of people's attention.

In September 2012, *the Opinions of the Ministry of Education, the National Development and Reform Commission and the Ministry of Finance on Deepening the Reform of Teacher Education* was proposed to promote the connotation development of China's teacher education, comprehensively improve the quality of teacher education, and cultivate a high-quality and professional teaching team. In August 2013, the interim measures for the qualification examination of primary and secondary school teachers were promulgated and implemented nationwide this year. It requires applicants to improve their qualifications, requiring them to be from "ordinary institutions of higher learning". Normal university students and non-normal university students are subject to the same standard of national unified examination. In high school education, it guarantees the quality of high school teachers in the future by raising the entrance threshold of the teaching profession. The above policy documents to a large extent reflect the importance of the party and the state on improving the quality of teachers in different periods, indicating the country's desire for high-quality teachers.

2. Teachers' ethics. In the early days of reform and opening up, the "gang of four" counter-revolutionary organization was just defeated. China urgently needs a large number of red and specialized socialist construction talents, and the cultivation of talents needs to start with education. For the primary and secondary school teachers, including high school teachers, there must be a red and specialized proletarian teacher team. Therefore, in this period, the improvement of teachers' political literacy has become a very important task, and even in the relevant provisions of teacher training policy, it is regarded as the goal and direction of training together with the professional level. For example, in the opinions on strengthening in-service teacher training in primary and secondary schools issued by the ministry of education in December 1977, it was clearly stated that the relationship between politics and business, between red and professional should be correctly handled, and neither should be biased against the other. The emphasis on political literacy was reflected in subsequent policies. Until now, qualified political literacy is also a prerequisite for qualified teachers (Li, 2020; Li et al., 2020; Zhao, 2019).

With the success of the socialist cause and the emphasis of the society on teacher ethics, the "political level" in the teacher training policy has been changed to "teacher ethics level". In September 1999, the ministry of education issued the regulations on continuing education for primary and secondary school teachers in order no. 7, which included ideological and political education and teacher ethics cultivation into the content of continuing education for primary and secondary school teachers. Since then, the important objectives and contents of teacher training stipulated in the policy of our country must include ideological and political education and teacher ethics cultivation, especially the emphasis on teacher ethics, which has become one of the important training objectives and contents stipulated in the policy. Issued in our country every primary and secondary school teachers professional ethics in all aspects of the political in the teachers' professional ethics, so "improve the level of teacher's ethics" is not to raise the level of negative political just revised goal not only emphasizes the teachers' political orientation, also begin to pay close attention to the teacher to the student, the teaching level of morality and education closely related. In November 2017, the 19th central leading group for comprehensively deepening reform adopted the opinions on comprehensively deepening the reform of teacher team building in the new era (hereinafter referred to as the opinions), which is the first landmark policy document specially designed for teacher team building since the founding of the new China. In the opinion, the following measures are emphasized to comprehensively strengthen the construction of teachers' ethics and style: (1) strengthen the construction of teachers' party branch and party member team, given top priority to the party's political construction, and earnestly implement the requirements of strict party governance to every teacher's party branch and party member; (2) improve teachers' ideological and political quality, innovate teachers' ideological and political education, and enhance the pertinence and effectiveness of ideological and political work. In the process of the construction of high school teachers' ethics, we should establish a perfect supervision and management system, set up diversified supervision subjects, and form a close responsibility management network. In the process of school development, we should enhance the importance of the construction of teacher ethics, enhance the professional ethics and ideological concept of college teachers, form a teaching system of teacher ethics education in education, and determine a clear work goal and work system.

The socialist nature of China's fundamental political system and the people's character of its purpose determine the ultimate goal and fundamental value of the government management system. At the same time, the fair value choice of the fundamental political system also determines the orientation of the value pursuit of education. The embodiment of government management system as a fundamental political system will inevitably affect the realization of educational equity. To understand China's educational equity from the perspective of politics, although it is only one aspect, it is impossible to complete it, but at least it can be seen that the progress of China's educational equity is largely dependent on China's political development, and its effect also depends on the effect of political development and economic development.

Educational equity is an eternal concept pursued by human beings. As a social ideology, the essence of educational equity is people's evaluation of the interest distribution between people in the field of education. It contains the thought of human rights, embodies the subject value, and is manifested as the fair distribution of the educational rights and educational resources of the whole society. It emphasizes the equal share of educational rights and resources held by an educated group relative to other educated groups, and it is the premise for individual educated people to get the corresponding equal share. The educational equity is a mirror of social equity and an extension and embodiment of the value of social, political and economic equity in the field of education. It has become the basic idea in the modern education system and the starting point for countries in the world to formulate educational policies and systems. With the development of The Times, the issue of educational equity has become one of the focuses of Chinese scholars. In recent years, the policy of teacher education has been strengthened to favor rural areas, which reflects China's efforts in education equity (Li, 2020; Li et al., 2020; Sun & Lin, 2014; Tan & Liu, 2016; Zhao, 2019).

Since the reform and opening up, the rural teacher policy in different stages also presents different characteristics because of the social environment at that time. Policy adjustment period (1978–1984), which is the stage of the restoration and reconstruction of the educational order in China, is the preparatory stage of the educational reform. After the cultural revolution, there are two main problems in the development of rural education, that is, a large number of non-qualified teachers and the number of teachers cannot keep up with the development. Therefore, strengthening the construction of rural teachers became an important issue of rural education policy at that time. The ministry of education has issued a series of policy documents to train rural high school teachers. From 1985 to 1992, China's rural education entered a new stage. The decision of the CPC central committee on the reform of the education system was promulgated in May 1985. The decision "pointed out that" the development of teacher education and the training of in-service teachers as a strategic measure for the development of education. In the 1990s, China's teacher training has been standardized, scientific and institutionalized. During this period, China also promulgated a series of laws and regulations to provide legal support and guarantee for the development of rural high school education. From 1993 to 2002, China's education policy mainly carried out the deepening of education reform in accordance with the requirements of the market economy system, political system and science and technology system. During this period, the party and the state attached great importance to teacher education and issued a series of policy documents to promote the process of teacher specialization. At the same time, the reform of rural basic education management system has also entered a new stage. In 2001, the decision of the state council on the reform and development of basic education stipulated: further improve the management system of rural compulsory education. We will put in place a system under the leadership of the state council, with local governments in charge and counties at the top. In October 2003, the third plenary session of the 16th central committee of the communist party of China (CPC) put forward the guiding ideology of China's social development—scientific development concept. The 16th national congress of the CPC was the first to put forward the thought of "overall planning for urban and rural development", which is an important part of the scientific outlook on development. Due to historical reasons, narrowing the gap between urban and rural education development has become an important issue. Centering on the theme of "balanced development between urban and rural areas", the state has promulgated a series of supporting policies for the construction of rural teachers. In 2007, China passed the implementation measures of free education for normal university students directly under the ministry of education (trial), which has made an important contribution to the selection and training of teachers in rural education. In 2010, the outline of the national program for medium - and long-term education reform and development (2010–2020) clearly stated that promoting equity is the basic national education policy. In 2015 through the "rural teacher support plan (2015-2020)" is the policy for rural teachers first to the highest level of guidance documents, the provinces have established to promote rural teacher "had to go to, to retain and a better teacher" of specific measures, from urban and rural development as a whole to the integration of urban and rural development, rural teacher policy to narrow the gap between urban and rural, to realize the balanced development of steering special support, promote the rational allocation of teacher education resources (Li, 2020; Li et al., 2020; Sun & Lin, 2014; Tan & Liu, 2016; Zhao, 2019).

In different periods, the status of teachers is also different, and has a close relationship with the politics, economy, culture and so on. But on the whole, the status of teachers is undoubtedly improving. After the reform and opening up, the state adopted a series of measures to help teachers walk out of the shadow of the "cultural revolution" and improve their status. In March 1978, Deng Xiaoping made it clear at the national science conference that intellectuals, including teachers, were part of the working class. In terms of social propaganda, the positive understanding of teachers' image and the social prestige of teachers are improved. In 1992, Deng Xiaoping's speech in the south and the 14th national congress of the communist party of China (CPC) held in the same year fully launched the construction of China's socialist market economy. The traditional exam-oriented education has been criticized more and more, and the voice of carrying out quality-oriented education has become increasingly louder. With the change of the social cognition of education and the introduction of a large number of foreign educational thoughts, the government and the society have changed their evaluation criteria for teachers, paying more attention to teachers' teaching and research ability, professional quality and professional ethics. In the twenty-first century, the process of globalization is accelerating, the knowledge economy is developing rapidly, and the international competition is becoming fiercer. It has become a common understanding of education in various countries to reverse the excessive emphasis on knowledge imparting and emphasize the cultivation of innovative lifelong learners. In order to meet the globalization and the era of knowledge economy, to cope with the increasingly fierce international competition, and to comprehensively improve the national quality, China formally launched a new round of basic education reform in 2001. Under the new historical background, China is committed to improving relevant policies and regulations, standardizing the behavior of social members, and ensuring that teachers' legitimate rights and interests are not infringed upon. The social status of teachers is confirmed by the law, that is, the law guarantees the social status of teachers by the equality of rights and obligations, the equality and fairness of modern laws, and at the same time, the expectation and evaluation of teachers are reasonably adjusted to continuously improve the status of teachers.

2.2.3   The Economic Perspective

With the rapid development of China's economy, party and state leaders are increasingly aware that the quality of Chinese people has fallen far behind the development level of China's economy. In order to balance the two and make China's development sustainable, the state must pay attention to the improvement of the quality of its citizens. The most effective way to improve the national quality is to improve the quality of teachers in national basic education. In order to achieve this goal, the party and state leaders have formulated relevant policies according to the current specific situation of education in China. The idea of this paper is that for the cultivation of high-quality teachers, the policies introduced are mainly divided into two stages of teacher training: pre-service training in the early stage (the cultivation of normal university students) and in-service training (the expansion of teacher quality). The policy is shifted to rural teachers, mainly because of the introduction of rural teachers living allowance and related welfare policies; The improvement of teachers' system mainly includes the further improvement of senior high school teachers' professional title appraisal, retirement system and performance system.

The construction of high-quality teachers. There are two main systems of teacher education in China: one is pre-service training. In the system, the training of high school teachers is mainly in normal universities and normal colleges, and the graduates are mainly with a bachelor's degree or above. Another system is in-service teacher training. In the past, it was mainly the responsibility of provincial and municipal education colleges and local teacher training schools. But now colleges of education and extension schools are disappearing.

Training of normal university students. In terms of the training of normal university students, we have made a general survey of the development of the whole group of normal university students, and found that since 1997 when the normal university changed to charging fees, the number of outstanding students applying for the examination of normal university has decreased significantly, and the outstanding students of normal university graduates do not engage in education. Because in the same to pay fees, under the conditions of independent career, the teaching profession is more and more not to be valued by people. The fewer excellent talents choose the teaching profession, the more restricted the development of education. Even those who are willing to teach are desperate to move to economically developed areas. Rural primary and secondary school teachers in poor areas are in serious shortage, and the situation of education in poor areas is very sad. In recent years, the regional differences and inter-school differences caused by the unbalanced distribution of teachers in education have triggered a lot of criticism on education, and the voice of the society for educational equality is growing louder and louder (Li, 2020; Li et al., 2020; Sun & Lin, 2014; Tan & Liu, 2016; Zhao, 2019).

In 2007, the policy of free normal university students returned again in this context. Compared with the previous free education for normal university students, this time six normal universities directly under the ministry of education were selected as the pilot of free normal education. The "return" of free education for normal university students, the more profound significance is that it contains the profound thinking of national leaders on the equality and balanced development of education and the overall development of the country. Although higher education is an education category with more attributes of private products, compared with other professional education, normal education still has an obvious attribute of public products, which is determined by the public characteristics of compulsory education. Compulsory education is the education that every citizen must receive in modern society, and it is the starting point for every citizen to realize upward mobility. Only when everyone enjoys high-quality education equally, can the quality of the whole society be improved. The quality of education must depend on the quality of teachers. At present, the state regulates the development of normal education through the intervention mechanism of public finance, which is fundamentally conducive to ensuring the public product attribute of education. The main performance of the country's annual expenditure on education. By observing the fiscal expenditure of countries in 14–18 years, we can find that the national expenditure on education is the largest and the annual increase is huge. Nowadays, with the increasing treatment and social status of teachers, free education for normal university students not only provides opportunities for poor children to go to university, but also attracts more excellent talents to join the teaching team. However, the employment system of normal university students implemented with free education is conducive to ensuring the quality and relative stability of the source of primary and secondary school teachers in poor areas and weak schools. This means that the balanced development of education and educational equity will be more guaranteed (Li, 2020; Li et al., 2020; Sun & Lin, 2014; Tan & Liu, 2016; Zhao, 2019).

Vocational training for teachers. The traditional system of teacher training is a closed, independent and segmented system. Closure refers to the fact that teacher training is not subject to external intervention at the provincial and municipal education colleges, prefecture-level education colleges and county-level education schools. Independence refers to the system of resources, funds and personnel of teacher training with special sources and independent budget under closed conditions. Segmental type refers to the system in which teachers receive training in the bottom-up institutions in primary schools and secondary schools. However, the traditional training mode is a kind of trading mode, which is often conducted by teachers from other schools, and the school gives them a certain salary. Moreover, the traditional teacher training is often linked to teacher welfare, and the form is "tourism+training". The present teacher training is from the closed to the open change. In 1999, the state stipulated that teachers could be trained not only in normal colleges, but also in all universities with the conditions and qualifications to train teachers. After the school is opened, the diversification of subjects and specialties can enable students to learn more knowledge beyond the scope of the curriculum of primary and secondary schools, so as to improve the quality of teacher training.

Pre-service teacher education and in-service teacher education towards integration. The so-called integration refers to the continuous training of pre-service and in-service teachers in normal colleges. Now, it's not exactly the same but I've changed it and I've integrated it in some ways. For example, the on-the-job master's and doctor's degrees in education are produced by normal universities and some comprehensive universities. But some are off-job, which is now free normal education. And the investment funds are increasing year by year. The state allocates only a small part of the money, with the local authorities holding the lion's share. As a result, the opportunities for teacher training have increased, not only with the national training program, but also with the provincial training program (Li, 2020; Li et al., 2020; Sun & Lin, 2014; Tan & Liu, 2016; Zhao, 2019). The policy deviation of our rural teachers is mainly reflected in their subsidies and salary increases, and the intensity of these policies will directly determine whether they will stay in the countryside to teach.

Teachers' expected salary. Theory of compensating wage differentials (going to compensating wage differential) think, seeking to maximize utility when choosing teachers, students will be considered wages and working characteristics of two kinds of factors. Students are willing to go to the country to teach depends on two factors, one is to teach in rural teaching will than urban gained by the additional salary compensation (compensating wage) and incentive policy, the second is the individual mental reservation price (reservation price), namely, if let students go to the original don't want to go to poor working conditions of rural schools, he will be asked to pay the minimum additional salary. However, only when the additional salary compensation provided to rural teachers in the western region exceeds the psychological reservation price of normal university students will normal university students choose to teach in rural areas. The higher the expected salary of normal university students is, the higher the psychological reservation price is. According to the theory of compensatory wage difference, the higher the psychological reservation price is under the given compensatory wage level, the lower the willingness of normal university students to teach in the countryside is. Therefore, the state formulates and implements the living subsidy policy for rural teachers and the support plan for rural teachers, which involves a number of supporting policies for rural teachers, such as further implementing the living subsidy policy for rural teachers, tuition compensation and loan remission for normal university students. As for the expected salary of teachers, Chinese scholars have found that both the willingness of teachers to change schools and the willingness of teachers to quit schools are closely related to the salary of teachers. For rural teachers, the subsidy of living allowance is also one of the important factors affecting their change and withdrawal from schools (Li, 2020; Li et al., 2020; Sun & Lin, 2014; Zhao, 2019).

National policy. In policy terms, the state issued in 2013 rural teachers' living subsidies policy on the implementation of 2013 central no. 1 files required to work in the continuous destitute areas in rural subsistence allowances, teacher give notice required the government at the county level in the continuous destitute areas of township and village schools and school work of rural teachers offer certain allowance for living expenses. In 2015, the support plan for rural teachers once again emphasized the further implementation of the living subsidy policy for rural teachers and encouraged aspiring young people to devote themselves to rural education in many aspects, such as the salary of rural teachers, tuition compensation for college graduates and student loan repayment.

According to the data released by the general office of the ministry of education on the implementation of living subsidy for rural teachers [2018] no. There were 84,700 rural schools and 1.319,200 rural teachers in 725 contiguous counties in poverty-stricken areas, of which 82,500 were subsidized schools and 1.2718 million were rural teachers. The coverage of subsidies for rural schools and teachers was 97.37% and 96.41%, respectively. In 2017, the per capita monthly subsidy for all regions was 322 yuan, an increase of 38 yuan or 13.38% over 2016. Among them, 27.27% of the regions received per capita monthly subsidy of 400 yuan or more, and 68.18% received per capita monthly subsidy of 200–400 yuan.

In order to make teachers more focused on teaching, the state has improved its pay performance system so that excellent talents can be rooted in the education industry. The specific measures include the assessment of professional title, the system of teachers' performance and the improvement of the related welfare system after teachers' retirement.

Professional title system. In order to mobilize the enthusiasm of teachers' work and improve their welfare, the state has established the teacher title system. In 1986, the central professional title reform work leading group forwarding state education commission of the republic of secondary vocational schoolteachers' position and other documents, established the system of secondary vocational schoolteachers' titles. In this reform, we found that the evolution of primary and secondary school teachers' professional title policy showed a trend of unified professional title grade and evaluation standard, the proportion of professional title structure referring to the post setting standard of public institutions, from focusing on teachers in big cities to favoring teachers in rural areas.

Criteria vary from elementary school to the primary and secondary school teachers unified regulation of "moral, intellectual, physical," three basic requirements, that is, love education career, teachers' qualification and teaching ability, physical and mental health, of each grade teachers made specific provision, not only covers the education and teaching experience, teaching ability, also includes the literacy education theory, education teaching research ability and education teaching achievements. The higher the professional title level, the stronger the requirements of all aspects. For rural teachers, professional title evaluation and employment is the "lifeline" of rural teachers. Due to the deviation of the national policy, supporting teaching in the countryside is regarded as an important part of evaluating teachers' professional titles, so more rural teachers can get higher professional titles. And the teacher's title is directly linked to the teacher's performance bonus, so this can better mobilize the enthusiasm of rural teachers.

Merit pays. As for teachers' merit pay, the merit pay system was gradually popularized to schools at all levels after the implementation of the system in 2009. Nowadays, high schools (regular high schools and vocational high schools) also generally implement the merit pay system. In 2018, "on deepening the reform of the new age teachers team construction implementation opinion" clear requirements: the fixed linkage mechanism, primary and secondary school teachers' salaries in the verification performance of total payroll to plan as a whole to consider the local civil servants actual income level, to ensure that primary and secondary school teachers income level is not lower than the average wage level or higher than the local civil servants of average wage income. On February 24, 2019, the general offices of the CPC central committee and the state council issued the implementation plan for accelerating the modernization of education (2018–2022), which set out ten key tasks for promoting the modernization of education. Among them, the fifth key task is to comprehensively strengthen the construction of teachers in the new era., according to the documents to guarantee teachers' salary, the fixed linkage mechanism of the primary and secondary school teachers' salaries, total performance salary of the approved plans as a whole to consider local civil servants actual income level, realize the synchronous with the local civil servants wages adjustment, improve the total primary and secondary school teachers' performance salary allocation system of check and ratify and internal allocation system (Li, 2020; Li et al., 2020; Sun & Lin, 2014; Tan & Liu, 2016; Zhao, 2019).

Retirement system. To improve the treatment of teachers, we should extend the time limit of subsidy on the basis of the existing policy design. According to the current policy, living subsidy is the subsidy for teachers' jobs, which is not included in the calculation base of five social insurance and one housing fund and retirement pension. Teachers are entitled to it when they are on duty, and it will disappear naturally after they leave the post. This policy design has its rationality and matches the current financial resources of different places. Looked from the long-term development of rural teachers, rural teachers at ease rural roots, remove their worries, real should be synchronized to consider its retirement benefits to some extent, such as: the lifetime or exceeds a certain year in remote rural school and school teachers teaching, it is necessary to extend life subsidies to retirement. That is to say, we should not only pay attention to their benefits while on duty, but also pay attention to their benefits after retirement. If the salaries of in-service teachers and the basic pensions of retired teachers plus subsidies for projects other than overall planning are lower than the standards for similar personnel in primary and secondary schools run by the enterprises that have not yet been handed over to the local governments to run primary and secondary schools, the enterprise shall calculate and issue the salaries according to the standards for similar personnel in primary and secondary schools run by the governments. The above - mentioned expenses of the enterprise are allowed to be included in the expenses and deducted before the income tax. According to the standard for the same kind of people in primary and secondary schools run by the government, loss-making enterprises with real difficulties shall be provided with appropriate financial subsidies at the same level. The central loss-making enterprises shall be appropriately subsidized by the central finance.

2.2.4 The Social Perspective

Education is not a natural activity, but an artificial social activity after the development of human society. Education plays a special and unique role in the whole human society and plays a very important role in the development of human society. It cultivates people through the imparting of knowledge and experience between teachers and students and teaching by words and deeds to meet the needs of the development of human society. The relationship between education and society is mutually reinforcing. On the one hand, education is a social activity. The education system is placed in the big system of the society and is influenced by all aspects of the society. Throughout the ages, the system, purpose, content and policy of education are all related to the contemporary social environment and are restricted by the social development. On the other hand, education, through its cultivation of people, sends a batch of talented people with knowledge and quality to the society, improves the moral quality of the people throughout the country, and thus promotes social development. In modern society, teachers have a variety of roles in educational activities, which can be divided into: (1) the role of teaching and educating people: disseminator of knowledge and educator of words and deeds; (2) the role of administrative management: the leader of students' collective, the manager of classroom discipline; (3) the role of psychological guidance: interpersonal relationship coordinator and mental health workers; (4) the role of self-directed: the learner of lifelong learning and the agent of the parent of the student. Teachers are a kind of professional personnel in charge of education that has been differentiated with the development of society. Therefore, the positioning of the role of teachers cannot be separated from the concept of society, and the analysis of high school teachers should focus on the social environment of this group and the relationship between social environment and high school teachers (Li, 2020; Li et al., 2020; Sun & Lin, 2014; Tan & Liu, 2016; Zhao, 2019).

1. Attach importance to the cultivation of teachers' ethics and improve the quality of the teaching staff. Teachers are the disseminators of knowledge, the managers of students, the nurturers of students' minds, and the organizers of teaching activities. Teachers as students values guide, coordinator of the interpersonal relationship and social label, in the teaching activities of the need to improve the understanding of their role, due to the effect of the implicit of the teachers, in order to better cultivate students' good moral character, social requires teachers in professional teaching ability and accomplishment, requires teachers to have more noble virtue and good strengthen.

Teacher's morality refers to the professional ethics of teachers. It is the moral code and code of conduct that all educators must observe in their teaching activities, and the moral concept, sentiment and quality that are compatible with it. Our country from the ancient society, attaches great importance to the moral quality of teachers, teachers in addition to having profound knowledge, but also have a noble sentiment, do with virtue touching, as a teacher. As a result of more than two thousand years of cultural influence, now the society still requires teachers to have noble ethics. Since the reform and opening up, with the development of the economy and the improvement of people's living standards, the state, society and families have paid more and more attention to children's education. Most of the teachers at this time were the outstanding talents and advanced intellectuals trained in the society at that time, and the teachers also kept themselves clean and were teachers. Most of the teachers cared about students and worked conscientiously in the front line of education, which was respected by people. However, in recent years, due to the decreasing of the training level of new teachers and the lowering of the threshold of teacher occupation, the teaching team gradually becomes uneven, and some teachers' moral quality declines. "Class lectures, suggest that students paid tutor", "gift" from parents corporal punishment or corporal punishment in disguised forms such as news, led to the majority of parents, the social from all walks of life to teacher's reputation gradually decreased, and with the development of the education situation and the social public opinion, from all walks of life to teacher's professional ethics requires a higher demand.

Morality is the first step in teaching. Teachers in educational activities are representatives of the society, and they are entrusted by the society to cultivate talents needed by the society, so as to infuse the society with excellent construction power in line with the expectation of social development. The implementation of teacher ethics training and the practice of virtue cultivation are the expectations of the society for teachers under the development of the new era, and the transformation of such expectations into actual actions of teachers depends on the promulgation, implementation and practical implementation of relevant teacher policies.

In 2014, the Ministry of Education issued *the Measures for Dealing with Violations of Professional Ethics by Primary and Secondary School Teachers*, which drew "ten red lines" for primary and secondary school teachers. This policy was the first to standardize teachers' professional ethics with high standards and strict requirements, which laid the foundation for teachers' moral cultivation and set a new social trend. In 2018, the Ministry of Education issued *the Ten Guidelines on Teachers' Professional Behavior in the New Era*, and in 2019, the Ministry of Education and other seven departments jointly issued *the Opinions on Strengthening and Improving the Construction of Teachers' Ethics in the New Era*. All these documents show that the current society attaches great importance to the cultivation of teachers' ethics. And in full to deepen the reform of the new age teachers team construction put forward "outstanding virtue, improve teachers' ideological and political quality and professional ethics level in the first place," the basic principle, embodies the national attention to the height of the teachers' quality, further standardize the teacher working behavior, promote the teachers' ethics strengthen construction enthusiasm.

2. Policy shift to rural teachers, improve the living treatment of rural teachers. To analyze the reasons for the deviation of education policy from rural teachers, it is necessary to connect rural teachers with the social environment at that time. Since the founding of the People's Republic of China to the present, the number of Chinese teachers in urban and rural distribution is very uneven, on the whole, the quality and quantity of rural teachers is far lower than that of urban areas. Since ancient times, the mainstream concept of the Chinese public is that the urban infrastructure conditions are good, the life is convenient, the development opportunities are more, the comprehensive conditions are many times better than the rural areas, many people engaged in education work mostly choose to work in the city, which leads to the rural areas with fewer teachers and poor teaching standards. At the same time, the status of urban teachers is vastly different from that of rural teachers. The society generally respects urban teachers more, while rural teachers are often treated with contempt and indifference. Rural teachers have low social status and poor pay, so it is difficult to attract excellent teachers to teach in rural areas. Although a small number of people voluntarily choose to go to the countryside to teach, it still does not change the status quo of excellent educators gathering in cities. Under the influence of this social environment, more and more excellent teachers go to work in cities, while fewer teachers stay in rural areas. Moreover, with the widening gap between urban and rural education hardware facilities and software, the education level in cities is getting higher and higher, and the gap between rural education level and urban education is getting bigger and bigger. However, the cost of education is still sinking in the economically developed urban areas. Due to such problems as poor rural conditions and insufficient funds, rural teachers still have such problems as insufficient survival guarantee, great economic pressure, heavy teaching tasks, unbalanced allocation of subjects and lack of professional training. By the beginning of the twenty-first century, the inequality, injustice and unfairness of urban and rural education in China had become more and more prominent (Li, 2020; Li et al., 2020; Sun & Lin, 2014; Tan & Liu, 2016; Zhao, 2019).

Since the beginning of the twenty-first century, the social voice for educational equality has been growing louder and louder. In this era, China's education policies follow the concept of people-oriented and educational equality, and various education policies gradually incline to rural education and rural teachers, leading to the rapid development of rural education. For example, the decision of the state council on further strengthening rural education issued in 2003 reflects the government's concern for rural education and the importance of educational equity. Although educational equity has gradually become the consensus of the whole society and the government has been making efforts to this end, the development speed of rural education still cannot keep up with the speed of social development due to the high development of social economy in the information age, and the problem of education imbalance still exists. In the problems of rural education, the most important factors hindering its development are the small number of teachers and the low teaching level. Therefore, to develop rural education, the problems of rural teachers should be solved first. After entering the new era, the goal and theme of social construction is to complete the building of a moderately prosperous society in all respects, and the current situation of rural teachers is an important factor restricting the integration of urban and rural education development, and also becomes an obstacle on the road to complete the building of a moderately prosperous society in all respects. At this stage of reform and development, the government's policy towards rural teachers has been continuously deepened, and the policy focus has become more specific, effective and comprehensive. Various policies are flexible and coordinated, and each policy has its own emphasis, thus a relatively complete policy system for rural teachers has been established. For example, the general office of the state council issued the support plan for rural teachers (2015-2020), implemented the support plan for teachers in the central and western regions, and expanded supplementary channels for rural teachers.

3. Improving the salary and welfare system for teachers and improving their social status. Since the reform and opening up 40 years ago, in the development process of China's teacher policy, an important feature of the teacher policy is to enhance the occupational attraction with the status and treatment of teachers, which promotes the professional development of teachers and the prosperity of the national education cause through the supplementary approach of attracting excellent talents. But in recent decades, due to the rapid development of economy, the teachers group of average wage growth rate is low, the welfare system hasn't caught up with the pace of social development, teachers' treatment in the social labor industry no longer has the advantages of not only failed to attracting talent teaching effectively, some teachers also choose to resign from the work, change other professions to develop.

At the same time, the family education concept of modern society, great changes have taken place in today's society is even more important than any time before the emphasis on respect for students, student rights maintenance, when conflict, teachers and students prefer to maintain public opinion students, teachers and the construction of individual, family, social relationships between closely linked, when society too much emphasis on students' rights, influence gradually reduce the teachers in the education activities, and even appeared in some places and the school teacher can't tube student, afraid to criticize the phenomenon of education students, let students, teachers' professional status has been challenged. Teachers are only a part of social division of labor. Like other members of society, they need each other functionally, and those who are needed by the society need certain rights and status from the society. The decline of teachers' social status not only affects the rate of teachers' career choice, but also has a negative impact on education and teaching activities.

Teachers assume the function of teaching and educating people in the society. The value of teachers' labor does not directly create social wealth but cultivates people who need social development through educational activities. As a social spokesman, the role played by teachers is always a reflection of the social development, cultural background, interpersonal relationship, organizational form and other factors in a specific period. In the current era, knowledge, talents, innovation and technology have become the main driving force of social development, so the value of teachers is closely linked with the degree of social development. Teachers professional with public attribute, bear the national mission and duty of public education services, but the teacher is, first and foremost, as a person, then as a social spokesperson exists, therefore, requires teachers to fulfill public responsibilities before, should first ensure that the teacher as a person need good work environment and salary welfare level. Only by enhancing teachers' political status, social status and professional status, can teachers give full play to their social value of teaching and educating people, achieve the unity of their social value and personal value, and promote the development and progress of the society.

From the perspective of the development course of China's education and teacher policy since the reform and opening up, the formulation and implementation of teacher policy are closely related to the social environment at that time. Policy formulation is to solve the problems that exist in the society, teacher's professional development and the construction of teachers in our country must be focused on the problems existing in the teachers' professional development, give full consideration to the social reality and the future society to the needs and expectations of teachers group, make reasonable and effective policy, building integrated flexible and gradually perfect the policy system, promoting the development of the education teachers in China.

2.2.5 The Cultural Aspect Analysis

The teacher policy of Chinese high school education has many characteristics, but from the perspective of culture, we can see that it is historic, unique and social. Chinese culture is extensive and profound, especially in education, so teachers also play a very important role, and teachers are also one of the oldest human occupations. The word "teacher" first appeared in the book of learning: "the teacher therefore learns for the king." In ancient times, teachers were called "teachers". The teacher policy of Chinese education has undergone many changes. For example, in ancient times, teachers were generally not very high in economic status, which was inseparable from the social form. Teachers were divided into official and private teachers. In modern times, the main feature of teacher education policies is that they highlight the characteristics of teachers and attach importance to the cultivation of moral quality of normal university students. In some policies, advanced ideas such as gender equality, student autonomy and democratic management emerged (Li, 2020; Li et al., 2020; Sun & Lin, 2014; Zhao, 2019).

During the "cultural revolution", under the wrong guidance of the policy, the cause of teacher education in China reached a difficult position. From 1966 to 1977, the national normal education colleges and universities did not recruit students for several consecutive years. Many schools have been forced to close, and teacher education and the rule of law have largely ground to a halt. After the reform and opening up, the country pays more and more attention to the legal construction of teacher education policy. In 1978, the ministry of education issued the opinions on strengthening and developing teacher education, emphasizing the centenary plan of flourishing teacher education. In 1980, the national conference on normal education was held to face up to the chaotic situation of normal education during the cultural revolution, summarize the experience of teacher education construction in China in the past 30 years, and further clarify the training objectives of normal colleges at all levels through actions.

The reform of the education system promulgated by the former state education commission in 1985 is an important milestone in the historical development of teacher education in China. The decision stipulates that "the development of teacher education and the training of in-service teachers is a strategic measure for the development of education". Thus, China's teacher education policy gradually becomes mature and even rises to the height of laws and regulations. The 1993 teachers' law of the People's Republic of China gives teachers their own special law. Subsequently, the regulations on teacher qualifications promulgated and implemented in 2000 ensured the large-scale implementation of the teacher qualification system in the country in the form of administrative regulations.

Teachers have made a great contribution to the cause of education in China, so in order to recognize the teachers' pay and the generation of teachers' day. In the modern history of China, there have been many different dates as teachers' day, and until 1985, the ninth session of the sixth National People's Congress standing committee passed the state council on the establishment of teachers' day proposal, determined the annual September 10 as China's teacher's day. Since teachers' day is not a traditional Chinese program, there will be different celebrations every year, there is no unified, fixed form. School, teachers' day will be held on the day of teachers' day to celebrate the general assembly, teachers issued certificates, held activities; Students will spontaneously prepare flowers, paintings and other surprises for the teacher, and the teacher took photos, to express the sincere wishes and sincere greetings to the teacher.

The social value of teacher's labor refers to the significance and function of teacher's labor in the process of education and teaching. It is the main attribute of the value of the teacher's labor, and it is also the symbol of the teacher's social status and personal value. The work of teachers has great social value. Teachers play an irreplaceable role in the growth of individuals and the continuation, progress and development of human civilization. The specific performance in the following aspects: first, the teacher's labor to the continuation and development of human society plays a link and bridge role in the past and the future; Second, education is a work of value guidance, representing the pursuit of a social ideal and the direction of progress. Teachers play an important role in participating in social life and serving the society.

To analyze the teacher policy of Chinese high school education from the aspect of culture, the emphasis is on the relationship between teachers and culture, and the contribution of teachers to cultural inheritance and cultural development. Therefore, the characteristics of teachers in the aspect of culture should be analyzed first. First of all, teachers are the product of culture, and they undertake the main task of spreading culture. His prerequisite is to receive cultural edification and cultural education, so as to basically master the main ideas of culture, master the knowledge of the subject and specialty, and cultivate the sense of belonging of the national culture. Therefore, as a product of culture, teachers are often unconsciously restricted by mainstream cultural values, and their acceptance of cultural values requires both conscious awareness and more unconscious awareness. Secondly, teachers promote the development of culture, but teachers can promote the development of culture through labor. Moreover, the promotion of culture by teachers should be comprehensive, including two aspects: the handling of the relationship between teachers and society and between teachers and nature, because culture itself is the result of conquering society and conquering nature. The above can be concluded that the relationship between teachers and culture is mutual integration.

In the context of contemporary culture, the labor characteristics of teachers are divided into the following aspects: first, teachers and the main body of learning - students in mutual communication. Students' life, wisdom, health, character, will and mental outlook, as well as students' happiness in school, all depend on teachers' level and ability, responsibility and wisdom. Second, education is a long-term task, today's teachers do the education results, not the day or tomorrow to see, but through a long process to see the results. What the teacher does, what he says, and what he makes the students learn, can only be revealed through the accumulation of time. Three, teacher's mission is to use your personality to the student's personality is the most effective, the most magical and most benefit and the effect of each student's background environment is different, so the teacher wants to know in advance the children's growth environment, and everything they had experienced, so as to influence students, from the source to develop their unique personality; Students are always changing, is always new, today and yesterday may not be the same. Therefore, teachers should always pay attention to students' emotions, consciousness and mental state, and keep up with the pace of changes in students' "ideological era".

In the context of multiculturalism, when confronted with many educational policies, teachers should have good cultural quality, including profound professional knowledge, extensive cultural knowledge and theoretical basis of teaching, high professional ethics, strong educational research quality and teaching research ability. Teachers should not only have extensive knowledge, but also be familiar with the basic social science, natural science and other aspects of knowledge, so as to be knowledgeable. To carry out quality-oriented education and cultivate students' comprehensive quality and innovation ability, it is of vital importance for teachers to have a wide range of knowledge. With the reform of teaching materials, the relation between adjacent subjects is strengthened day by day, and the arts and

sciences permeate each other. Therefore, teachers should pay attention to the communication with other subjects, create an open teaching situation for students, and
cultivate students' innovative consciousness and ability. The more profound the
teacher's knowledge, the more can inspire students' innovative thinking. The key
is to modernize the educational concept and set up the people-oriented educational
concept.

Teacher culture is the core part of the school culture, is also the key to Chinese
high school education, is a teacher in the process of long-term education practice,
on behalf of the teachers group which is formed by the common value orientation
and professional behavior characteristics, become the key and the groups of teachers
a kind of spiritual strength, it even decides the development trend of school and
its teachers and students. Usually the teacher culture displays the unique, has the
traditional color characteristic. Teacher culture refers to "the values, behavior habits,
knowledge skills and language symbols of teachers that are different from those
of other professional groups". According to culture, teacher culture can be divided
into material culture, institutional culture and spiritual culture. Teacher culture can
be divided into surface teacher culture, middle teacher culture and deep teacher
culture. The deep teacher culture is the core and soul of the teacher culture, which
reflects the deep values, ways of thinking and moral trends contained in the teacher
behavior. The teacher culture comes from the teacher's life scene, which is the value
concept and behavior pattern formed in the teacher's life scene. The teacher's life
scene is unique, it is difficult to form the teacher culture without the teacher's life
scene. Teacher culture reflects the survival, growth and development of teachers. The
process of teacher development is the process of teacher culture development (Li,
2020; Li et al., 2020; Sun & Lin, 2014; Tan & Liu, 2016; Zhao, 2019).

The purpose, significance and value of the cultural conscious pursuit of human
development and the pursuit of human freedom and liberation is the reflection of the
rational spirit in the process of human's pursuit of their own survival and development
and arrival at the kingdom of freedom. Cultural consciousness pursues the development of human beings as an end rather than a means. Teacher's cultural consciousness
is the extension of cultural consciousness in the study of teacher's culture, and also
the deepening and development of cultural research in the study of teacher's culture.
Teacher's cultural consciousness refers to the behavior process of teacher's professional cultural belief, rational understanding and code of conduct formed by teacher's
reflection on himself and his teaching culture in the field of education and teaching
life. Cultural consciousness is the self-awakening, self-reflection and self-creation
of culture. The core of teachers' cultural consciousness is rational reflection and
conscious practice. In terms of culture, teachers' cultural awareness is manifested
in their rational attitude of conscious practice, in practice, it is manifested in their
autonomy of cultural selection and creation, and in cultural creation, they realize the
life growth and independent development of teaching subjects.

In terms of culture, teachers have made great contributions to Chinese high school
education, which is full of great enlightenment. Patriotism is the ideal goal of teachers
and one of the sources of motivation. Patriotism is the humanistic care of Chinese
intellectuals. Patriotism constitutes the core content of teachers' personality ideal.

The teacher culture also needs to broaden the vision, insist on the unity of inheritance and innovation, treat and choose the traditional culture needs to carry on the dialectical choice, for the cause of education in our country to a higher level.

2.3 Problems and Suggestions of High School Teachers

2.3.1 The High School Teachers Education Status

The highest proportion of graduate students is in Beijing, where 30.1% of high school teachers have a graduate degree or above. Xinjiang has the lowest proportion of postgraduates, at 4.2%. In the proportion of graduate students, the first few accounted for a ride in the dust. The top four were Beijing (30.1%), Shanghai (24.0%), Tianjin (17.7%) and Jiangsu (17.4%), while there were no provinces even above 15%. However, in the traditional sense, the big provinces in the college entrance examination, such as Henan and Shandong, have almost no advantage in this index. It can be said that the ratio of graduate students reflects the imbalance of the teaching quality of high schools in China remarkably, which needs to be solved in the future. In 2018, only 9.8% of all high school teachers in China had a master's degree or above, far below the level of top provinces. This shows that the talent of graduate teachers has a very obvious trend of concentration in big cities. At the micro level, this is a matter of course and hard to avoid

First, we need teachers trained under the normal university student policy to be more professional. However, at the same time, we also need graduate students of various professional levels to join the teaching team, so that the same teaching content, can present more angles, more diversified, more levels of understanding, to promote the training of students with stronger comprehensive quality.

This problem should be solved from several aspects: (1) Under the existing normal university student policy, many teachers who have become teachers through normal university students can continue to study for on-the-job pedagogy graduate students according to the policy. But at the same time, the threshold can also be opened, for this part of teachers of non-normal university students, open the opportunity to study in the pedagogy graduate school, promote the in-service teachers more professional quality. In particular, many experienced teachers who have been teaching for many years encourage them to continue learning. To promote the development of teacher education research and make "front line" experienced teachers join the teaching and research team, so that "teaching" and "research" can promote the development of each other.

However, for teachers in some areas, the teaching staff in schools is already insufficient. Many teachers are busy with their work and find it difficult to find time to continue their professional study. And for many teachers with long working hours, their working and living patterns are basically fixed. Therefore, under the corresponding policies, the policy effect needs a long time. Therefore, synchronous assistance is needed to introduce graduate teachers from outside.

(2) For students of non-normal majors, the industry requirements cannot be lowered, but they are actively encouraged to participate in the work of teachers. In the case that the salary of teachers cannot change too much, we can establish a channel between the school and the society, introduce a part of graduate students who are interested in teaching and work in all fields of society and all industries, build a platform, implement the method of individual employment, and participate in teaching activities. The plan requires the school to improve the teaching mode simultaneously, and at the same time, the requirements of the social staff also need to have the corresponding norms, such as whether to require teacher certification, etc. But in many relatively underdeveloped regions, the proportion of graduates in the social work force is usually small. Schools may not be able to bring relevant talents into society. This requires cooperation across regions.

(3) Online teaching has emerged in Sichuan province. But at the same time, many problems have arisen. For example, there are differences in the difficulty acceptance of courses in different regions, differences in the course progress, the follow-up after the course, such as the follow-up of exercises after the class, and the delineation of teachers' functions under the video. Therefore, the network teaching method still needs to be further coordinated and improved. Now, there are support programs, support programs. In contrast, as a program that can rapidly change the areas with backward education and poor teacher resources, it is necessary to further improve the policies related to the incentives for supporting teachers and alleviate the concerns of more teachers. At the same time, for the very poor areas, teachers can be strengthened to work in the mobile, do not need to stay in the area for a long time to teach, so that more excellent teachers can be relatively attracted to join them.

2.3.2 Suggestions on the Teacher System

On January 22, 2018, the Ministry of Education released *the Key Points of the Department of Teachers' Work of the Ministry of Education in 2018,* pointing out that: "the reform of teachers' professional titles will start in the middle vocational schools, and then be carried out in major universities after relevant results are achieved. Later reforms may include job-by-job employment, contract management, and the elimination of existing subsidies and subsidies." However, there has been no relevant reform in primary and secondary schools, and I suggest that secondary schools should include the teacher performance appraisal system under the employment system.

Performance evaluation refers to a set of formal, structured system, used to measure the effect, evaluation, teachers' work related system characteristics, behavior and result, examine the actual performance of teachers, understanding of the potential development of teachers, in order to obtain the common development of teachers and organization, is to adopt a series of scientific method, according to work goals or performance goals, to assess the teachers' working condition, such as work situation, the development of the degree of job responsibilities, work, etc., finally will assess the results of the feedback to the process of teachers.

For teachers themselves, through the performance appraisal of teachers, teachers can not only see their own achievements, but also see their own shortcomings and shortcomings, so as to adjust their teaching methods, class management, etc., in order to do better. Performance appraisal can identify the potential of teachers by objective methods and can provide guidance for teachers' career direction according to their different characteristics, so as to enable teachers to give full play to their potential. At the same time, after the completion of performance appraisal, the school can organize targeted learning according to some common problems. For "good prospects", provide opportunities for additional training to improve teacher performance.

Performance appraisal can also improve the work efficiency of teachers, such as the following two: first, set work goals. The goal itself has a great incentive effect, can prompt people to change the need into motivation, let the behavior toward a certain direction, and finally achieve the goal. And in the design of the goal, can go to the achievement center, design multi-level goal. Second, merit pay. Link the salary with the result of performance appraisal to stimulate the work motivation of teachers.

For schools, it can improve the level of school culture construction and teachers' internal information exchange. Involvement in the process of performance appraisal should be teachers, from performance appraisal target, forming performance appraisal plan, the process of information feedback, the performance appraisal, as well as to the use of the assessment results, requires teachers to participate in, to teachers and administrators communicate with each other, form a "participatory" management, fully embodies the respect for teachers, improve the level of the school culture construction and internal communication.

All teachers in the whole process of performance appraisal, performance appraisal and assessment must promote take the student as the main body of education as a prerequisite, in all links of performance appraisal, from the formulation system, to evaluate job performance, and a series of links, is always around the target, which can guide teachers to work hard in the direction of education goals, finally to make teachers more a sense of belonging and a sense of achievement.

Therefore, performance appraisal must be teacher-centered and education-oriented in the end. At least achieve the following objectives: (1) promote the development of the teacher profession. Fair, fair and scientific performance appraisal is an effective means to promote teachers' professional knowledge and improve their professional skills. The appraisal results are timely and positively fed back to the evaluated teachers, so that teachers can accept and recognize them and have an objective and comprehensive understanding of themselves. To improve performance appraisal, teachers should fully recognize their own shortcomings, timely adjust their teaching behavior, improve teaching methods and methods, strengthen the training of learning professional knowledge and professional skills, and promote the development of professional ability of teachers. (2) improve the professional ethics of teachers. The professional ethics of teachers should be included in the evaluation scope, and a diversified evaluation system should be established to promote teachers to continuously improve their own professional ethics. Dedication and patriotism, as a teacher, respect students, with The Times and so on. (3) to promote the harmonious development of teacher-student relations. Through performance appraisal, it can reflect students' learning attitude, understand their needs, understand students' personality differences, and understand teachers' teaching level in students' mind, so as to enhance understanding, trust, mutual respect and encouragement, and provide possibility for the establishment of teacher-student relationship of mutual learning and friendship. (4) promote the exchange and reflection of education. Performance appraisal requires teachers' participation, that is, teachers' self-evaluation. Teachers' self-evaluation is conducive to arousing teachers' enthusiasm and initiative. Through the analysis of behaviors in the education process, teachers can actively reflect on their own behaviors in the education and teaching process, discover the root causes of problems, and make clear the direction of improvement and development. Performance appraisal can promote teachers to actively communicate with students and colleagues and have a comprehensive understanding and grasp of themselves, so as to do better in future educational performance activities (Li, 2020; Li et al., 2020; Sun & Lin, 2014; Tan & Liu, 2016; Zhao, 2019).

In the process of teacher appointment, it is necessary to establish a strict appointment procedure and establish a reasonable and standard appointment procedure. In accordance with the principle of two-way selection, the establishment of posts according to demand and the establishment of recruitment procedures: the first stage of intra-school employment, the second stage of inter-school employment, the third stage of the education committee to organize two-way negotiations, the fourth stage will be employed staff recommended to the school not hired. The employment system is conducive to the flow of excellent teachers and the competition among teacher groups. At the same time, in the aspect of salary, the autonomy of the school can be increased within a certain range. Relative to a career, you can be more flexible in terms of salary. The salary welfare of hire system teacher is paid by the unit, undertake adjusting appropriately according to the difference of teacher job content, holiday welfare is similar with in making up teacher, but allowance, salary can be lower than in making up teacher.

The implementation of the recruitment system, the former staff and workers to distinguish, different management, the implementation of full floating, break the egalitarianism distribution system, according to the post responsibility and workload of the pay structure salary system, the individual income of the staff and their own labor quantity and quality closely combined. Under the employment system of teacher performance appraisal system, the promotion opportunities of teachers are fairer. Under the enterprise establishment, the number of teachers with various professional titles is determined according to the number of assessments. There is a corresponding fixed relationship among the organization, establishment, post and personnel. In the case of limited number of places, the professional title evaluation and promotion opportunities refer to the teaching age, seniority, and it is difficult for new teachers to be promoted. Under the employment system, the number of teachers is no longer limited by the superior but depends on the number of people who have reached the performance score standard, which provides a fairer opportunity for teachers to be promoted and makes the profession of teachers full of new vitality. At the student level, the employment system and performance appraisal system also help to help underachievers and reduce educational inequality. Under the current education system, students whose academic performance is "not up to par" tend to be marginalized, get little attention from teachers, have low test scores for a long time, have low self-esteem and are less motivated to learn. Compared with the previous single salary index that only considers teaching years and educational background, the performance appraisal system takes into account the students' performance, average score, and passing rate, etc., which encourages teachers to pay attention to the students' overall academic level, makes teaching plans comprehensively and fairly, and helps underachievers.

At present, some regions in China have tried out the teacher performance appraisal system of the employment system. There are still many problems in the system, but it can be optimized and improved continuously. Among them, the most crucial is the establishment of performance appraisal. If there is deviation in this link, it will deviate from the direction under the magnification of employment system and performance. On compulsory education in 2009 since the implementation of performance pay policy, perfecting the performance appraisal system optimization, in addition to the legal responsibilities and ethics considerations, constantly to join the other indicators, comprehensive measure of teaching level, and through the adjustment of each index proportion and collective bonuses and other measures to solve possible wage inequality in the process, affect the team cooperation and other issues. Performance-based pay implementation plan in Shanghai as an example, the teacher's ethics, attendance, serious degree of teaching, scientific research achievements, the teaching quality, personal counseling, and all kinds of allowances, assessment index elaboration to the performance of the amount and proportion, through self-evaluation, mutual, students and parents feedback, reply and set up comprehensive evaluation in the form of the inspection team's help to the further implementation of the policy.

References

Li, J. (2020). Compulsory educational policies in Rural China since 1978: A macro perspective. *Beijing International Review of Education, 2*(1), 159–164.

Li, J., Yongzhi, Z., Eryong, X., & Zhou, N. (2020). Faculty ethics in China: From a historical perspective. *Educational Philosophy and Theory, 52*(2), 126–136.

Sun, D. F., & Lin, Z. F. (2014). Status quo and suggestions on the survival and development of rural teachers. *Research on Teacher Education, 26*(06), 40–46.

Tan, H. L., & Liu, Y. (2016). Characteristics, problems and Suggestions of rural teacher policy development. *Teaching and Management, 16*(16), 13–15.

Zhao, G. W. (2019). Research on the necessity of teacher ethics construction for improving teachers' quality under the new situation. *Career, 19*(25), 60–61.

Chapter 3
An Analysis of the Curriculum and Textbook Policy in Chinese High Schools

This chapter focuses on an analysis of the curriculum and textbook policy in Chinese high school. In particular, the analysis of curriculum and textbook policy in Chinese high school education, the analysis on the causes of curriculum and teaching material system in senior high schools in China, the current situation of high school textbooks and curriculum, and questions and suggestions on high school curriculum and textbooks have been offered in this chapter to explore the rationale of the curriculum and textbook policy in Chinese high schools.

3.1 An Analysis of Curriculum and Textbook Policy in Chinese High School Education

3.1.1 Reform and Change of High School Education Curriculum and Teaching Materials

Education is the cornerstone of social progress. Since the reform and opening up, China has made remarkable achievements in the fields of economy, science and technology, culture and education. The development level and quality of basic education is the basic symbol to measure the overall quality of the people and the degree of civilization of modern society, and also the fundamental symbol for China to become a talent power. High school education is the continuation of compulsory education and plays an important role in the basic education stage. The adjustment of curriculum structure is an important task in the reform of basic education curriculum, which is related to the speed of China's economic development and the achievement of socialist construction. The innovative progress of education has undoubtedly positive significance for human progress and the development and progress of all industries. Curriculum reform refers to the transformation of curriculum and teaching materials according to a certain point of view. The high school curriculum reform is the

J. Li and E. Xue, *Education Policy in Chinese High Schools*, Exploring Education Policy in a Globalized World: Concepts, Contexts, and Practices, https://doi.org/10.1007/978-981-16-2358-5_3

pioneer of the elementary education curriculum reform and vane, lead the development direction of our country elementary education curriculum reform, curriculum structure as the text form of curriculum reform idea, bearing and affects the value and function of the course, reflect and change the way of driving the ordinary high school education, is the high school curriculum reform idea and mode of educational intermediary bridge.

"Curriculum structure" is an important term to describe school curriculum and an important indicator to reflect the demands of educational reform. Since the founding of new China over the past 70 years, from the national curriculum mainly to the tertiary course pay equal attention to, from a single subject to subject curriculum and activity curriculum, integrated course diversity coexist, from academic and compulsory course to common and meet the demand of students on the basis of multi-level kinds of optional courses, ordinary high school curriculum structure in the reform of our country gradually optimized, perfect. The reform of high school curriculum structure is not only the embodiment of the educational concept, curriculum concept and student concept of Chinese educators, but also the curricular reflection of the development of China's education, the orientation of the nature of high school education, and the changes in the goals and tasks of high school education.

The historical evolution of the curriculum plan. The "seventeen years" after the founding of new China is an exploratory period of socialist construction, and also a transitional period of reforming the old education system and creating a new socialist education. During this period, by absorbing, transforming and drawing lessons from the educational experience of the liberated areas and the Soviet Union, the national unified and subject-centered curriculum structure system was gradually established in ordinary high schools. However, the eager pursuit of success and departure from national conditions exposed many problems in this educational revolution. Back in 1963, the Ministry of Education proposed *"Full-time Middle and Primary School Teaching Plan (draft)"*, summarizes the work since the founding of the people's education, and on the setting of course type has made a major breakthrough, allowing high school on the basis of the compulsory course action set elective courses, can according to the voluntary and hobby grade three choose a door, door or two courses without examination. This regulation is of great significance for getting rid of the compulsory course structure model in the early Soviet system. However, during the following decade of "cultural revolution", school education suffered a severe blow, and the achievements of curriculum reform in the early stage of new China failed to continue and develop (Choe et al., 2004; Guo & Wang, 2019; Li & Li, 2019; Liu, 2020).

In May 1977, Deng Xiaoping, in a speech entitled "respect for knowledge, respect for talent", stressed that "education should be conducted on two legs, with attention paid to both popularization and improvement", and put forward the idea of "concentrating the best people in key middle schools and universities through rigorous examinations". After the cultural revolution, chaos was brought to an end and the curriculum reform of high school education began. Starting from the pilot program (draft) of the full-time ten-year primary and secondary school teaching program issued by the ministry of education in January 1978, the fifth curriculum reform since the founding of the People's Republic of China was initiated, in response to the call of talent construction at that time. By the end of 1979, there were more than 5,200 key middle schools with about 5.2 million students.

In the early days of reform and opening up, school curriculum paid special attention to and emphasized the dominant position of subject curriculum and the systematisms of subject knowledge in view of the educational problems during the "cultural revolution". The "pilot draft of the full-time ten-year primary and secondary school teaching plan" issued in 1978 restored the tradition of "seventeen years", mainly focusing on academic subjects, and offering 10 courses in politics, Chinese, mathematics, foreign language, physics, chemistry, history, biology, agriculture and physical education in senior high schools. The curriculum structure of this period was still dominated by a single subject, and music and art had not yet appeared. Although the teaching plan of 1981 has been in use for a long time, it still has the problem of "unreasonable proportion". The scope of elective courses is relatively narrow, and it is not enough to cultivate students' adaptability to modern social life and production. Music and art are still not included in the plan (Choe et al., 2004; Guo & Wang, 2019; Li & Li, 2019; Liu, 2020).

After the sixth curriculum reform, high school education has made remarkable achievements, but there are still some problems, such as the curriculum is mainly compulsory courses, compulsory courses are mainly subject courses, mainly for the promotion of the establishment. In the implementation is not satisfactory, the proportion of high school elective courses is too small, and no restrictive provisions, there are many schools did not implement the situation. Sixth with better condition of the curriculum reform focuses on key middle school and high school, the problems such as the widening gap between resources in the middle school, according to these conditions, the state education commission has carried out the "ordinary high school curriculum reform research and experiment", in 1990 and awarded the adjustments of the current ordinary high school teaching plan, as a transitional teaching plan, in March 1996 and officially issued by the "ordinary high school course (test), teaching plan changed its name to lesson plans, again in 2000 promulgated the" full-time ordinary high school curriculum program (experimental revised) ", this is the seventh time high school curriculum reform. After this reform, the curriculum structure of high school has been optimized. On the basis of compulsory courses, students have set up limited elective subjects and any elective subjects. In addition to the subject courses, additional activity courses, extracurricular activities and social practice activities have been added to meet the development needs of different students.

General High School Curriculum Plan (experiment) was issued in 2003, and general high school curriculum plan (2017 edition) in 2017, on the basis of the 2003 edition, fully absorbed the experience and lessons of school curriculum practice, further optimized the curriculum structure, and made it more stable, more operable and more flexible. In terms of subject setting, foreign language planning is adjusted on the basis of retaining the original learning subjects. In terms of typesetting, the course category is changed to "compulsory course, optional compulsory course and elective course", in which the required course is "all courses taken", the optional compulsory course is "elective test", and the optional course is "study without examination or study for examination". In terms of proportion setting, the proportion of elective courses is increased while the total credits of graduation remain unchanged, which not only guarantees the foundation, but also gives consideration to the selectivity. On the whole, the curriculum structure under the new revised plan not only greatly guarantees the foundation and unity, but also provides space for students' independent choice, which also greatly satisfies the personalized and diversified demands of local, school and students.

As can be seen from the above, the curriculum reform in China has made great progress, but also has some problems, mainly displays in: first, all previous curriculum reform are consciously or unconsciously the guidance of political factors and restriction, with relatively strong political orientation, this feature in the previous class changes are reflected particularly, in many cases reflects the leader's personal will. Secondly, how to carry out the curriculum reform, what problems may occur, how to solve them, etc., all need the curriculum theory as the support. The previous curriculum reform lacks the guidance of scientific curriculum theory and curriculum reform theory, which has certain blindness and arbitrariness. And the development of the curriculum focuses on academic courses, especially the three instrumental subjects of language and Numbers, and the reform of the discipline takes adjustment as the main strategy to pursue relative stability (Choe et al., 2004; Guo & Wang, 2019; Li & Li, 2019; Liu, 2020).

The new curriculum reform of senior high school is the need of training high-quality talents to adapt to the era of knowledge economy. We are now in the era of knowledge economization, globalization and sustainable development. Knowledge is increasing and updating at an unimaginable speed. The focus of education is no longer to teach students fixed and systematic knowledge, but to firmly adhere to the concept of "student-oriented development" and to shape a free personality with rich connotations. Therefore, it is necessary to establish a whole set of new curriculum system to enable students to acquire the knowledge and ability needed for their own development. Therefore, the curriculum reform of senior high school is the only way to train qualified talents in the new historical period. The new curriculum reform of senior high school is in line with the development trend of international education reform. Since the mid-1990s, countries all over the world have started large-scale national education reform at the same time, which constitutes a global wave of large-scale education reform which is still continuously upgraded and deepened until now, among which curriculum reform is the focus of this wave of change.

The changes in course structure. The curriculum structure bears and influences the value and function of the curriculum, and the curriculum structure is the essence of the curriculum plan. On the basis of compulsory education, ordinary senior high school curriculum further improves the comprehensive quality of students, focuses on the development of students' core qualities, and enables students to have ideals and beliefs, social responsibility, scientific and cultural literacy, lifelong learning ability, independent development ability and communication and cooperation ability. China's curriculum structure has been adjusted and reformed for many times, but academic courses have always occupied a dominant position. However, the proportion of the three instrumental subjects, namely language, mathematics and foreign language, has decreased obviously, but it also tends to be stable, accounting for about 30% in the arts and science. Compared with Chinese and mathematics, the status of foreign languages has been significantly improved. Since 1981, the elective course system has become a system of curriculum construction in China, and the proportion of elective courses has gradually increased, which reflects the diversification of high school courses in China. Compulsory courses are set by the state according to the needs of students' all-round development, and all students must complete them. It is the common foundation for the development of ordinary high school students. The "common foundation" here is not only the common foundation of subject knowledge, but also the common foundation of social life and the common foundation of students' self-development. Elective courses by the school according to the actual situation of the overall planning to open, students choose to study. Among them, one part is the expansion, improvement and integration courses designed by the state on the basis of compulsory courses and selective compulsory courses. One part is the school-based curriculum developed by the school according to the diverse needs of students, the needs of local social, economic and cultural development, and the characteristics of the school. In the 1980s, a number of high schools that took the initiative to reform emerged in response to the problems of single curriculum types, the "unified world" of compulsory courses and the neglect of the development of students' personalities. For example, on the basis of the required courses of the affiliated high school of northeast normal university to establish the "course" and "of course" two classes and will course is in the history, geography, physics, chemistry, biology, a door you choose five courses, of course, including new science technology lectures, basic science and the history of science, art style, the second foreign language, a total of four categories of 37 courses; The affiliated high school of Nanjing normal university has carried out the experiment of "four types of senior high school curriculum model". The curriculum structure is composed of compulsory courses, elective courses, labor technology education courses and social practice courses. These curriculum experiments at the school level laid a practical foundation for the overall reform of the curriculum structure in the later ordinary high schools (Choe et al., 2004; Guo & Wang, 2019; Li & Li, 2019; Liu, 2020).

In 1981, the Ministry of Education, in accordance with Deng Xiaoping's guiding spirit of "to run key primary schools, key middle schools and key universities", issued *the Teaching Plan of Full-time six-year Key Middle Schools (revised draft) and the Revised Opinions of the Pilot Draft of Full-time five-year Secondary School Plan* ", and the sixth curriculum reform began. In this curriculum reform, senior high school only opened elective courses, and stipulated two forms of elective: one is the "one-class elective", that is, elective a certain (some) courses; The other is the "elective", that is, the arts and sciences; In the course categories, we have opened 12 courses, including elective courses and labor technology courses, and restored the structure of the course which is mainly subject courses. Promoting diversified development is an inevitable requirement for the connotation development of ordinary high schools. At present, to promote the diversified development of ordinary high schools, it is necessary to firmly grasp the core of the reform of talent cultivation mode and create a good reform environment based on the support of system and resources. How to better adapt to the objective requirements of the economic and social development of our country for the diversification of talents, and how to better meet the diverse educational needs of students, is a prominent issue facing the reform and development of ordinary high schools. To face up to and solve this problem, we must vigorously promote the diversified development of ordinary high schools and constantly deepen the comprehensive reform of ordinary high schools. It should be said that "diversification" is an inevitable requirement of the connotation development of ordinary high schools. The training goal of secondary vocational schools is to cultivate high-quality laborers and skilled talents who can work in the production and service lines. The main outstanding abilities are employment-oriented: good professional ethics, professional awareness, as well as more skilled professional knowledge and professional skills, but also need to have a certain degree of employability and entrepreneurial ability, with the ability to adapt to the work of production line comprehensive quality. Ordinary high school education training target is based on the characteristics of high school students body and mind, cultivating outstanding ability is geared to the needs of the university entrance exam, the specific contents: one is to cultivate students to master modern society needs the common cultural science basic knowledge and basic skills, has consciously learning attitude and the ability to study independently, 2 it is to cultivate students and habit of taking physical exercise consciously, have good will quality and certain strain capacity. The third is to have the ability to continue to study, in order to enter the higher education for learning reserves.

The changes of high school textbooks. Teaching material is the carrier of classroom teaching, the basic material of teachers' teaching, and the medium of students' understanding of the world. More importantly, every curriculum reform changes, will inevitably be reflected in the construction of teaching materials. In the past 40 years of reform and opening up, the textbook publishing work of primary and secondary schools has accumulated rich experience, and the textbook publishing system has made great progress, which guarantees that "before class, one book for each person", and provides important support for the establishment and improvement of the socialist education system with Chinese characteristics. In 1977, the Ministry of Education decided to set the 10-year system as the basic schooling system for primary and secondary schools and formulated a national unified teaching plan. To the people's education publishing house elementary and secondary school textbook editors as the basic force, and from the national selection of a number of experts and teachers to constitute the compilation team, in the form of the national primary and secondary school textbook compilation work began to compile work. Under the circumstances of a hundred wastes waiting to be revived, a hundred industries to be promoted and a great many difficulties to be solved, through comrade Deng Xiaoping's personal intervention, the personnel of the China people's education association scattered in four places during the "cultural revolution" were transferred back. Deng Xiaoping also believed that the import of textbooks was more urgent than the import of steel. He directed the relevant departments to allocate special funds from the very scarce foreign exchange to introduce textbooks from developed countries for editors to study, learn from and refer to (Choe et al., 2004; Guo & Wang, 2019; Li & Li, 2019; Liu, 2020).

In the fall of 1978, the first volume of textbooks for all subjects in primary and secondary schools was simultaneously made available throughout the country. This is the "cultural revolution" after the end of the first set of universal primary and secondary school textbooks. In 1978, the third plenary session of the eleventh central committee of the party made a strategic decision to shift the focus of the work of the party and the state to the socialist modernization drive. Under the guidance of this strategic decision, the people's education press compiled and published a series of textbooks for primary and secondary schools of 12 years, which began to be supplied to the whole country in the autumn of 1982.

The formal establishment and improvement of the examination and approval system of teaching materials. With the deepening of the reform and opening up, in order to adapt to the reform of the economic system and the reform of the scientific and technological system, the reform of the education system has also been put on the agenda. In order to implement the 1985 "decision on reform of the education system of the central committee of the communist party of China" and in 1986 enacted the law of the People's Republic of China compulsory education law, to adapt to the regional economic development level and the needs of different students starting point, China's decision to formally establish teaching material system, on the premise of unified requirements, unified examination and explore the diversification of teaching materials. In September 1986, the national primary and secondary school textbook examination and approval committee was formally established, which marked the establishment of the separate compilation and examination, textbook examination and selection system. This is the new China after the establishment of the first set up specialized examination and approval of primary and secondary school textbooks authority. In November of the same year, the national primary and secondary school textbook review committee held an expanded meeting, reviewed and approved the revised primary and secondary school curriculum of 18 subjects. According to the regulation of new outline, each discipline teaching material undertook again big revision, some teaching material rewrite, reduce difficulty appropriately. The new edition of the textbooks began in 1986 and was published in 1987. At the same time, from 1987 to 1988, "primary and secondary school textbook examination and approval standards", "primary and secondary school textbook examination and approval measures" and "the national primary and secondary school textbook examination and approval committee work constitution" have been issued. In order to adapt to the reform of the education system and the needs of nine-year compulsory education, the state education commission formulated the draft teaching plan for compulsory education in primary schools and junior middle schools, and from April to November 1988, it successively compiled and issued the preliminary examination draft of the nine-year full-time primary schools and junior middle schools' teaching syllabuses, which served as the basis for the compilation of teaching materials. The state education commission has decided to compile four types of compulsory education textbooks: one is the "six-three" system of textbooks in most regions of the country; the other is the "five-four" system of textbooks in most regions of the country; the third is the textbooks in developed coastal areas; the fourth is the textbooks in less developed areas (Choe et al., 2004; Guo & Wang, 2019; Li & Li, 2019; Liu, 2020).

Approved by the state education commission, a total of eight sets of half textbooks (half of which are only primary school textbooks) were ready to be launched, and the people's education association undertook two sets of them, namely, one for each of the "six three" and "may four" systems in most regions of the country. Since 1989, the people's education association has compiled and published textbooks on the "six-three" system and the "five-four" system of compulsory education. For the implementation of the central committee of the communist party of China in 1993, the state council issued by the spirit of "Chinese education reform and development compendium", the state education commission held a high school education work conference in 1995, issued the several opinions about to do a good job in ordinary senior middle school ", at the same time commissioned to lead pep, organize the drafting of the cohesion and compulsory education phase high school syllabus in all the subjects. In March 1996, the state education commission issued the curriculum plan of full-time ordinary senior middle school (experiment). At the same time, the people's education association started the compilation of new high school textbooks.

The reform of textbook publishing system in primary and secondary schools since the new curriculum reform. In accordance with the spirit of the decision on the reform and development of basic education and the outline of the reform of basic education curriculum successively issued by the state council and the ministry of education in 2001, the ministry of education issued the curriculum plan of full-time compulsory education, the curriculum standards of various subjects (experimental draft) and the interim measures for the compilation, examination and approval of primary and secondary school textbooks. Many publishing houses are involved in the construction of teaching materials. According to the new curriculum standards, the people's education association has been actively involved in the establishment, compilation and submission of new textbooks. In the autumn of 2001, a total of 14 subjects in the standard experimental textbooks for compulsory education were approved by the ministry of education, and experiments were conducted in the national experimental areas. In 2006 and 2010 respectively, the ministry of education issued a notice on the selection of textbooks in experimental areas of new curriculum, standardizing the ways and methods of the selection of textbooks. In 2010, according to "national medium and long-term education reform and development plan outline (2010-2020)" proposed "to promote the curriculum reform, strengthen the construction of teaching material", in order to better meet the needs of the country's long-term development of talent training, perfecting the basic education curriculum decision-making procedures, improve the level of curriculum construction, the ministry of education established the national basic education curriculum expert advisory committee and working committee. In December 2011, the ministry of education issued the curriculum standards for all subjects of compulsory education (2011 edition), and the people's education association launched a new textbook, which was revised and improved on the basis of summarizing the experience of compiling and publishing textbooks of all subjects since the new curriculum reform.

The new textbooks carry out the spirit of the outline, uphold the concept of quality education, adhere to moral education as the first, education-oriented, ideological, innovative, basic, appropriate and other aspects are more perfect (Choe et al., 2004; Guo & Wang, 2019; Li & Li, 2019; Liu, 2020).

The cause of teaching materials for socialism with Chinese characteristics has entered a new era. Since the 18th national congress of the communist party of China (CPC), comrade Xi Jinping has issued important instructions on the work of teaching materials on many occasions, proposing that we should cultivate people with morality and promote core socialist values in teaching materials, classrooms and minds. In October 2016, the office of the CPC central committee and the office of the state council issued the opinions on strengthening and improving the construction of textbooks for primary and secondary schools under the new situation. In March 2017, the ministry of education established the teaching materials bureau. In July, the national teaching material commission was established in Beijing with 10 expert committees to coordinate the work of teaching materials nationwide and to study and solve major problems in the construction of teaching materials. In September, the ministry of education organized a unified compilation of compulsory education textbooks on ethics and the rule of law, Chinese and history, which were examined and approved by the national textbook committee and published by the people's education association. At the beginning of 2018, the people's education association officially published the curriculum standards for all subjects in ordinary high schools (2017 edition) issued by the ministry of education. The compilation of new textbooks for senior high schools is under way in a tense and orderly manner. Since the reform and opening up 40 years ago, the publishing of textbooks for primary and secondary schools in China has adhered to the correct political direction and developed rapidly with The Times. The leadership of the new era party over textbook publishing will be further strengthened, the ideological attribute of textbook will be more prominent, and the cause of socialist textbook with Chinese characteristics will present an extremely broad development prospect.

3.1.2 The Implementation of the Latest Curriculum Reform Plan

The new curriculum and new textbooks will be fully implemented in regular high schools by 2022. The ministry of education held a press conference today (June 20, 2019) to interpret the guidelines on promoting the reform of education methods in ordinary high schools in the new era just published by the state council. The ministry of education has organized experts to revise the curriculum plans and standards of ordinary high schools, and the compilation and review of textbooks on Chinese, history and ideological and political subjects has been basically completed and will be put into use by 2022. It is understood that in view of the diverse learning needs of high school students and the requirements of the college entrance examination, the new curriculum and new textbooks have appropriately increased the selectivity of the curriculum, providing students with a choice of courses in different development directions. The new curriculum specifically revised the language and other subjects 17 curriculum standards, new German, French and Spanish 3 curriculum standards, a total of 20 curriculum standards. The newly revised curriculum standard mainly includes two parts: the core accomplishment and the academic quality standard. For the first time, the core quality of each discipline is put forward concisely, and the correct values, essential characters and key abilities that students should form after learning the course of this discipline are made clear. The newly revised curriculum standards make it clear that academic quality is a comprehensive measure of students' development in various aspects, and help teachers better grasp the teaching requirements and teach students according to their aptitude. Recently, the general office of the state council issued the guidelines on promoting the reform of education methods in ordinary high schools in the new era (hereinafter referred to as the opinions). The opinions make it clear that by 2022, the comprehensive training system for moral, intellectual, physical, and aesthetic labor will be further improved, and the mechanism for the implementation of moral cultivation will be further improved. Ordinary high school new teaching material, the full implementation of the new curriculum to adapt to the students' comprehensive and personal development education teaching reform deepening, elective basic improve class teaching management mechanism, scientific education evaluation and examination recruitment system basic establishment, effectively ensure the teachers and educational condition, the development of the diversified features of average high school pattern basic formation (Choe et al., 2004; Guo & Wang, 2019; Li & Li, 2019; Liu, 2020).

We will improve school curriculum management and strengthen the construction of distinctive courses. Third, innovate the teaching organization management. Promote the orderly selection of classes to meet the needs of students of different development; Deepen the reform of classroom teaching and promote the in-depth integration of information technology and education; The teaching management should be optimized, and it is strictly prohibited to exceed the teaching standards, to catch up with the teaching schedule and to finish the course in advance. Fourth, strengthen student development guidance. Pay attention to the guidance effect, help students to establish the correct ideal and belief, correct understanding of self; We should make use of all kinds of social resources to build a cooperative guidance mechanism among schools, families and society. Fifth, we will improve the examination and enrollment systems. Standardize the academic level examination and deepen the reform of examination proposition; We should steadily advance the reform of college enrollment and gradually change the tendency to evaluate students solely on the basis of their test scores. Sixth, we will strengthen teachers and conditions. We focus on strengthening the construction of teachers and innovating the way of teacher training; We should improve the conditions of school buildings and improve the mechanism for funding them.

Press interpretation of the policy. Recently, the general office of the state council issued the guidance on promoting the reform of education methods in ordinary high schools in the new era. This is the first important programmatic document on promoting the education reform of ordinary high schools issued by the general office of the state council since the new century. The general high school education is an important part of the national education system, which plays a key role in the talent training. What important influence will the introduction of guiding opinions have on the running of general high school education, enhancing the development of high school education, and improving the overall quality of the nation? Authoritative experts read about it.

We will set the goal of education reform in ordinary high schools. Based on the training of the new generation to assume the responsibility of national rejuvenation, the guidance of the general high school education reform system design and comprehensive deployment. The guideline sets out the goal of the reform. By 2022, the comprehensive training system for moral, intellectual, physical, and aesthetic labor will be further improved, and the mechanism for the implementation of moral cultivation will be further improved. Ordinary high school new teaching material, the full implementation of the new curriculum to adapt to the students' comprehensive and personal development education teaching reform deepening, elective basic improve class teaching management mechanism, scientific education evaluation and examination recruitment system basic establishment, effectively ensure the teachers and educational condition, the development of the diversified features of average high school pattern basic formation. The new curriculum and textbooks will be fully implemented by 2022. According to the guideline, all provinces (autonomous regions and municipalities directly under the central government) should formulate new curriculum implementation plans for ordinary high schools in combination with the comprehensive reform of the college entrance examination, and fully implement the new curriculum and use the new textbooks by 2022.

3.2 Analysis on the Causes of Curriculum and Teaching Material System in Senior High Schools in China

3.2.1 The Analysis from Political and Economic Aspects

A country is composed of four elements: territory, people (nation, inhabitant), culture and government. In a broad sense, a country is a social group that shares a common language, culture, race, lineage, territory, government, or history. In a narrow sense, the state is a community form formed by a certain range of people. High school education curriculum and teaching material in China set up the first meaning is the basic value of the People's Republic of China, let the students know that the People's Republic of China is led by the working class and based on the alliance of workers and peasants of the people's democratic dictatorship of socialist countries, the five-star red flag as the national flag, the march of the volunteers, as the national anthem, is one of the Han nationality as the main body, composed of 56 ethnic groups united multi-ethnic country, lets the student identity exists significance in China. Therefore, the textbook "socialism with Chinese characteristics" in high school ideological and political courses mentioned this part of content.

China's development path and political system. As mentioned above, China is a socialist country under the people's democratic dictatorship led by the working class and based on the alliance of workers and peasants. The fundamental meaning of the curriculum and teaching materials in China's senior high school education is to educate students to support China's development path and political system. The development path includes the political development path, the economic development path, the cultural development path, the social development path and the ecological progress path. The political system includes the fundamental political system—the people's congress system and the basic political system—the system of multi-party cooperation and political consultation under the leadership of the CPC, regional ethnic autonomy, and the system of self-government at the grassroots level. Only by understanding and supporting the development path and political system with Chinese characteristics can students better serve our country and society and become qualified Chinese citizens. Therefore, in the high school ideological and political curriculum "socialism with Chinese characteristics" and "politics and the rule of law" these two textbooks put forward. Introduction to the ideological and political textbooks of ordinary high schools published by the ministry of education mentioned that the compilation of textbooks should adhere to the guiding position of Marxism, organically integrate socialist core values, guide students to love the party, patriotism and socialism, strengthen the "four self-confidence", and form a correct world view, outlook on life and values. Through teachers' teaching and self-learning, students can form their own understanding of these contents and gradually accept and support China's development path and social system (Choe et al., 2004; Guo & Wang, 2019; Li & Li, 2019; Liu, 2020).

The initial intention of the comprehensive reform of college entrance examination is to train national talents and develop education healthily. At that time, as the chief architect of the reform and opening up, comrade Deng Xiaoping decided to resume the college entrance examination in order to cultivate talents for the reform and opening up. Since the 18th National Congress of the CPC, the CPC Central Committee and the State Council have attached great importance to the comprehensive reform of the college entrance examination. *The Outline of the National Plan for Medium and Long-term Education Reform and Development (2010-2020)* mentions "comprehensively improving the comprehensive quality of ordinary high school students. We will push forward the reform of the curriculum, fully implement the curriculum plan, and ensure that students fully complete the study of all the subjects stipulated by the state, including arts and science. Create conditions to set up a variety of elective courses, to provide more choices for students, to promote the comprehensive and personalized development of students. Gradually eliminate the phenomenon of large shift. We actively carry out research study, community service and social practice. We will establish a scientific education quality evaluation system, and fully implement the high school academic level test and comprehensive quality evaluation." In other words, it is necessary to clarify the diversification and characteristics of the general high school, to achieve the diversification of the development of ordinary high school education, to promote the diversification of talent training model. For a long time in the past, China's high school curriculum education implemented the system of liberal arts and science division, which is not only conducive to reducing the learning burden of students and promoting the development of students' personality, but also conducive to improving the efficiency of talent cultivation and conveying more professional talents to the society. Such a curriculum system has indeed provided a large number of talents for China in the past many years. According to statistics from the ministry of education, the number of high school students reached 39.347 million in 2018, among which 9.75 million applied for the college entrance examination, and the actual enrollment reached 7.9099 million, with the acceptance rate reaching a record high of 81.13%. It can be seen that the diversified courses and teaching materials have contributed to the large number of talents being imported into universities and society (Choe et al., 2004; Guo & Wang, 2019; Li & Li, 2019; Liu, 2020).

3.2.2 The Policy of Curriculum and Teaching Materials in High School Education

The high school curriculum and its reform are influenced by policies. Throughout the 100-year history of education in the twentieth century, "the three major changes in the field of education all began with the curriculum reform". Especially since the 1980s, the curriculum reform of the scope of the third world, not only affects all aspects of the curriculum system, the curriculum reform of the guiding ideology, objectives, contents, structure and organization methods, implementation, evaluation and management and so on various aspects has carried on the system and overall reflection transformation but also affects the broad participation and leadership of the government, governments from national level put forward the corresponding policy of curriculum reform, a series of related study of curriculum reform, curriculum reform, related laws and policy documents, the extensive influence on national education field, its influence continues today. In this context, it is found that as the curriculum reform gradually moves towards systematization and integration, the planning, design, implementation and organization of the curriculum reform cannot just stay in the field of professional discussion but need to involve more policy arrangements at the national level. Today, our country is still diligently seeking better high school education curriculum, carrying out a series of reforms on high school education curriculum and teaching materials, and most of these reforms are issued and implemented in the form of policies. Thus, high school curriculum and its reform are greatly influenced by policies.

The high school curriculum reform policy breeds political ecology. Political environment is an important aspect of public policy making and implementation, which usually includes "the sum of political system, political structure and political relations". Political environment has an important influence on public policy, which fundamentally determines the political nature, democratization and legalization of policy. The reform of political system as an important component of China's comprehensive reform, involving the political value system, organizing system, institution system and the transformation of the power relations, is a system of political transition, it must affect the generation and development of public policy in our country, also will be important influence on curriculum reform policy, constitute the curriculum reform policy's main political ecology. As mentioned in the course reform policy process: conceptualization, review, implementation and evaluation, the reform of the education administration system that emphasizes hierarchical management and division of responsibilities is the first step to change the current situation that China's education administration is too centralized and unified and the local government's administrative capacity is not strong through streamlining administration and delegating power. Secondly, the policy environment of curriculum reform also implies the struggle between old and new political concepts and political culture. Under the condition of the political system reform, the emergence of new political culture constantly challenging political ideas, try to change us about "political thinking ways, including our faith in the political process, political right purpose, and appropriate behaviors" politicians, reflects a certain social historical period of the popular social political culture and psychology.

3.2.3   The Economic Significance of Curriculum and Teaching Materials in High Schools

The possible labor education into the reality of labor, when a person has no knowledge of any production and labor skills, he can only is a kind of potential and potential labor force, it is only through education and training to make this possible, potential labor force into reality, at the same time, the direct labor education is an important approach to science knowledge of reproduction, scientific knowledge is a kind of productivity, and the reproduction of productivity, also want to achieve through education, education in the aspect of scientific knowledge to reproduce the role played by, first performance in terms of its inheritance, reproduction of through the school is a kind of expanded reproduction, it makes the original The scientific knowledge that is mastered by a few is mastered by more people, and the scope of its dissemination is constantly expanded. This is especially true of high school education. Senior high school education plays an irreplaceable role in the inheritance and reproduction of knowledge. Senior high school education enables the dissemination of basic scientific and humanistic knowledge and lays a foundation for the training of qualified modern workers.

It is of great value and significance for high school students to study political economy. First, let the students adapt to the development needs of modern economy and society. Modern society has begun to shift from the traditional manufacturing economy to a new society with diversified economic development, and various industries are constantly promoting the development of modern society. Students can effectively improve their cognition of the social political and economic situation through the study of political and economic courses. Modern political and economic teaching is closely related to consumption, life and people's livelihood. Only when students master the development factors and the development situation of economic development at the root can they make better self-development planning and later major selection. Therefore, the study of high school political economy is not only the demand of modern economic and social development, but also the demand of students' self-development. Secondly, improve students' cognitive ability of political economy. In high school political and economic teaching, teachers can answer the meaning of economic development and economic life for students in a simple way. These questions can help students understand social development more deeply and effectively improve their political and economic cognition. At the same time, through the study of these theoretical knowledge, students can develop many good consumption habits, reduce the pressure of family life, reduce the psychology of keeping up with the joneses, and help them establish correct values. Finally, change students' consumption concept and promote the development of students' personality. Political and economic course is students life values and the main way of consumption idea, political and economic teach students to be able to live within our means, the appropriate consumption, avoid blindly follow, rational consumption, etc., can let students under the existing conditions of deep cognition to the hard-earned money, can let students cultivate good character thrifty. There will also be solidarity between students, mutual help, help each other pull the friendly phenomenon. The fundamental purpose of high school political and economic education is not only to improve students' high school political performance, but also to cultivate students' personal quality and stimulate positive social energy (Choe et al., 2004; Guo & Wang, 2019; Li & Li, 2019; Liu, 2020).

3.2.4 The Influence of Economic Ecology on High School Curriculum and Teaching Materials

Since the 1980s, China has entered the era of building a socialist market economy system and reforming production technology and industrial structure. Curriculum reform is a gradual process, which is deeply influenced by the economic circle. Under the influence of the environment change, the new curriculum policy is imperceptibly pregnant with the change of external conditions. Corresponding to the transformation from planned economy system to market economy system, China's high school education curriculum and textbooks have also undergone a transformation in the course selection, course management mode and textbook resources. The first is the change of course selection, which recognizes the broad differences and uniqueness of students and recognizes the potential of diverse development of students, which directly leads to the direct direction of course selection to the development of individual students. In addition to the required basic courses, students can choose the elective courses they want to take. Secondly, the mode of three-level curriculum management is developed gradually, which promotes the differentiation of power. Finally, the development of curriculum resources is also gradually decentralized, the introduction of market competition mechanism, the central monopoly of textbooks and teaching reference materials and the distribution of administrative mandatory resources, the concept of curriculum resources has been expanded.

After entering the post-industrial society, the era of "knowledge economy", a new economic form, has arrived. Knowledge has become the direct resource and driving force of economic development replacing land, labor, raw materials, tools and capital. First of all, the sustainable development of knowledge economy, as a kind of economic strength, let us begin to get rid of a dynamic civilization mode control technology, to "to the person's nature, innovation, talent cultivation and the application of high and new technology and new economy growth way deep reflections on the relationship between", which is realized under the new economic form of education must be used as a breakthrough value and tool state of "nonhuman", the liberation of students in the education teaching activities and social life of the object position, to rethink the "human development as the fundamental purpose" education aim, let the students to participate in their real life and social public life In theory, the consciousness of this new educational concept has brought about the concrete and thorough changes in the content, structure, teaching and evaluation of the curriculum. Finally, the development of knowledge economy and go beyond the pursuit of quantity to quality excellence, quality and efficiency to become the number one priority for the new economic environment, reflected in the teaching, on the one hand, from the past as much as possible in a limited time on knowledge teaching of education ideas and thinking about how to select the teaching content, how to create conditions for real effectively help students to autonomous learning and development. On the other hand, this effectiveness and quality is guaranteed through the specialization of the curriculum area, including the specialization of the basic modes and processes of curriculum policy operation and the specialization of the curriculum personnel.

The conceptual category of "society" and the process of its influence. There is a clear historical clue in the history of the change of Chinese educational curriculum policy from 1978 to today, that is, from "double bases" to "three-dimensional goals" to "core literacy". "double-base" education emphasizes the basic knowledge and basic skills of teaching content, reflects the emphasis on "knowledge and skills", and from June 8, 2001 by the Ministry of Education issued the "basic education curriculum reform outline (try out)", put forward the new target of curriculum reform: "change course too pay attention to the tendency of knowledge, emphasize the form active learning attitude, make the process to acquire basic knowledge and basic skills become the process of learning to learn and form the correct values at the same time." "Students are encouraged to take the initiative to participate, to be inquisitive and to be hands-on, to cultivate their ability to collect and process information, to acquire new knowledge, to analyze and solve problems, and to communicate and cooperate." The cultivation of students' specific learning process and methods, as well as the cultivation of students' learning attitudes and values have become the same important curriculum objectives as "knowledge and skills", and the development of Chinese education has undergone a great transformation. After that, the establishment of textbook examination and approval system, the new basic education curriculum system composed of compulsory courses, elective courses, activity courses and other curriculum arrangements, and the proposal of "core quality" in the next stage are all based on such a document (Choe et al., 2004; Guo & Wang, 2019; Li & Li, 2019; Liu, 2020).

It can be seen from the historical process mentioned above that the curriculum reform in China takes the policy document issued by the central government as the symbolic event and the central event. Before and after the release of such policy documents, leaders, experts' groups and social figures make policy documents and implement policies. In the "decision of the state council on the reform and development of basic education. In 2001, it proposed to "implement the three-level curriculum management of national, local and school". Such a statement is often mentioned in subsequent and previous documents. The so-called "three-level curriculum management" means that the state formulates a master plan, local governments can develop local curriculum suitable for their own regions on the basis of ensuring the implementation of national curriculum, and schools can develop or select courses suitable for their own characteristics. Therefore, it can be judged that the process of social factors playing a role should focus on the course management and practice of local and school, and the problems found in these two processes will affect the formulation of the overall plan of the country.

In order to further explore the specific influence of social factors in the process mentioned above, it is necessary to make clear the category of social factors and, more accurately, the category in which social factors should be discussed in this article. In the curriculum and textbook reform as the core to promote the overall reform of senior high school education published by Shanghai municipal education commission in 1995, it put forward that "the guiding ideology of curriculum reform program design based on 'social demand', 'subject system' and 'student development' and taking comprehensively improving the quality of students as the core is determined. The "society" in the "social demand" mentioned here is an oversized and overbroad concept, which refers to the expectations and requirements of the whole Chinese society on the educational curriculum for its own development and further modernization. Today, what is referred to here as "social demand" has been more clearly stated, that is, the state and society require education and educational courses to meet their demand for talents in the context of the competition of comprehensive national strength. Therefore, education to meet the "social needs" is education to cultivate enough quantity and quality of talents for the country. In addition, some scholars classify economic, political, cultural and other contents into the society, believing that the so-called society is the development stage and overall level of the society. This article as part of the team cooperation, consideration should be given to the concept of "social" in with the "political, economic and cultural concept of the three phase of the category, that is to say, this article discussed the range of" social "including should start with" political, economic and cultural "included in the scope is quite different. Therefore, the social category stipulated in this paper excludes the factors related to "politics, economy and culture" and focuses on the individuals in each society, that is, the social subject. In the process of curriculum reform, every individual more or less related to it has participated in it and made their own choices. The main trend that emerges from the numerous choices of these subjects, namely the influence of the so-called social concept on the educational curriculum and teaching material system, is the focus of this paper. At the same time, it is worth noting that the social concept mentioned here is not just an abstract and spiritual thing, because their carrier is the practical choice made by each social subject, and these choices together are undoubtedly an important part of the social reality under the background of educational curriculum reform (Choe et al., 2004; Guo & Wang, 2019; Li & Li, 2019; Liu, 2020).

According to the basic education to the public in the Ministry of Education website on June 10, 1986 to January 17, 2020 in all of the files, only the general office of the Ministry of Education on collect basic education course reform teaching research results notice (teach 2 hall letter [2010] no. 2) and the general office of the Ministry of Education on hold a national work conference on high school education popularization crucial notice (teach hall letter [2017] no. 6) the two documents mentioned called social main body participation. Among them, the former extensively collects "the curriculum development results, and teaching reform experimental results formed by systematic practice and exploration around the key and difficult issues of basic education curriculum reform", which can be in the form of papers, teaching cases, courseware, software and other forms. The latter is mainly limited to government officials in local education bureaus. Department according to the teaching material to open on March 7, 1986 to December 2019. 19 all files, including the social main body participation in policy making teaching process of the review of documents, a total of 7, article is mostly about the ministry of education basic education curriculum experts working committee and the establishment of the foundation education course teaching material expert advisory committee and write the articles of association. Write on the textbook, whether on June 7, 2001, the interim regulations on primary and secondary school textbook examination and management made in article 3 of the general rules of "the state encourages and supports the conditional units, groups and individuals writing meets the needs of teaching reform of primary and secondary schools of high quality, distinctive teaching material, especially the teaching materials for use in rural areas and minority nationality areas." On December 16, 2019 in the third chapter put forward the measures for the management of the primary and secondary school textbooks article 13: "experts textbooks written by the team and related disciplines, teaching and research staff, a gleam of primary and secondary school teachers and so on, all kinds of writers should maintain a reasonable structure and relative stability, each book core writers in principle no more than eight people." All indicate that the compilation of teaching materials depends on the relevant people in the society to a considerable extent. These social subjects participate in the compilation of textbooks, which makes Chinese high school textbooks more diverse and flexible, and more suitable for China's national conditions with a large gap between regions. In addition, we should not ignore the research results of many scholars in the aspects of high school curriculum reform, textbook compilation and approval, etc., most of which in the form of papers and investigation reports have a significant impact on the decision-making of relevant government departments.

From "double-base" to "three-dimensional goal" to "core accomplishment", with the curriculum reform of high school, students' personality development and culti-vation of core accomplishment have been paid more and more attention, and even been placed in the key position of comprehensively deepening the curriculum reform. However, there is always a big distance between the reality and the ideal. Various social subjects, especially teachers, students, parents and other groups, make their own response to the part divorced from the reality in the policy, thus playing a role of resistance. Their forms of resistance varied from mild to violent. For example, the elective program listed in the "curriculum plan" was explicitly violated, the national education policy was simply copied without any policy decomposition and local innovation, or the curriculum reform was fiercely criticized on social media. These protests may seem like a huge obstacle to education policy and curriculum reform, but at the same time, they are the most profound and beneficial collective reflection on these reform policies. Teachers, students and parents of students who have been there before are most aware of the advantages and disadvantages brought to them by the education curriculum and teaching material system. Only when they protest and speak out can the government and scholars find out the problems in the practice of education policy and curriculum reform. Even if their ideas are backward or even wrong, they still reflect the reality, the actual situation of Chinese education and Chinese society. This is why the reaction of social subjects in the process of policy implementation, as a social factor, has a great enlightening effect on the curriculum and teaching material system in China.

For example, both the outline of the national program for medium—and long-term education reform and development (2010–2020) and the key plan for the popu-larization of high school education (2017–2020) have put "universal employment integration" on the agenda and placed high priority on it. It also pointed out that the government should pay more attention to the training of teachers and the sharing of teaching resources and strengthen the cooperation between schools and enterprises. Although there is no clear evidence of a link between the two, in the national imple-mentation plan for vocational education reform on January 24, 2019, these ques-tions have been answered to some extent. We should promote high-quality develop-ment of higher vocational education, reform the system of running schools in higher vocational colleges, improve the quality of running schools, and build a number of higher vocational schools and key majors (groups) that lead the reform and support development, with Chinese characteristics and at world levels. "It is necessary to take multiple measures to create a" double-qualified "teaching team, strengthen the construction of vocational and technical normal schools and specialties, explore the establishment of a high-level and structured teaching innovation team, organize and select key teachers for overseas study and training, and promote the two-way flow of school-enterprise personnel. "Vocational training should be carried out extensively for students and members of the society, and vocational skills upgrading activities should be actively undertaken to guide the in-depth participation of enterprises in the industry." We need to promote the high-quality development of higher vocational schools can enable secondary vocational students to obtain better opportunities for further study and further study after graduation, which is conducive to them to strive for broader development opportunities, so that the problem of inequivalence between general and vocational schools will be alleviated to a certain extent. The construction of "double-qualified" teachers and the advocacy of the cooperation between vocational schools and enterprises will help secondary vocational students to receive better and more comprehensive education and increase the attractiveness of vocational education. From this example, it can be seen that the behavior of the social subject exposes the loopholes and problems of the education policy, which is beneficial for the government and scholars to reflect on the curriculum and textbook system, propose specific measures to improve it, and promote the adjustment or transformation of the policy (Choe et al., 2004; Guo & Wang, 2019; Li & Li, 2019; Liu, 2020).

Generally speaking, the social main body in the process of policy making process and textbook compilation the social main body in the process of participation and policy implementation in response to these two kinds of social factors on the main approach to influence our curriculum and teaching material system respectively occurred before the policy after the policy and practice, but in many cases, both are in the synchronized. That is to say, on the one hand, while discovering problems, scholars and researchers are also trying hard to find better ways to solve these problems; On the other hand, in the process of accepting the test of social reality in practice, the policy before it is also in the process of revision, and the policy after it is being questioned and discussed by cadres, experts and scholars as a possibility. Therefore, in general, social factors are an important mechanism for the self-reflection and self-adjustment of educational policies, whose function is to expose and solve problems. Under such a mechanism of reflection and adjustment, China's curriculum and teaching material system can be truly formed, as the ministry of education documents often say when describing the teaching material, this system has a certain degree of stability, but also has the timeliness (or time). In addition, it needs to be stressed again that although we often say that the current situation of the society and the needs of the society determine the educational curriculum and teaching materials system of a country, for example, the curriculum system under the background of comprehensive national strength competition has to emphasize the cultivation of students' core qualities.

3.3 Current Situation of High School Textbooks and Curriculum

3.3.1 The Current Situation of High School Curriculum

As one of the four ancient civilizations with a long history of 5,000 years, China has attached great importance to education since ancient times. With the development of The Times, education has also undergone many reforms and continuous development. Education determines not only the present but also the future of mankind, xi said. The human society needs to continuously cultivate talents needed by the society through education, and it needs to impart known knowledge, update old knowledge, explore new knowledge and explore the unknown through education, so that people can better understand the world and transform the world, and create a better future for mankind. Since 2004, the reform of China's experimental promotion of ordinary high school curriculum has been carried out for 16 years through preparation, initiation, promotion, summary and adjustment. The curriculum reform of senior high school is mainly reflected in the curriculum structure, curriculum plan, curriculum standards and other aspects. It is gradually carried out in the whole country through the way of "experiment first, promotion later". Up to now, the curriculum reform of senior high school in China has been continuously improved in practice and achieved some results, but there are still some problems in the reform. The curriculum reform of senior high school in China is progressive and creative. In view of the long-term problems in senior high school education in China, this paper puts forward the corresponding reform measures from the aspects of curriculum structure, curriculum plan and curriculum standards to improve the teaching level of senior high school and to adapt the teaching quality to the growth of China's comprehensive national strength. Its basic characteristics are as follows:

First, it breaks the traditional curriculum model of liberal arts and science, and constructs the curriculum structure of "two vertical and one horizontal" ("two vertical "refers to the professional foundation and scientific and technological accomplishment, and" one horizontal "refers to the scope of knowledge), which is conducive to the all-round development of students. According to the new college entrance examination reform plan, most provinces choose the mode of "unified examination + selective examination" in the calculation of college entrance examination results, that is, the results of the unified examination of language, mathematics and foreign subjects plus the results of the three grades of high school academic level examination subjects selected by students.

Secondly, the high school curriculum reform in view of the contradiction in our society and education aspects of the outstanding problems, students in the process of development for the high school curriculum more accord with China's national conditions and social transformation needs, such as in the ideological and political course to enhance cultural consciousness, cultural self-confidence education, increase the modern title in the language teaching material, etc. Three high school curriculum is based on high school students' cognitive characteristics and learning needs, will be the goal of teaching reform, direct representation for "creating conducive to guide students to active learning curriculum implementation environment, to improve students' autonomous learning, cooperation and communication, and analysis and problem solving skills", further advocate teachers teaching reform from the front, to encourage students' autonomous learning, for students to create opportunities and conditions of the "learning to learn". The curriculum reform of senior high schools in China is a comprehensive and systematic reform, which challenges the traditional school-running model and curriculum structure. It not only improves the students' independent choice to a certain extent, but also stimulates the students' learning enthusiasm and initiative.

3.3.2   The Problems Faced by High School Curriculum Reform

China's high school curriculum reform has its own unique, but the reform needs to be gradual and continuous improvement, as far as the present stage is concerned, there are still some problems in China's high school curriculum reform. First, the differences between urban and rural areas are obvious. The survey found that there have been significant differences between cities, towns and rural schools. Due to the differences in the basic conditions, teaching environment, teachers' level and students' foundation, teachers in different regions have different understandings of the course content and difficulty. The curriculum reform in urban schools is progressing smoothly, while there are some difficulties in towns and villages.

Second, the shortage of educational resources and regional differences. Due to the unbalanced economic development, there are obvious regional differences in educational resources of high schools in China. In terms of class amount, the average class amount of ordinary high schools in China is as high as more than 50 people, far exceeding the amount of high school classes in developed countries. In addition, there is a phenomenon that the amount of class amount is as high as 70 or even hundreds in the economically backward areas such as Hebei province. Lack of resources and regional differences in high school curriculum reform form a great resistance.

Third, the implementation of high school curriculum reform is seriously restricted by the college entrance examination. Due to the pressure of the college entrance examination, there is a phenomenon of "teaching what is tested" in many regions, which makes some PE classes, experimental classes and social practice activities in the curriculum reform of high schools become mere forms and even canceled by some schools themselves. In addition, the curriculum of many schools focuses on the second year of senior high school and the third year is all used to focus on review. This teaching mode and curriculum design do not meet the requirements of quality education, which violates the original intention of curriculum reform in senior high school and is not conducive to the long-term development of students. Moreover, according to some front-line principals and teachers from provinces where the reform of the college entrance examination is piloted, the implementation of the high school academic level examination requires middle schools to implement the system of walking classes, but some middle schools are deficient in teacher reserves, curriculum and other aspects, so there is a situation of "walking cannot go on" (Choe et al., 2004; Guo & Wang, 2019; Li & Li, 2019; Liu, 2020).

3.3.3 The Curriculum Plan and Curriculum Standard of High School

The implementation of high school curriculum reform needs the support of supporting policies and programs. The next step is to comprehensively revise the curriculum plan for compulsory education and the curriculum standards for all subjects, study and formulate the 2020 plan for the reform of ideological and political theory courses in schools in the new era, and focus on the implementation of the curriculum plan for ordinary senior high schools and the curriculum standards for all subjects. The curriculum plan and curriculum standards of senior high schools have been constantly improved and revised, providing a direction for the compilation of textbooks and further promoting the curriculum reform of senior high schools in China. The current curriculum standards and curriculum plans for ordinary senior high schools in China will be released in January 2018, which will be the basic compliance and weathervane to lead the teaching reform of senior high schools in the future. This curriculum standard has important guiding significance for the revision of new textbooks and the adjustment of teachers' teaching. Featured high school refers to the national ordinary high school featured project school. Its curriculum reform is different from that of the senior high school. The curriculum reform of featured high school is the overall characteristic design of the school curriculum, which should comprehensively reflect the requirements of the construction of featured high school and form the overall characteristic curriculum system of the school. The curriculum reform of featured high schools focuses on the all-round development of students and emphasizes quality-oriented education. At present, the main work of curriculum reform is the integrated curriculum, namely "national curriculum + local curriculum + school-based curriculum + activities".

At present, the formal use of high school textbooks in China needs to go through four stages: preparation, revision, review, publication, distribution, selection and use. China's curriculum materials are compiled and revised according to the national curriculum materials construction plan, curriculum plans for primary and secondary schools and curriculum standards. The local curriculum materials should be compiled and revised according to the corresponding curriculum materials construction plan or compilation plan, based on the regional talent training needs, and make full use of the local unique economic and social resources. After the completion of the compilation and revision of textbooks, the corresponding institutions will audit, strictly check the pass, adhere to the principle of "every compilation must be approved", "every selection must be approved", "the combination of management and construction", to ensure the improvement of the quality of Chinese high school textbooks. In addition, our country teaching material audit implements the system of separating the compilation and examination of the teaching material, follows the principle of avoiding, changes from once the country custom to the examination and approval system, this has certain guarantee to the teaching material quality. The textbook can be published and distributed only after it has passed the examination and approval, and the textbook can be selected and used in an open, fair and just environment.

3.4 Questions and Suggestions on High School Curriculum and Textbooks

3.4.1 The Problems and Suggestions of High School Textbooks

Textbooks are materials for students to study. What we hope the textbooks can bring is that students can broaden their horizons, enrich their knowledge, and train and develop their cognitive abilities through learning the textbooks. Although since the founding of the People's Republic of China, China has carried out a number of reforms on high school textbooks, which are closer to China's requirements for basic training of talents in the new era, there are still some problems in the current high school textbooks. Practice has proved that only by taking into account the logic system of subject knowledge, the system of teacher's teaching and the system of students' receptivity, can a qualified textbook be compiled. Otherwise, the quality will be affected. However, most of the problems in high school textbooks at this stage arise from the failure to coordinate the reasonable proportion of the three major systems, leading to the failure to make the textbooks play a full role in the education of students. Here are some of the problems found in high school textbooks

The high school textbooks are still fragmented, fragmented, not a complete logic system of subject knowledge. One of the reasons why high school textbooks are becoming more fragmented is that textbook writers hope that textbooks can stimulate students' innovative thinking, so some important contents in the logic system of knowledge are deleted, and some important contents are expanded by practical examples and innovative thinking. One of the trends of contemporary education development is to attach more and more importance to enlightening students' thinking and improving their abilities in various aspects. Especially now more and more attention is paid to cultivate students' interest in the subject, so as to make students truly interested in the subject, stimulate students' innovation, exploration thinking, which is the new era of comprehensive and innovative talent requirements. Therefore, in the current high school textbooks to add innovative thinking to expand and link the real-world practical examples. But because the energy of the students is limited, that is, the length of the textbook is limited, in addition to the expansion of a knowledge point, will inevitably lead to shorten the length of some other knowledge points, or even directly delete a knowledge point. As a result, the logical relationship between subject knowledge points is broken due to the lack of some knowledge points, which makes the whole logic system of subject knowledge not complete, that is, the systematic destruction of teaching materials. However, education is a systematic engineering, which must be considered comprehensively and systematically from the perspective of system theory. According to the view of system theory, the sum of the parts is greater than the whole, and the premise is that the parts are interrelated and promote each other, and the whole that is full of vitality should have a level problem, a problem of coherence. For the use of textbooks for students in learning because of the lacking of teaching material systematically, can lead to students for understanding between knowledge and knowledge of associative scientific memory method cannot be implemented, only mechanical memory, rather than a systematic understanding of memory, it is against the original intention of subject education, cultivate students' basic ability of discipline. Moreover, when students do not have the basic subject ability, it is impossible to train students to innovate at a higher level. On the premise of not having a solid foundation, it is difficult for students to further explore and expand the subject knowledge they have learned (Choe et al., 2004; Guo & Wang, 2019; Li & Li, 2019; Liu, 2020).

The second reason that leads to the fragmentation of the logical system of the subject knowledge in the teaching materials is the system that over considers the students' receptivity. It is indisputable to consider students' receptivity in a certain learning stage to make textbooks, but the current high school textbooks pay too much attention to students' receptivity, so the knowledge points in the blood multidisciplinary knowledge system are deleted, so as to reduce the learning burden of high school students. But too brief teaching materials to students is not to reduce the burden, for high school students, but is a form of another increase in the burden.

First of all, in order to make most of the students understand, especially the science textbooks, the knowledge points mentioned are almost superficial and superficial. However, as for the college entrance examination for talent selection, what it examines is not only the superficial knowledge. This has high requirements on teachers' teaching level and students' exploration ability. When teachers' teaching ability and students' exploration ability are either deficient, it will lead to students' dilemma that "they can understand the knowledge in class and textbook, but they are totally ignorant of the practical application". In this way, the dependence of some students on after-class tutoring or the ineffective abuse of after-class teaching AIDS is increased, but the negative effect is not achieved. This will also lead to students and teachers to have a sense of distrust with the teaching materials, so that in the learning process to abandon the teaching materials, teachers to choose their own teaching materials or teachers to write their own handouts, do not let the teaching materials play their due role in education, but for teachers and students to a certain extent. Second, the college entrance examination as the examination of talent selection, shrink scope of knowledge, in order to reduce the ability of appraisal of knowledge reduction, the college entrance examination for some knowledge can only be deep mining, if the teacher can't accurate grasp dig "degree", will appear a few schools themselves out of the volume of distracting, strange questions, students in the class will also continue to explore these deviations, the blame for this problem, but off the cultivating students' subject ability this purpose.

In order to adapt to the training of talents in the new era and consider the system of students' acceptance ability, China's current high school textbooks are not satisfactory. In order to alleviate this problem to a certain extent, our team makes the following Suggestions:

For the addition of teaching materials to cultivate students' innovative thinking, we believe that for each discipline, innovative thinking is indispensable, but must consider the students' acceptance ability and the examination content of the college entrance examination. Therefore, for students majoring in arts and science, taking science students as an example, physics, chemistry and biology are subjects that require in-depth understanding of students, that is, innovative exploration. As for history, politics and geography, science students need to have a comprehensive but not in-depth understanding of the knowledge system of these subjects, and they do not have to demand their ability of innovation and exploration. Therefore, we can divide the teaching materials into two books, one is the basic knowledge system, the other is the innovation and expansion of combining with the actual life. The textbook for the basic knowledge system is divided into an introductory section and an expansion section. The expansion section will be marked with "*". In the school of science living, for example, students need to learn is a basic subject system teaching materials (including the introduction section and expand section) and innovation to expand the teaching material of physics, chemistry, biology, basic subject system of the teaching material (including the introduction section only) the history, politics, geography, for the development and innovation under the condition of the study interest and spare capacity will be able to understand and communicate with the teacher after class.

In the high school chemistry teaching material, for example, on REDOX teaching in the beginning, the teacher usually starts with the experimental phenomena, tough and then asked the students memorize the chemical equation, the student to carry on the chemical equations to recite after six months, the will of the REDOX reaction equation of ion is the essence of the REDOX reaction—electronic transport in teaching, the students of REDOX reaction system of the first break; After the students entered the next teaching stage, they were told that the REDOX reaction was not a one-way reaction, but a two-way reversible reaction, and their cognitive system of REDOX reaction was overturned. Most students learn in the process of building a new body of knowledge by continually building a simple system, learning it, and then overturning it, telling it that it is wrong. And this teaching method not only through the entire high school teaching, but also through almost every student's learning life. From the primary school start learning basic addition, subtraction, multiplication, and division, for example, the teaching material on since the beginning did not directly introduced to the whole system, so convenient for students to understand the teacher, some teachers will conduct such extended to the teaching material, cannot be minus the larger Numbers, with smaller Numbers are fundamentally denied the existence of a negative number; In the later math learning, some teachers denied the existence of irrational Numbers in order to understand rational Numbers. In order to let the students better understand the real Numbers, and the existence of imaginary Numbers. After the students have established a simple system, they will be overthrown again and build a more complex new knowledge system.

Although the present teaching material on this teaching method makes students' learning pressure relief, but for students, sometimes repeatedly in the knowledge system and to overthrow and to establish the process of students tend to be confused, because the correctness of the knowledge has doubt attitude, will also hit the students' innovation enthusiasm. To this, our group's advice is, based on the modeling idea in the knowledge of economics, has certain difficulty in the need to simplify the knowledge points, teaching material should be active on the equivalent of a virtual model of the knowledge system, was built in order to facilitate understanding, in practice should pay attention to its applicable scope, must not abuse, misuse. Teaching materials should pay attention to inform the use of any knowledge points is a certain range of knowledge, cannot be easy to understand and ignore the knowledge points need to be in a certain range of application will be correct. At the present stage of teaching materials, a large area of space in the simple introduction of knowledge, let students remember, understand, but for the scientific thinking methods, advanced ideas and a variety of ability to cultivate a small amount of space. Scientific thinking methods include analysis, synthesis, generalization, reasoning, contrast, dialectical, forward and backward, convergence and divergence, and other thinking methods. Advanced ideas include concept of benefit, concept of competition, concept of time, concept of information, concept of connection, concept of whole, concept of system, etc. Ability includes self-study ability, ability to distinguish right from wrong, ability to collect information for comprehensive generalization, hands-on ability, creative ability and so on. These methods of scientific thinking are the abilities of the talents needed in the new era of China. Only after cultivating these methods of scientific thinking, can we develop our own thinking and innovate better after mastering them (Choe et al., 2004; Guo & Wang, 2019; Li & Li, 2019; Liu, 2020).

Taking high school physics as an example, in addition to introducing the basic formulas, basic principles and operations of physics, the history of physics is an important part of high school. However, most textbooks at this stage only show the history of physics in a straight line, and most students do not read it carefully. In recent years, in order to let students, understand the scientific thinking methods used by physicists to explore the physical world, the college entrance examination of physics integrates the history of physics into the college entrance examination questions, so that students attach importance to the history of physics. But the college entrance examination way also is relatively rigid, usually in multiple choice list several options to let the students to choose, makes the student to the physics history is "a man who knows the table, the", just hard to know a few famous scientist some of the more important scientific discoveries or inventions, the achievement of learning can't before its scientific thinking method, movement to use their own learning and exploration of innovation. These abilities are also to prepare for future undergraduate higher education and lay a solid foundation for national innovation and talent training.

After our group discussion, we think that the training part of students' scientific thinking in the textbook should not be rigidly filled in and the assessment method should not be rigidly used. This kind of scientific innovation ability can achieve relatively good results only by education and examination. Still in high school physics, for example, needs to be a physicist's scientific thought let students understand and apply to the real innovation to explore, to make teaching material after fully explain the principle of physics experiment, in the case of study students spare capacity, in the teaching practice after class, you can set up some more flexible, the topic of investigation. Accordingly, in the examination of college entrance examination and daily examination, the examination part of this list of questions should also be added, so that the proportion of questions that are rigid, rigid and set formulas should be reduced, and the number of such flexible and innovative questions should be increased, such as the experiment of redesigning similar principles according to the original physics experiment and so on.

3.4.2 The Questions and Suggestions on High School Curriculum

Over the past 70 years of reform and opening up, China's high school curriculum system has undergone several stages of development. At present, China's high school curriculum system is mainly established in the 2003 edition of the general high school curriculum plan and is taking the general high school curriculum plan (2017 edition) as the program for a new round of curriculum reform. The new curriculum reform changes the curriculum structure and content of the high school classroom, so as to make teaching and learning, learning and examination adapt, conducive to the overall development of students and personalized development, and better fit the training objectives of ordinary high schools, to achieve the role of high school education on the society.

Compared with the 2003 edition of "the ordinary high school curriculum plan", the curriculum reform in 2017 the biggest bright spot is that increased the "selective compulsory module", implement compulsory "complete test", selective compulsory "optional choose to take an examination of," courses "learning without examination or study and the reference appendix" pattern, at the same time, with the university entrance exam "3 + 3", "7" 3 plan, "3 + 1 + 2" scheme. The 2003 edition of the general high school curriculum plan divides the high school curriculum into three levels: learning areas, subjects and modules. In general, the curriculum structure is relatively loose, and the learning areas are not closely related. In addition to the way of the college entrance examination, the examination paper is called "comprehensive literature" and "comprehensive science". In fact, there is still a basic separation between subjects, and the phenomenon of division between subjects is more serious. This clear distinction between disciplines, on the one hand, is not conducive to the construction of high school students' learning knowledge system, the destruction of the integrity of high school learning, on the one hand, students after entering the university for further study causes certain restrictions. Therefore, the curriculum structure of the 2017 edition broke the original paradigm and no longer separated disciplines artificially, but only differentiated compulsory, compulsory and elective courses according to the learning level. From the perspective of curriculum structure, the degree of subject integration has been improved. In addition, the adoption of the "3+3" college entrance examination method is also conducive to the promotion of interdisciplinary integration. The advantages of subject integration are as follows: first, it is conducive to students' knowledge transfer. Students can use the knowledge or methods of a certain subject to solve problems in other subjects. Second, it is conducive to the construction of students' knowledge system, to better shape students' world view and values. Third, it is conducive to the overall development of students and the improvement of their comprehensive quality. Therefore, the direction of curriculum reform should be the direction of subject integration. This thought can be embodied through the design of teaching materials and permeated into the teaching content. At the same time, research-based learning can also focus on interdisciplinary issues, or set up lectures, etc. to cultivate students' comprehensive thinking at the school level.

According to the General High School Curriculum Plan (2017 edition), high school students are required to complete 144 credits upon graduation, with only 60% of them taking exams, continuing a downward trend. With the development of high school education in China, it is an inevitable trend that the proportion of examination subjects decreases, which is also the requirement of quality education. But at the same time, this curriculum plan in the implementation of some resistance, deviation. Main show is: currently, most of the university entrance exam of high school students are as far as possible in order to get high as study target, part of the high school courses also favor subjects, lay particular stress on the test requirements of the module, the so-called "learning without examination or study and the reference appendix" electives often stop driving, reflects not value to teachers and students from the school. Therefore, quality-oriented education is sometimes superficial, and the essence of high school education still returns to exam-oriented education oriented to the college entrance examination, failing to achieve the goal of students' free choice of courses and comprehensive quality cultivation. Based on the reality that college entrance examination is still the main way of college enrollment, we believe that the problem of high school education excessively favoring examination subjects is still difficult to solve. A feasible measure is to broaden the way of college enrollment, such as the recent "strong foundation plan" put forward by the ministry of education, for students to choose the corresponding subject courses, carry out in-depth study, improve their own subject ability to promote the role. The "comprehensive evaluation enrollment" currently implemented in some regions is also conducive to promoting the development of relevant courses in high schools. In addition, each region, high school can adjust measures according to local conditions, in addition to the national curriculum plan, set up a certain number of local courses, school-based courses, etc., in order to broaden students' horizons, develop students' interests and hobbies.

The content of high school curriculum should change with the reform of the curriculum system, which is reflected in the changes of textbooks and teachers' classroom teaching. At present, the main forms of high school teaching are still teachers' teaching and students' memory. This kind of classroom form exists for a long time, which is the main classroom form for exam-oriented education, but it is not suitable for the development of quality-oriented education. On the one hand, this kind of classroom teaching lacks feedback, which makes it difficult for teachers to understand students' mastery of knowledge and leads to the disconnection between teaching and learning. The lack of interaction between teachers and students also tends to lead to dull classes and students' loss of interest. On the other hand, this kind of classroom is mainly for the transmission of knowledge, less teachers on the cultivation of students' subject quality and values. Therefore, this way of curriculum development has a certain inhibitory effect on students' learning enthusiasm, and the nature of class that only emphasizes knowledge and not literacy is not conducive to the improvement of students' comprehensive quality. Measures should be taken to improve students' participation in the classroom, increase the frequency of classroom interaction, and develop a variety of teaching methods based on multimedia, so as to improve students' status in the classroom, ensure students' interest and concentration, and thus contribute to the development of students' emotional attitude and values.

In the college entrance examination as the vast majority of high school students study goal today, test-oriented teaching problems cannot be avoided. Although the general high school curriculum plan (2017 edition) stipulates credit hours and elective courses for various subjects, the courses actually taught in teaching practice do not fully conform to the plan. The main performance is: in some cases, the number of non-examination subjects is not up to the standard, the occupation of examination subjects, the non-examination subject teachers teaching requirements are relatively low, the students in class at will; The elective courses in the examination subjects have fewer or no courses, only pay attention to the examination points and difficulties rather than the subject system structure, and the content of the class is knowledge based and ignores the process of inquiry. In some areas, the exam-oriented teaching based on the college entrance examination annihilates the individualized and diversified characteristics of education, which runs counter to the requirements of the program. It is difficult for us to ask all high schools and students to leave the focus of teaching in the national college entrance examination. If the present college entrance examination system does not make corresponding adjustment, it is difficult to realize quality education. The fundamental means of reforming the current "exam-oriented education" is the reform of the talent selection system. First of all, we should broaden the way of college enrollment, such as in recent years "independent enrollment" way, launched in January "strong foundation plan", some colleges and universities adopted "comprehensive evaluation of enrollment", etc., conducive to guide students to develop disciplinary expertise or comprehensive development. Secondly, for the college entrance examination itself, we can change the idea of proposition, attach importance to the subject core quality proposition, the proposition reflects the subject system and the course of subject development, and increase the breadth of knowledge, so as to play the role of the "baton" of college entrance examination, and prevent the phenomenon that knowledge is more important than process in teaching practice.

References

Choe, Y. H., Ke, Z., & Lin, Y. Z. (2004). The historical evolution of the ordinary high school curriculum in China. *Journal of Education Research, 4*(01), 86–91.

Guo, H., & Wang, L. L. (2019). A 70-year exploration on the reform of curriculum structure in Chinese senior high schools. *Journal of Education in China, 19*(10), 9–16.

Li, J., & Li, J. (2019). Educational policy development in China in the 21st century: A Multi-Flows Approach. *Beijing International Review of Education, 1*(1), 196–220.

Liu, B. (2020). Current situation and thinking of the reform of the new college entrance examination system: The perspective of institutional change. *China Higher Education Research, 20*(01), 35–41.

Chapter 4
An Analysis of the School Layout Policy of Chinese High School Education

This chapter concentrates on an analysis of the school layout policy of Chinese high school education. High school education is an important part of basic education. The state has also issued many relevant policies on the layout of high school. Here, we will enumerate and analyze the current policies. This paper will analyze the logic behind the current school layout policy from political, economic, cultural and social perspectives. Then, starting with the cities and counties, the author will analyze the current situation of the layout of high schools, find the deficiencies of the current layout and put forward some opinions and suggestions on the existing problem.

4.1 The School Layout Policy for High School Education

The location of primary and secondary schools should follow certain basic principles. Can be listed as the following: (1) the principle of balanced development: refers to the location planning must be considered in the various factors. Such as population size, distribution and density, traffic, quality of students and other factors. (2) The principle of nearby admission: that is, to ensure the convenience of students' admission. (3) The principle of intensification: in the process of using educational resources, the cost should be saved as far as possible, which requires the school to have a certain scale while meeting the standard requirements. (4) Safety principle: site selection should consider the safety of students. (5) The planning and layout of sub-areas should be carried out, and different areas should be treated differently: urban development will result in inconsistent land conditions in new and old urban areas. In the process of planning educational resources, it can be integrated through a variety of measures, including relocation, withdrawal and merger, so as to ensure the standardization of schools. Due to the shortage of land in the old city, schools in the old city must be considered from the following aspects in terms of planning: first, meet their needs based on the space distribution point. If the school is relatively small, it should adopt the transformation method such as relocation and school

J. Li and E. Xue, *Education Policy in Chinese High Schools*, Exploring Education Policy in a Globalized World: Concepts, Contexts, and Practices, https://doi.org/10.1007/978-981-16-2358-5_4

merging. As for the new urban area, the conditions of land use are easy to be satisfied, so the school planning in the new urban area must be considered from a long-term perspective. (6) Long term combination, combination of rigidity and elasticity: for the development of primary and secondary schools, must be implemented in accordance with the relevant national standards, but also based on specific actual needs, so that the elasticity and rigidity can be effectively met. For the short-term goals, it is necessary to pay attention to the predicted population, distribution and specific scale, so that the school's consistent layout can be effectively adjusted, and the basic indicators can be appropriate and advanced. As for the long-term goal, we should pay attention to the long-term development of the school. So, under the guidance of these principles, our country will formulate what kind of policy to make the school construction site rationalization, scientific layout? Through the search and sorting of the network, we found some relevant policies, which play a very important role in the layout and location of the school.

4.1.1 The Evolution and Development of China's Policies on the Layout of Basic Education Schools

Since the founding of the People's Republic of China, China's education policy is constantly changing, and the reasons behind it are the change of educational concept, social development, demand and so on. According to the time division, China's basic education school layout policy can be divided into the following periods: "New-democratic to a socialist transition" period (1949–1955), "the comprehensive construction socialism" period (1956–1965), during the "cultural revolution" (1966–1976), under the background of reform and opening up "efficiency first, balance equity" as the main orientation of the new era (1978–2000), since the twenty-first century to "scale" to the orientation of the period (2001–2011) and 18 since the "fair and quality" as the orientation period (after 2012). The educational orientation is different in different periods, and the policies promulgated are also different.

The period of "transition from new democracy to socialism". During this period, the new China was just established, and all walks of life were in a state of waiting to be developed. The main task facing education is to reform the educational institutions in the old society. It is vital, then, to receive and transform the old social schools. The main policy based on this work was the department of education's 1951 directive on the treatment of missionary schools and other institutions of education receiving United States subsidies, which proposed the gradual conversion of missionary schools to public or private on the basis of ideological preparation. Of course, taking over the old schools is not all the work, there is a more important work is literacy. Therefore, many policies at that time emphasized the construction of part-time schools such as literacy classes, night schools, and accelerated middle schools for workers and peasants.

At the same time, the government is encouraging private schools to address the pressure on public schools, which is also increasing the number of people educated. For example, in 1949, the ministry of education issued the instructions on carrying out this year's winter schoolwork, and in 1955, the state council issued the regulations on industry and mining, enterprises running their own middle schools, primary schools and kindergartens. In addition, in 1953, the ministry of education issued the opinions on the success of some middle schools and normal schools in key areas. During this period, educational resources were very limited and educational tasks were very heavy. At this time, educational policies mainly encouraged the construction of primary and secondary schools and paid little attention to the layout and site selection.

The period of "comprehensively building socialism". During this period, the educational policy was characterized by two points, namely, the emphasis on basic education, the encouragement of various forms of running schools and the emphasis on the construction of key schools. As a result, there were also these characteristics in the layout problem at that time, which were embodied as follows: We attached importance to basic education and promote its development on a large scale. The relevant education policies all emphasize the development of compulsory education, but do not attach much importance to the high school education which is also the basic education. For example, the outline of the 12-year national education program proposes to make compulsory education universal within seven years, and the instruction of the CPC central committee and the state council on education proposes to eliminate illiteracy and make primary education universal within three to five years.

The state planning commission and the ministry of education issued a notice in 1962 on the problems that schools at all levels should pay attention to in their enrollment plans in 1962 and the opinions on several issues concerning rural primary schools and "private schools" issued in 1963. It is worth mentioning that these two policies put forward the requirement of allowing students to enroll nearby as far as possible in the school layout. Of course, in this period, the education policy paid more attention to the construction of key schools.

During the cultural revolution, the society was relatively chaotic, and under such a social background, the education industry was also greatly impacted. In my opinion, the education policies during this period were somewhat grandiose. Relative deviation from reality. For example, a series of policies such as the minutes of the national meeting on education work issued in 1971 and the notice on opening schools issued by the education and science group of the state council and the ministry of finance in 1974 all proposed that schools should be located at the door. Such policies have led to a rapid expansion of basic education. This blind expansion has seriously affected the quality of education. At this time the layout policy is as close as possible to the doorstep of the proletariat, the pursuit of schools everywhere.

The period in which "efficiency first and fairness" is the main orientation. After everything back on track, the layout of education policy and before the cultural revolution is not a very big difference, such as the following features is just little difference with before the cultural revolution, the construction of key schools, for example, in January 1978, the Ministry of Education issued the "on hold a number of key primary and secondary schools of the implementation of circular, 1980 the Ministry of Education about done by the decision of the key middle school" can be found. In 1985, the central committee of the communist party of China issued the decision on the reform of the education system. In 1999, the decision of the CPC central committee and the state council on deepening educational reform and comprehensively promoting quality-oriented education and other documents all expressed the idea of encouraging various forms of school running, hoping that the layout and forms of school running could adapt to the production and life of the masses. Of course, there are also many new goals to make the basic education layout policy more perfect and closer to life. For example, the renovation of dilapidated houses built and reserved during the promotion of universal compulsory education to ensure the safety of teachers and students. The state education commission's notice on the repair and reconstruction of dilapidated primary and secondary schools in 1989 and the regulations on the comprehensive elimination and elimination of dilapidated primary and secondary schools issued in November 1992 are policies specially formulated for this issue. And at the same time, policies to build key schools are also aimed at improving weak schools to reduce the gap between schools. Released in 1995 on the printing of ten measures to strengthen the construction of weak ordinary senior middle schools (trial) notice "about to do a good job in ordinary senior middle school's several opinions are aimed at strengthening the construction of the weak school, reduce the gap, 1996" about issued by the national education career and development plan in 2010 the "ninth five-year plan" period of notice also mentioned this point.

And very importantly, there was an emphasis on economies of scale in education policy. Such as the aforementioned "about the printing ten measures to strengthen the construction of weak ordinary senior middle schools (trial) notice is put forward to remove scattered layout, the small size of school, out of 1998 units on the acceptance of the" two basics "earnestly strengthen improve work several opinions are reasonable layout is presented to increase the size of the request.

The "economies of scale" oriented period. In pursuit of economies of scale, our approach is mainly to "remove the points and merge schools". Due to the great economic pressure on county-level governments caused by the education management system dominated by counties, and the reduction of school-age population due to the implementation of family planning, school and class sizes have shrunk. At this time, there was the layout adjustment of "removing points and merging schools", and relevant policies followed: for example, the decision on the reform and development of basic education and the tenth national education cause were issued in 2001.

The annual plan proposes to optimize the allocation of educational resources, make rational planning and adjust the layout. Then there is the problem: too much focus on economies of scale makes it harder for many students to get to school because they are too far away. Therefore, starting from 2006, the state began to rectify partial policies. In June 2006, the ministry of education issued the "notice on adjusting the layout of rural primary and secondary schools in a practical and practical way" on the principle of seeking truth from facts, steadily advancing, and facilitating schooling to implement the layout adjustment of rural primary and secondary schools. In 2010, the outline of the national medium- and long-term education reform and development plan (2010–2020) and opinions on further promoting the balanced development of compulsory education by implementing the scientific concept of development also mentioned such requirements as "reasonable planning" and "scientific planning".

At the same time, education policy is strengthening the construction of weak schools. In 2003, the Ministry of Education issued "on further strengthening rural education work decision", introduced in 2004, the energy department, the department of education in 2003–2007 education revitalization action plan of the notice, in 2007, the Ministry of Education issued the "11th five-year plan" national education career development planning outline, more than a lot of policy document the promulgation and implementation of greatly improved conditions of weak schools especially rural small ones and reduce the unfair of education.

In this period, compared to the previous period, we began to encourage characteristic education. In 2002, the ministry of education issued the notice on actively promoting the reform of evaluation and examination system of primary and secondary schools, which proposed that schools should meet the requirements of quality education and reflect the school's characteristics of the school-running goals and development plans. In 2010, the CPC central committee and the state council issued the outline of the national program for medium- and long-term education reform and development (2010–2020), which explicitly encourages primary and secondary schools to develop their own characteristics and standards. To sum up, we can find that the layout policy in this period gradually developed towards the direction of intensification, which is conducive to the maximization of economies of scale.

The period with the orientation of "fairness and quality". After the 18th national congress of the communist party of China (CPC), basic education entered the era of "reversion and integration". This era has several characteristics as follows: focus on improving the running level of small-scale schools in rural areas and boarding schools in towns and villages. In 2017 promulgated by the State Council "about" much starker choices-and graver consequences-in "issued by the national education career development planning of notice, in 2018 promulgated by the State Council" about strengthening rural small schools and the construction of rural boarding school guidance, "published in 2019, the Ministry of Education" in 2019, the Ministry of Education work points put forward the reasonable layout, vigorously construction of rural small schools, rural boarding schools, improve the school. Efforts should be made to eliminate the phenomenon of "large class sizes" in urban schools. The notice of the state council on the issuance of the 13th five-year plan for the development of national education issued in 2017 proposed to basically eliminate the "large class size" with more than 56 students by 2020, which has a certain impact on the layout of classes in the school. Characteristic school construction. In 2018, the ministry of education issued the notice of the general office of the ministry of education on the establishment of special schools for youth football in schools, the creation of pilot counties (districts) (2018–2025) and the selection of "full star" training camps in 2018, proposing to establish 30,000 special schools by 2025. In February 2019, the general office of the CPC central committee and the general office of the state council issued the implementation plan for accelerating education modernization (2018–2022), which proposed to promote the high-quality and distinctive development of ordinary high schools. To sum up, in this era, the school layout strategy is mainly to strengthen the construction of small schools and boarding schools in the countryside and weaken the integration of schools. Reduce class sizes in cities. At the same time, we should strengthen the construction of special schools.

4.1.2   The Policies Generally Considered in the Current School Layout

The policies mentioned before are generally guidance, mainly reflecting the guidelines and strategies of the layout. Therefore, the policies to be considered in the real layout of the school will be more specific and more complex. In the aspect of layout, primary and secondary schools and other education facilities is the important public service facilities in urban and rural areas, is the main content of the urban and rural planning, clear requirements according to the urban and rural planning act to coordinate development strategy of urbanization, population size and distribution, the rational allocation of urban and rural public service facilities and land use layout, including primary and secondary schools and other kinds of education facilities. So, in the planning layout is bound to refer to the urban and rural planning law. In addition, the design code for primary and secondary schools and the construction standards for urban ordinary primary and secondary schools specify the service radius, school size, class size, functional housing and site layout of primary and secondary schools, secondary schools and nine-year schools. It is also a policy that must be considered in the planning of the school.

In terms of the selection and guarantee of urban school land, the urban and rural planning law clearly requires that before the transfer of state-owned land use right, the planning conditions such as the location, nature of use and development intensity of the transferred land should be put forward according to the detailed urban control planning, including the requirements for the construction of supporting educational facilities such as primary and secondary schools. Methods for the compilation of urban planning and methods for the compilation of controlled detailed planning for cities and towns require the layout of land for primary and secondary schools to be arranged according to the population size of residential areas and relevant standards. These relevant standards not only guarantee the land use of primary and secondary schools, but also make requirements on their location and scale. In addition, document no. 40 [2016] of the state council clearly requires all regions to formulate the layout plan of compulsory education schools in cities and towns according to the urbanization plan and the size of resident population, and reserve enough school land according to the changing trend of school-age population and the construction standards of primary and secondary schools. General Office of the State Council on strengthening rural small schools and the construction of rural boarding school guidance "(countries do hair [2018] 27) is also a special emphasis on the layout of rural school should not only to provide students with a fair, with quality education, and to respect the minors' physical and psychological law of development, and convenient neighborhood school students; Not only to prevent the rapid withdrawal of schools and lead to overconcentration of students, but also to avoid the emergence of new "hollow schools". According to the information on the official website of the ministry of education in 2018, we can know that the ministry of education will also work with relevant departments to promote the unification of urban and rural standards for the construction of ordinary primary and secondary schools, and the formulation of unified standards for the construction of ordinary primary and secondary schools between urban and rural areas, so as to promote the fair and balanced development of urban and rural basic education facilities. We will guide local governments in actively optimizing the distribution structure of ordinary high schools, establish a mechanism for quality schools in provinces to help poor schools in poor areas, and promote balanced allocation of quality education resources.

In December 1980, *The Party Central Committee and the State Council Focusing on Some Issues of Universal Primary Education Decision* is put forward for the first time about the provisions of the "school": given the economic and cultural development is very uneven in our country, the natural environment, living condition difference is very big, must from set out actually, adjust measures to local conditions, take various forms of running a school, makes every effort to make the layout and form of running school adapted to mass production, living, to facilitate students to go to school. While running a good full-time school, there should be more simple primary schools or classes in various forms, such as half-day, alternate day, traveling, morning, afternoon and evening classes.

One of the main goals of the key plan for the popularization of high school education (2017–2020), issued by the Ministry of Education in 2017, is to popularize high school education nationwide by 2020, so as to meet the needs of middle school graduates to receive good high school education. The national and provincial gross enrollment rates reached more than 90%, and the gross enrollment rates in the central and western regions increased significantly. The structure of general high school and secondary vocational education is more reasonable, and the enrollment scale is roughly the same. The conditions of the school have been improved to meet the basic requirements of education and teaching. The mechanism of funding input has been improved, and the system of funding per student has been fully established. The quality of education has been significantly improved, the characteristics of running schools have become more obvious, and the appeal has been further enhanced.

Since the 18th national congress of the communist party of China (CPC), China's senior high school education has made great progress on the whole. However, due to various reasons, there are still many shortcomings in high school education. Some poor areas, ethnic minority areas and remote areas are short of educational resources, and their popularity is low. The development structure of general high school education and secondary vocational education is not coordinated and balanced. Many schools are too weak to meet basic teaching requirements. The funding mechanism of high school education is not perfect, and the debt problem of ordinary high schools has not been effectively solved. There is a shortage of specially assigned teachers in some subjects and "double-qualified" teachers in secondary vocational education in ordinary high schools. The quality of education is not high. Ordinary high schools lack characteristics and secondary vocational education is not attractive. These problems and difficulties have seriously affected the balanced development of high school education.

First, the main responsibility for promoting the balanced development of high school education lies with the government. From the current situation, promote the development of high school education in our country before strategy is a balanced development strategy, namely, local government and the administrative departments of education in high school education has taken on the way such as financial support, policy tilt, priority to promote some places, some schools take the lead in development, the formation of a batch of high-quality high school education resources, through these high quality education resources to promote the overall growth of high school education. Although the starting point of this development mode is high, on the one hand, it will form a batch of high-quality high school education resources, but on the other hand, it will artificially widen the gap between regions and schools, which is not conducive to the balanced development of high school education.

On March 2, 2000, China issued *The Notice of the Central Committee and the State Council of China on the Pilot Reform of Rural Taxes and Fees*, which abolished the administrative fees specifically levied on farmers such as township planning fees and rural education fund raising. On March 24, 2001, the State Council issued *A Further Completing the Rural Reform of Taxes and Fees Pilot Work of the State Council Notice*, by the township government and the local farmers to raise the school, organized by the government at the county level and management of rural education, instead of education funds incorporated in the county level, and establish and perfect the mechanism for ensuring adequate funding for rural compulsory education, strengthen the government at the county level for teachers management and payroll functions as a whole. On May 29, 2001, *The Decision of the State Council on the Reform and Development of Basic Education* pointed out: "adjust the layout of rural compulsory education schools according to local conditions, and rationally plan and adjust the layout of schools according to the principles of primary school enrollment nearby, relatively concentrated junior high schools, and optimized allocation of educational resources. Rural primary and secondary schools and teaching points in the convenience of the nearby students to choose the appropriate combination of the premise, in the areas with transportation difficulties still need to retain the necessary teaching points, to prevent the layout adjustment caused by students to drop out. The adjustment of school layout should be planned as a whole with renovation of dilapidated houses, standardization of school system, urbanization development, migration and relocation. Assets such as school buildings after adjustment should be guaranteed to be used for the development of education. Boarding schools may be held where there is a need and a condition." In September 2003 the State Council on further strengthening rural education work of the decision "points out:" in primary and secondary schools continue to push forward the layout structure adjustment, and strive to improve managerial condition, the finish to strengthen rural and remote mountainous areas, ethnic minority areas, construction of boarding schools, improve school health facilities and student accommodation conditions, and improve the equipment level of experimental instruments and equipment and books. After that, local governments at all levels issued documents on the layout adjustment of primary and secondary schools one after another, which took the school layout adjustment as an important work. The school layout adjustment swept across the country and was stipulated to be completed within the tenth five-year plan period.

From 2001 to 2005 is the first stage of school layout adjustment work, this stage layout adjustment policy has the following characteristics. First, the objective needs, the government to promote. In the reform of taxes and fees and the request of the education management system reform, in the face of practical problems such as urbanization, rural population decline, due to compression education team personnel, rational allocation of education resources, national policy adjustment layout, the provinces, cities and county (city) where the layout of the corresponding adjustment policies and measures, is dominated by the government, in accordance with the administrative measures, layer upon layer. Second, interest driven, local blind. The central committee of the CCP, the State Council notice about the conduct of the pilot reform of rural taxes and fees, "dangerous house reconstruction funds arranged by the budget of primary and secondary schools", "the State Council on further completes the notice of the pilot reform of rural taxes and fees," the central and provincial governments to enhance the support to rural education, education through transfer payments support poverty-stricken counties, and set up a special fund for dangerous house renovation and building construction of rural elementary and middle schools in poverty-stricken areas. The central government set up "special funds for primary and secondary school distribution adjustment" and supporting measures, while local governments often make layout adjustment without scientific planning and argumentation in order to maximize profits. Third, the national advance, the grassroots passive. At this stage, the layout adjustment is fully advanced, with provinces, prefectures, cities and counties (cities) fully rolled out, and government-led, profit-driven, and movement-oriented; In some places, the work of grassroots administrative and educational departments is very passive. People at the grassroots level do not know enough about the layout adjustment policies and have difficulty adapting to them. At the same time, they are also very passive and even resistant to such practical problems as the distance and difficulty for children to go to school.

From the analysis of policy documents, it can be seen that the value orientation of the layout adjustment policy at this stage is to pursue benefit and give consideration to fairness. The pursuit of efficiency is mainly manifested in two aspects: first, "reduce personnel", "streamline and optimize the staff of primary and secondary school teachers", mainly is to dismiss substitute teachers, dismiss unqualified teachers, reduce non-teaching staff in rural schools, and eliminate temporary workers. Second, "rational allocation of educational resources" to improve the use of educational resources. The Ministry of Education, Ministry of Finance on primary and secondary schools of planning layout structure adjustment notice in illustrates the development of primary and secondary school layout adjustment planning goals: "by adjusting the distribution network of primary and secondary schools, the rational allocation of education resources, not reduce the number of primary and secondary schools, expand the scale of places, to improve the teaching quality and benefit of education investment, gradually realize the school layout is reasonable, optimize the education structure and mechanisms of choose and employ persons, funds using efficient target, the promotion of basic education sustained, steady and healthy development." It should be said that the layout adjustment policy at this stage also takes into account the fairness. After that, various relevant documents of the country all mentioned the issue of nearby school enrollment and the consideration of the burden of the people. Moreover, one of the motivations for the layout adjustment is to promote the popularization, consolidation and improvement of primary and secondary education, so that most children can go to school.

2006–2010 is the second stage of school layout adjustment. This stage, school-age population decreases, the urbanization process to speed up the deepened, more migrant workers to find jobs in cities, migrant children growth trend is obvious, national various measures to promote the development of balanced gradually implemented, the local government and education administrative department of the school layout adjustment of self-consciousness and initiative to enhance, the rational thinking to adjust the layout, the layout adjustment range from school, elementary school to junior high school and senior high school, even in the counties and cities within the scope of pre-school education to high school education, from normal education to vocational and adult education overall planning, rational layout. At this stage, the country adjusted the policy orientation to the layout prudently and steadily.

In June 2006, the Ministry of Education about seeking truth from facts to do a good job of rural primary and secondary school layout adjustment notice "issued, the "notice" that the layout of the previous phase adjustment, from the overall, layout adjustment achieved significant results, the conditions of primary and middle schools, the educational efficiency and quality of education has improved further. In February 2007, the Ministry of Education on further strengthening and improving comprehensive supervision inspections at the provincial level to realize the "two basics" opinions", the finish check layout is not reasonable, the large amount of small and medium-sized school, teaching instruments and equipment with the problem of insufficient, and facilities, construction of rural boarding schools, the application of the modern distance education equipment. In October 2007, the Report of the 17th National Congress of the Communist Party of China (CPC) focused on national rejuvenation and social equity, put forward the concept of "running the education that the people are satisfied with" and made clear plans.

In October 2008, *The Decision of the CPC Central Committee on Some Major Issues Concerning the Promotion of Rural Reform and Development* emphasized that "we should consolidate the achievements in popularizing education in rural areas, improve the quality of education, and improve the educational policy and funding guarantee mechanism". The national policy of "promoting balanced development of education" put forward at the 17th National Congress of the Communist Party of China (CPC) was upgraded to "promoting balanced development of education in urban and rural areas". In January 2010, the Ministry of Education about further push forward *the Opinions of Balanced Development of Education to Implement the Scientific Outlook on Development*, "stressed: local education administrative departments at all levels in the adjustment of layout of primary and secondary schools, to overall consideration of urban and rural economic and social development, the future changes in population and the people's real needs, be practical and realistic, scientific planning, both to ensure the quality of education, and convenient to students, avoid blind adjustment and simple operation. For the schools that have completed layout adjustment, we should improve the conditions of running schools, especially the conditions of boarding, so as to guarantee students' study and life. To further standardize the school layout adjustment procedures, the school must fully listen to the opinions of the masses, to avoid new contradictions caused by the layout adjustment.

It can be seen from the policy document that the policy characteristics of the school layout adjustment at this stage are as follows: first, highlight equity, pay attention to balanced development, and promote balanced education between urban and rural areas; Second, making prudent decisions and advocating steady progress; Third, layout adjustment policy combined with multiple education balanced development measures combine layout adjustment and balanced development efforts, the school layout and boarding school construction, standardization of school construction, teacher resources rational allocation of measures such as combination of the development of education in the development of rural public utilities, the school layout adjustment is incorporated in the policies and measures of education balanced development between urban and rural areas, rural education into the whole career development. The value orientation of school layout at this stage is to highlight fairness and promote balanced development of urban and rural education.

From the point of view of the current high school funds running situation, the education bureau of the salaries of teachers, basic construction fee, such as school, teacher's benefits, the temporary workers wages, daily spending by the school self-raised, rural high school is the only source of income for student's tuition and fees, few donations, donations from outside, this leads to the shortage of fiscal investment of high school education. In terms of the whole country, the fiscal income of high school education is far lower than that of primary school and middle school. The investment subject of the school and the main body of the school merge into one, from the institution reduced to a quasi-economic entity, the school capital shortage, development is difficult. The education bureau often refuses to invest in the school on the grounds of "non-compulsory education" and "tuition payment" in ordinary high schools, and the school has to resort to the two ways of enrollment and fund raising to seek financial support for the development of the school. In order to increase the school's income, the high school principal tried every means to expand the enrollment scale and recruit students, but still unable to do it. But this way of survival is already at the end of the road, because the main way for schools to increase income is to expand enrollment, and the state has regulations on the high school fees, the school's income is declining year by year. From the legal point of view, the ordinary high school is a public institution, which does not have the right to loan and the ability to finance, and all the assets of the school and its value-added part are owned by the state, so the government's role as the debt subject of the school is indisputable. In view of these two aspects, the state must attach importance to and strengthen the educational function and investment responsibility of the government, and actively use the financial channels at the central and provincial levels to solve the debt problem prevalent in high schools.

Moreover, with the popularization of compulsory education and the acceleration of the popularization of higher education, the development of ordinary high schools has been accelerated. According to the advantages of high-quality high school education resources, key high schools continuously improve the conditions of running schools, expand the scale of education, improve the quality of education, and further improve their influence in society. The state and society attach great importance to the education of key high schools and call for the expansion of high-quality high school resources. Governments at all levels attach great importance to the education of key high schools and give special support in human, financial, material and policy aspects. The school fees standard is high, the fee limit is big, the development potential is big, the condition of running a school is good add good, some schools even reached the point of luxury; Admission priority, priority selection, students of good quality, is the general high school cannot compete with; The high quality and good treatment of teachers are more conducive to attracting high-quality teachers and forming a group of high-quality teachers. Key high schools have become the source base of undergraduate colleges and universities. On the contrary, the general high school is not taken seriously, the state appropriation funds are seriously insufficient, the school fee standard is low, the charge amount is small, the school condition is bad, the teacher level is low, the school scale is small, the student source quality is low, the student source is seriously insufficient. General high schools not only the college entrance examination rate is low, and its graduates are mainly admitted to colleges, vocational and technical colleges. In this way, the gap between key high schools and general high schools is further widened, and the trend of unbalanced development of ordinary high schools is further strengthened.

To explore the influence of social and cultural factors on the school layout policy of Chinese high school education, we should first understand the school layout policy of Chinese high school education. To some extent, we can use the layout situation of high school to reflect the school layout policy. Different from the interpretation of political and economic factors, this time we choose samples for analysis. We selected the distribution of high schools in Sichuan province as the representative for analysis. From the two aspects of time and space to carry out the analysis.

According to the horizontal and vertical comparison of the number of schools in Sichuan province, it can be found that there are certain differences in the number of schools in different time and space. It can be said that most of the differences in space come from the economic development of different regions. However, I think these differences are more or less directly or indirectly influenced by social and cultural factors. Social and cultural factors including all the activities of human beings, such as health habits, living conditions, living environment, population flows, customs, religious beliefs, social unrest, etc., also includes a person, a social group, a nation, a country's production and living habit of qualitative, namely basic culture quality performance. The following is an analysis of the cultural and social impact on the distribution of high schools in China.

There is a natural kinship between education and culture. On the one hand, education policy is based on culture, and on the other hand, education policy reacts on culture. Regional culture is an important cultural foundation of educational policy. The unique regional culture of the region has a great impact on the education policy. The regional culture includes the construction of the regional environment, the cultivation of humanistic styles and so on, which will permeate the education of the students in the region and make the school different from the similar schools in other regions and form its characteristics. For unique culture in national minority areas, the ethnic minorities have their own language, has its own unique traditional culture, and so on, these will make them and the Han nationality in the process of receiving education to form difference, such as on the degree of master of Chinese is different, and so on, so in ethnic minority areas, there will be and they adapt to the culture of middle school's distribution, and less on the distribution of the ethnic minorities, such as ethnic minority education of children of migrant workers, where he lived for their unique culture of the school might be less or even no. How to meet the special educational needs of these ethnic minorities is a problem to be considered in the future.

The new culture also has a great influence on the distribution of schools, including the new culture borrowed from others and the reflection on the emerging problems in the society. These emerging cultures often cause changes in the distribution of high schools. For example, with the development of economic globalization, English has become an increasingly important subject, and many foreign language schools have appeared in some big cities. And a lot of schools have international departments, and most of these students will finish university abroad. All these changes are related to the more frequent communication between big cities and the outside world. In rural counties or relatively backward areas, there will be fewer or no such middle schools, which is related to the close degree of cultural communication between the local and the outside world. Of course, it is also limited by other conditions, such as the local standard of living and the local teachers.

Cultural level should affect people's ideas and behaviors and other aspects. In the relevant research carried out in Ningxia during the summer vacation, we conducted a study on parents' cultural level and their children's educational level. We measured parents' cultural level according to their ability to help their children with their homework. The most time parents can help with homework is in elementary school, middle school, high school, or none at all. According to the questionnaire, 87.4% of the grandparent generation had not been coached by their parents for homework, and 8.3% had been coached for elementary school work. 82.5% of parents had no homework, 13.3% had elementary school homework, and 2.9% had junior high school homework. Only 1% of students of this generation had not been tutored in their homework, 47.6% had been tutored in their primary school homework, and 16.3% had been tutored in their middle school homework. It can be seen that the educational level of parents increases with each generation, and also changes significantly in the generation of students. According to the corresponding analysis of education background and parents' educational level of a single sample, there is no significant difference in education background of students corresponding to other options except that those who choose the option of "no counseling" have lower education background. Thus, it can be seen that parents' level is not the main factor affecting children's education background. In addition, we also explored the influence of gender on academic qualifications. By processing the data, we found that the education (expectation) of different genders in the first generation was significantly different. The specific performance is that the male education is obviously higher than the female education. In this part, we found that in the first generation (grandparents), gender has a significant impact on the level of education; However, from the second generation (parents' generation) to the third generation (high school students) today, gender factors have less significant influence on academic qualifications, or it can be said that from the second generation, in terms of academic qualifications, gender equality has been achieved. This suggests that earlier "son preference" affected women's access to education and, indirectly, that when this phenomenon lessened, girls' secondary schools would emerge, eventually increasing the number of schools without gender differentiation. This is the effect of literacy on school distribution. Chinese fine traditional culture has a great influence on education, especially on the ideological and moral education of students. China's fine traditional culture, Chinese revolutionary culture and Chinese contemporary culture are in one line, and they are unified in the inheritance and innovation of Chinese culture and in the great national spirit of China. In education, these cultures, spirits and qualities are passed on. The so-called society is a community of human life based on certain material production activities. The production of material materials is the foundation of social existence and development. The sum of the relations of production formed by people in the process of material production and corresponding to the development of certain productive forces constitutes the economic foundation of the society. On this basis, a superstructure corresponding to it is produced. I think the influence of society on the distribution of high schools can be seen from the following aspects.

4.2   Current Situation of Layout: A Case Study of Xiamen City in Fujian Province

Xiamen education will basically complete the modern lifelong education system by 2020, improve the quality of education and guarantee level comprehensively, significantly improve the ability to serve Xiamen's economic and social development, and basically form a modern education governance system, taking the lead in realizing the modernization of education. High school education, as an important bridge to transport high quality talents to higher education, has been widely concerned by policy makers and the public. In fact, the layout of high school is influenced by urban structure, urban land layout, urban traffic layout and other factors. The following part is to analyze and summarize the layout and configuration of Xiamen high schools through social investigation and consulting documents (Fang, 2014; Li, 2018; Shen, 2019).

4.2.1 The Overview of Xiamen City

Xiamen is one of China's five special economic zones and a leader in education in Fujian province. The development and construction of Xiamen's educational cause plays a leading role in the whole province. High school education is the hub between nine-year compulsory education and higher education, which is responsible for providing high-quality talents to higher education schools. High school education reform has also become the top priority in China's education reform. Xiamen city has also made continuous beneficial attempts in adjusting the layout of high schools, facing such problems as unbalanced development, incomplete implementation of the funding guarantee mechanism for some local public high schools, and the inadaptability of some local schools to the comprehensive reform of the college entrance examination. At present, Xiamen city has put forward some effective Suggestions on reasonably planning the layout of ordinary high schools and regional overall planning in some laws and regulations.

4.2.2 The General High School Layout Related Theories and Examples

Due to the paid use of land and the differentiation of land ownership, land rent is inevitable. The layout of high schools is also affected by the rent effect. On the one hand, the high school construction will increase the regional flow of people and promote the improvement of the surrounding land price; on the other hand, the high school covers a large area, has a low plot ratio, and belongs to the quasi-public goods, so the output benefit is not high. Therefore, the city managers need to balance the marginal benefit maximization of land investment and city income and find the best combination point. The location theory of service industry studies the location choice of service industry and the relationship between service industry and other urban functional space.

At present, there is a trend to expand the scale of ordinary high schools, especially the schools with outstanding school quality and famous reputation, which have a certain source of student's market.

According to the "2018–2019 basic information of Xiamen schools at all levels and of all types" released by Xiamen municipal education bureau, there are 32 high schools in Xiamen, 12 of which are located in Huli district and Siming district in the central city, and the remaining 20 high schools are located in the other four districts. Although there is no obvious difference in the average number of schools, from the perspective of popularity and strength of the schools, 9 of them are rated as provincial model high schools, 5 are located in the central city, and the remaining 4 are respectively located in Jimei district, Haicang district and Tongan district. Thus, it can be seen that most of the ordinary high schools with strong educational strength are located in the downtown area. Moreover, the high school located in the central urban area is closely related to the layout of residential land and traffic structure. There are at least two or more public transportation means and more than three residential areas around the high school. Although the living and transportation conditions are very convenient, there are two phenomena of large class size and less ground area per capita in high schools in the central city. However, most of the current high schools are located in the old city and their expansion scope is limited, which leads to land shortage and other problems.

4.2.3 The Distribution of Cross-Island Radiation High-Quality Resources to the Outside of the Island

The reasons for the early stage are as follows: according to the data, the primary reason for Xiamen high-quality high school to relocate or establish its campus at the beginning is the increase of the total number of students. The educational resources of the original campus cannot meet the educational conditions of students. At the same time, the middle and high schools are separated to improve the quality of teaching and students' living and learning. Now to introduce the present stage, the Xiamen municipal education bureau released by the Xiamen city "much starker choices-and graver consequences-in" special education career development planning (2016–2020) (hereinafter referred to as the "plan") is put forward to further enhance the level of ordinary high school education, optimizing the layout of average high school, the development of ordinary high school in rural areas, meet the requirements of high quality high school district at least 2. Because the island's junior high school has been very dense, so the education bureau hopes to through a high school, double ten, foreign language quality high schools outside the island to set up a substantive branch.

4.2.4 The Significance of Off-Island Layout

According to a 2019 four department of Fujian province (province education department, the provincial development and reform commission, the provincial financial department, the province people club hall) released the "Fujian province high school education quality improvement plan" points out that the average high school layout structure remains to be optimized, unbalanced development, also be the many existing conditions of running a school and teachers configuration can't meet the need of high school new curriculum implementation, the college entrance examination reform and other issues. So the ordinary high school teachers into the "county tube school hired" to reform limits, revitalize the county teacher resources, shortage of promoting disciplinary system of teachers "teaching", and encourage teachers to undertake more workload or outside part of part-time teachers or use the information means to close the gap between urban and rural education, teachers accept the municipal or district regulation and with the aid of education informatization make up the education resources also greatly help the integration of urban and rural education gap, effectively avoid the island hollowing out of high school (Fang, 2014; Li, 2018; Shen, 2019).

High quality high school resources are generally considered to have better conditions for running schools, a better learning style, a stronger teaching team, and a higher quality of education. The planning of the space layout of the ordinary high school is a regional plan of overall planning and coordinated development. The difference between the expansion of quality resources and the reconstruction of new schools is that the former can be accepted and recognized by the public more quickly, while the latter needs the influence of time and conditions to be accepted easily. The future urban development of Xiamen city is bound to have the form of "multi-center", so it is the objective requirement of urbanization development to expand the quality education resources to the suburbs. Xiamen city also encourages high-quality high schools to open branch schools in districts outside the island and sends high-quality teacher resources to each branch school. Since the 18th National Congress of the Communist Party of China (CPC), China's high school education has made great progress, with the scale of running schools continuously expanding. According to the national bureau of statistics, the gross enrollment rate of senior high schools reached 88.% in 2018, with 23.754 million students enrolled in senior high schools. School conditions have been gradually improved, the quality of education has been steadily improved, and the level of popularization has been constantly improved. However, there are still some structural and layout problems in the development of ordinary high schools in our country. Mainly reflected in two big aspects: one is the layout of regional imbalance, the second is the layout of the lack of long-term development considerations.

Another possible problem is that such uneven distribution can lead to the creation of "super high schools". For example, if there is only one key high school in a city, and a comparable high school is located in a neighboring city or county, it is likely that most of the children in the city will attend this high school, and the local investment in the construction of high school education will only be in this school, and then form a "super high school". The so-called "super high school" refers to the large-scale schools with a large number of educational resources. Its existence has certain positive effects, such as enabling more students to enjoy quality educational resources; But it also brings a lot of problems. It will increase the uneven distribution of educational resources: in the investment of funds, the super-sized high schools will surely account for a large proportion, which will make the inter-school differences develop more and more, and will aggravate the polarization of the ordinary high school education; In addition, the teachers will be uneven distribution of resources, because of the development of the school must have a greater demand for high quality teachers, at the same time, the school already occupy brand, capital, treatment, and the advantage of the opportunity, will attract high quality teachers, poor conditions even school teachers switch to big schools, thus making more barren area school lack of resources, lead to urban and rural, regional, intercollegiate unbalanced development of education. This is also an embodiment of the issue of educational equity (Fang, 2014; Li, 2018; Shen, 2019).

The regional imbalance of distribution not only refers to the uneven distribution of quantity, but also the uneven distribution of school quality and investment intensity. And the question that this raise is one of efficiency. The efficiency here refers to the degree to which educational resources play a role. In general, it is said that the school does not have benefits and guarantees the right of students to receive a good education. An important purpose of the layout adjustment is to make the limited educational resources play the largest role in the quantity and quality of children and adolescents, and to avoid the waste of human, material and financial resources. Investment in small schools, if the teachers, equipment conditions are too poor, may not make students good or even normal education, the quality of education must be greatly reduced, such investment efficiency is certainly very low. For example, the phenomenon of such small-scale "sparrow schools" in rural areas is quite serious. Meanwhile, the minimum size of small schools should be reserved according to the special circumstances of the educates, so as to guarantee the right of students with special needs to receive education.

There is also an imbalance, which may be reflected in the high schools in various regions, that is, there are ordinary high schools and key high schools, which is also a problem in the layout structure. Because there are so many issues involved in this situation. High school education should be both popularized and improved. Popularization means that the right students can receive a good education; Improvement refers to the improvement of the quality of education, the pursuit of the improvement of training level, training quality and students' physical and mental development level. These, and the government's attention and investment intensity are closely related. High school will get the priority to the construction of the corresponding amount of investment of resources, and this will also attract more high quality of teachers and students to focus on high school, high score of students will naturally choose larger better focus on high school teachers, students behind because can't be admitted to key high school and ordinary high school, the school selection problem also make these intercollegiate gap is more and more big. Students in ordinary high schools may not receive a high level of education and have low motivation due to the lack of school resources and weak teaching staff. As a result, the proportion of students admitted to key universities in ordinary high schools is very small. Although students in key high schools can get the best quality teaching, the competitive pressure is also very huge, it is easy to appear that students are not confident enough, self-abandonment phenomenon. Where there is a need to balance adjustment, not light stresses the investment and construction of some key high school, the other ordinary high school investment construction should intensify efforts to guarantee the teaching should have modern solid hardware devices and the faculty, let each qualified to enter high school students can get a good high school education; On this basis, we should focus on the construction of some key high schools, and invest in excellent teachers and teaching resources, so as not to waste too much, so as to achieve both popularization and improvement. This is a problem that should be paid attention to when the layout is adjusted (Fang, 2014; Li, 2018; Shen, 2019).

This problem is also an important aspect in the layout adjustment, the reason for its existence is also inseparable from the contradiction between the current needs and long-term development. In the process of trade-offs, people tend to focus only on the immediate urgent issues, leading to neglect of their long-term development, while focusing on the immediate needs will lead to the long-term waste of human, material and financial resources. At present, in many rural areas, there is such a phenomenon that in order to realize the task of universal compulsory education, a large amount of financial and material resources is invested to build schools. However, due to the remote location and shortage of students, many newly built schools and teaching buildings will have to be empty because there are no students, resulting in the waste of resources and property. Such a phenomenon is a typical result of focusing on the immediate problem without considering the actual situation and taking a long-term view.

Similarly, there is the consideration of the future policy direction, and then the balance between the elimination and merger of schools in some areas, the centralized management, or the increase of construction investment. In Jiangxi province as an example, in 2018 in Jiangxi province department of education issued by the "Jiangxi province high school education popularization crucial plan" explicitly mentioned, to optimize the structure layout, according to the trend of population change, new urbanization planning and industry development needs, and reasonable planning school layout, effective utilization of high school education resources, convenient students within the county school, do a good job in the necessary township high school. From this point of view, blindly remove and merge rural township areas of high school is not reasonable, centralized management is to make more centralized use of resources but may inconvenience part of the area students in its county region We will basically eliminate the phenomenon of large class sizes in ordinary high schools and reduce the number of super-sized schools. Optimize the allocation of resources to meet the requirements of the comprehensive reform of college entrance examination for students to choose courses and move classes and other educational and teaching reform. This is the problem of large-scale "super high schools" mentioned before, which needs to be solved according to the policy requirements. Therefore, the government's investment in large-scale schools will be reduced, and the focus will be relatively shifted to the construction of basic teaching conditions in ordinary high schools to improve the popularization level. And, to ensure that all the province ordinary high school in 2020 to achieve the basic conditions for offering education of Jiangxi province ordinary high school standard, also want to combine the region around the reality, on the basis of fully excavating existing education resources, in a planned way, the annual implementation of some construction projects, construction and reconstruction of a number of schools, for the weak school or necessary education teaching and living facilities. These are the measures to be taken in view of the problems existing in the layout and teaching structure, which also indicate that there are still corresponding problems to be solved. If we do not follow the policy direction, according to the future development situation and blind construction, it is easy to waste resources, the allocation of unreasonable problems. Some county in Hubei province one of the key high school is such a problem, for a long time they spend a lot of money on basic construction, which invested \$9.32 million in 2009 alone, but in the county bureau of education develop much starker choices-and graver consequences-in planning, because of the existing functional area is insufficient, cannot adapt to the needs of the development of the future education and inconvenience for further reform, so the final decision on the relocation as a whole. As a result, all the previous construction investment of the school has become a waste. Therefore, it is necessary to study the policy direction, judge the future development trend, choose appropriate solutions to solve the current problems, and carry out the school layout construction in a long-term perspective. In general, there are still a lot of problems in the layout of high schools in China that need to be solved. The second is the lack of long-term development considerations, including future regional development, population and student mobility, and policy direction. At an abstract level, there are unresolved issues of equity and efficiency, trade-offs between access and improvement, and, finally, concerns about the immediate and long-term. This is our country high school in the layout of some problems, urgently need to adjust and solve (Fang, 2014; Li, 2018; Shen, 2019).

4.3   Suggestions on the Distribution Status of High Schools in China

Under the background of entering a well-off society in an all-round way, the distribution of high schools in China still has some obvious problems, such as unbalanced supply and demand, insufficient popularization and large level difference. This part because of this, combined with the status quo analysis and reference to the central and local government policies, through the simulation in the process of the scheme idea for the current high school distribution problems puts forward corresponding Suggestions, aimed at thinking source and influence at the same time, explore and promote a fair and balanced development of education undertakings, promote education under the socialism with Chinese characteristics of road construction actively.

In recent years, China's high school education has been growing rapidly in the mode of efficient development. By 2017, the gross enrollment rate of high schools in many provinces had exceeded 90%, and it is expected to reach 90% in all provinces by 2020. Looking into the future, the construction of basic education is still the top priority of China's financial investment, and the comprehensive popularization of compulsory education is likely to include high school education or enhance the relationship between cultivation. The reform of college entrance examination and related policies and regulations on quality-oriented education have also been carried out in many provinces, which indicates that China's educational development standards have been actively transformed from "quantity education" to "quality education", and the educational concepts of "teaching students according to their aptitude" and "people-oriented" are increasingly prominent.

The continuous popularization of high school education and its development and progress are in urgent need of the close follow-up of high school allocation. According to the research report of scholars in the field of education, the current situation of imbalance between education allocation and demand exists in many cities (counties) within the province, and the problem of the distribution of existing high schools restricts the enrollment, development, management and innovation progress of high schools. Reasonable adjustment and investment in the distribution of high schools, starting with the two ideas of increasing educational resources by infrastructure construction and balanced allocation of existing educational resources, this paper analyzes and solves the distribution problem in two ways.

The following part is mainly on the basis of the following ideas modules: analysis summary the present distribution of the national high school and revealed the main problems, and presents preliminary schemes for assuming that idea, in view of the question to give advice on executive idea, absorb the education scholars in the field of statistical data analysis and conclusion, through the actual situation of the provincial, city and county and local solutions, for example, gives the education resource allocation optimization idea (Fang, 2014; Li, 2018; Shen, 2019).

4.3.1 The Overview of the Distribution of High Schools in China

It has been 70 years since the founding of the People's Republic of China, and more than 40 years since reform and opening up. Looking back on the arduous process, the basic principle of "rejuvenating the country through science and education" has been highly recognized by the public since the early days of the founding of the People's Republic of China. Over the past few decades, China's senior high schools (including ordinary high schools and technical secondary schools) have shown a qualitative leap in terms of the number of teachers, the level of students and infrastructure, and the education cause has been highly valued by the CPC central committee and local governments, and has carried the ardent hope of tens of millions of Chinese families.

According to the current data of the national bureau of statistics (updated in 2018), there are 14,091 high schools in China, with 7.927,063 million high school students, 7.828,452 high school graduates and 2.75 million high school staff. Among them, there were 7.792443 million high school graduates, 1.81 million full-time high school teachers and 23.794053 million high school students. In the statistics, the number of indicators in 2018 is close to or slightly higher than that in 2017.

Among the more than 14,000 high schools in China, there is a wide distribution of provinces, cities and regions. In terms of the number of high schools in various provinces, the number of high schools in southern regions is generally higher than that in northern regions, the central and southeastern regions are the gathering places, and the number of schools in western regions and autonomous regions is relatively low. According to the high school public praise, student source, graduation rate and multiple references of infrastructure, the distribution of high schools is corresponding to that of high schools. The concentration of high schools with strong comprehensive strength is located in first-tier cities such as Beijing and Shanghai and provincial capitals, and its occurrence probability has a positive correlation with the total number of high schools in this region. On the whole, the current situation of high schools in China presents the basic situation of decentralized establishment of various regions in the country, from northwest to southeast from sparse to dense, the density of some cities in regional provinces, the positive correlation with the level of regional economic development and population, and the uneven comprehensive strength (Fang, 2014; Li, 2018; Shen, 2019).

4.3.2   The Distribution Status of High Schools in China

According to the comparison of the number distribution and comprehensive strength of high schools in China, there is still a certain difference between the domestic status quo and the standards for the comprehensive popularization of high school education and the comprehensive improvement of school strength. Since China's reform and opening up led by the central and local government response, the national people's concerted effort to support, the increase in the number of high school in our country and the level of progress is indeed there for all to see, but is limited by time and manpower, and economic development of science and technology, population density, multiple factors such as geographical environment, also mainly exist the following problems.

First of all, there are some areas that do not fully reach the full coverage of high schools, which is particularly obvious in areas with remote areas, poor areas and economically backward areas as the core subjects. The insufficient number of senior high schools or the unsound number of senior high schools will force students to study in other places or even suspend their secondary school career, increasing the burden of normal education for local students and the resistance to the improvement of the level of education for all. It is urgent for local governments to establish schools, introduce teachers and optimize the allocation of education.

It is true that the establishment of a school is a century-old industry, but the source of teachers and students is fluid, in the influence of the role of the factor itself, more high-quality teachers and students tend to the comprehensive level of excellent middle school is human nature. Many cities already have their own famous high school signboards. Under the aggregation effect, the strength of excellent high schools in the front will be consolidated and improved, while schools with ordinary or even insufficient foundation may fall into the situation of gradual loss and decline. In addition, in the differentiation of the starting line, China's high school education philosophy, education policy, the trend of school cannot be ignored. Secondary schools in regions with low levels of education may still be in the basic stage of completing high school education and striving to enter universities. The middle school in the general level area has more chances to enter school, the comprehensive quality of teachers and students is better, and the teaching facilities are basically complete. In areas with both school density and population density, there may be polarization among the above assessment factors, such as excellent or quality decline due to the number of students exceeding the standard. The regions with high economic level and high school density themselves gather the top resources of each region and even the whole country. The concept of going to school is easy to be significantly transformed, the proportion of quality-oriented education is improved, the pressure of going to school is reduced, and the allocation of educational resources is more flexible and abundant.

Finally, apart from the improvement of infrastructure and the balance between regional level and quantity, China's senior high schools are also facing the milestone of innovation and reform of senior high school education. The "spatial mismatch" between the supply and demand of basic education facilities makes urban residents need to bear high monetary and time costs in order to enjoy the corresponding public services, which also generates a large number of social and economic costs. With the deepening of reform and opening up and the policy of "rejuvenating the country through science and education", all regions should, under the leadership of the party and the central committee, combine with local policies and educational levels, jointly conquer the problem of the existing distribution of high schools, and build a distribution system of high schools under the background of socialism with Chinese characteristics.

Eliminate the slogan of "egalitarianism". The people's political expectations are often "a bowl of water and a bowl of peace", which is the common people's understanding of the word "fairness". China is a socialist country under the people's democratic dictatorship, and the definition and requirements of fairness are more responsive to the voice of the people. Due to the uneven level of economic development and infrastructure construction capacity in various regions, the layout of senior high schools in cities (counties) in various provinces shows obvious differentiation, and the corresponding educational resources also show the characteristics of high-quality clustering and marginal evacuation. For a long time, the public has been more and more strongly calling for "educational equity", and the central party committee and the education bureau have successively issued the policy requirements for the fair popularization of local education. Meanwhile, educational scholars have been paying much attention to and discussing the issue of educational equity. The education law of the People's Republic of China was promulgated in 1995. Among them, the concept of educational equity is that Chinese citizens have the right and obligation to receive education regardless of ethnic group, gender, property status, religious belief, etc., and also enjoy equal educational opportunities. The report of the 19th national congress of the communist party of China proposed "fair and quality education", which is an upgraded version of China's educational fairness. In the new era of socialism with Chinese characteristics, people have new expectations for education (Fang, 2014; Li, 2018; Shen, 2019).

However, the public's doubts and anxieties need to be properly responded to and channelized. The so-called "equalitarianism" means that no matter the difference of labor paid and their respective significance and value, they all correspond to the same returns and benefits. This treatment mode that pays too much attention to the average itself but omits the core mechanism of social operation has long been proved to be eliminated by the people through practice. The law of our country guarantees and supports that citizens' right to receive education is equal and free from infringement. It does not accept that all citizens will receive education of the same quality, level and direction. Cities (counties) in poor areas still need to increase the number of high schools and expand the number of students to try to break through the threshold of 90% gross enrollment rate. The goal of eliminating the slogan of "equalitarianism" is to better analyze the substantive connotation and measure effect of "educational equity" to the public, clarify the starting point of policy implementation, and reasonably guide the public's attention. The vigorous development of China's education cannot be separated from the support, encouragement and supervision of the masses, but the public's concern should not be led astray or used by people with ulterior motives. The positive feedback to the public is to carry out the understanding and promote the real "educational equity" and effectively promote the progress of local education.

The balanced educational resources. In addition to increasing financial investment and infrastructure, and fundamentally improve the level of education and expand the scale of teaching, based on the existing education resources, led by the central and local governments in some provinces equilibrium, the equilibrium in the province, talent introduction, such as policy support, help under the condition of the existing high school layout reasonable adjustment, improve the shortages of the layout and the difficulty of the allocation of resources.

The innovation, reform and liberal arts and science. While the popularization of education infrastructure has been promoted in an orderly manner, the innovation experiment and reform of front high school education have not stopped. 18 by the third plenary session of "the central committee of the communist party of China on comprehensively deepen reform certain major issue decision", the core content is to recruit students and exam is separation, multiple choice exam students, the school in accordance with the independent recruitment of students, professional institutions to organize the implementation, the government macro management, social operation mechanism involved in supervision, fundamentally solve the disadvantages of a youngster. In view of this problem, the reform policy of the college entrance examination proposes to break the original pattern of "pure science" and "pure liberal arts", and adopt the "3 + 3" independent choice mode to flexibly test subjects, so as to give students more room for choice, respect their subjective interests and development possibilities, and realize the internal balance of the six subjects.

According to the distribution status of high schools in cities (counties) in different provinces in China, there should be self-digesting delay in the implementation of the college entrance examination reform policies in different regions. Regions with high average educational resources, teachers and students and relatively sufficient financial resources can give priority to educational reform after all the cities (counties) in the province actively interpret the policies and formulate follow-up work. In the provinces where the distribution of high schools is not enough to meet the demand of the basic college entrance examination model, or in cities (counties) where the distribution density of high-quality high schools is low, it is suggested that the local government should apply to the central government to delay the implementation of the reform after discussion. The deepening of the impact of education reform inevitably leads to an increase in the teaching demand of the original liberal arts. At present, the distribution of high schools with strong strength in liberal arts training is sparse, and even the high schools that can achieve the close enrollment of students of liberal arts and science are few. Based on the analysis of the cities (counties) in Jilin province, the high schools that meet the above two conditions are mainly located in the provincial capitals of Changchun, Jilin and Yanbian (north Korea autonomous region). According to the distribution characteristics of local high schools, the province can have policies to encourage high schools that support strong liberal arts to add branch schools or increase the enrollment scale, and each city (county) to promote the balanced setting of liberal arts and science, so as to ensure that each city (county) at least has a balanced distribution of liberal arts and science characteristics or liberal arts and science cultivation. Starting from the school's own training emphasis and teachers' tendency, it follows the central government's policies and encourages students to make their own choices and develops in a diversified and profound way in the new era of liberal arts and science.

Creating a high school education system with Chinese characteristics that is tailored to local conditions. The balanced development and continuous progress of urban educational resources are closely related to the allocation of regional public service facilities. The trend of population mobility is not only closely related to the local economic level and urban environment, but also an important factor for the introduction of foreign population and the retention of local residents. The optimal allocation of public service facilities is an important way to improve the livability and sustainable development of a city. The matching between supply and demand of educational resources in total amount and space is directly related to the quality of life of residents and the operation efficiency of urban transportation. Since the reform and opening up, under the leadership of the CPC central committee, we have jointly built and witnessed the completion and gradual improvement of the socialist system with Chinese characteristics. Since the high school stage of education popularization crucial plan (2017–2020) issued after the printing, in provinces, municipalities directly under the central government and autonomous regions in our country as the unit issued after deep research learning in the crucial plan the implementation of the province, according to the provincial conditions suitable for implementing the specific regulations in the province, selectively, preparation and planning to the crucial plan to realize the goal. Regional distribution and allocation of high schools also exist in every city in the province, which cannot be implemented uniformly. Relevant scholars have also conducted investigation and research on this issue. For the old city, the demand for facilities in the next few years is relatively stable. Therefore, when considering the infrastructure construction to increase the number of schools and expand the school scale, it can be considered to focus on the development and construction of new urban areas. In the old urban areas, by adjusting the flow of teachers and students or expanding the enrollment of students, the distribution of the original high schools should be appropriately balanced. The trend of education quantification to quality also reminds educators that they should not ignore the impact of the distribution of quality schools on the balance of education resources. Areas with high density of high-quality high schools can adopt the pattern of fixed-point support and joint training to realize the flow of resources within cities (counties).

Numerous experiences and lessons have pointed out that only by combining the education level and development status of the region in a practical and realistic manner, implementing the education work in accordance with local conditions, and taking the road of socialism with Chinese characteristics in line with China's national conditions, can we build a strong country in education. The problems existing in the distribution of high schools in China need to be solved urgently. However, the "one-size-fits-all" solution mode should be avoided by all means. By making good use of the existing resources, implementing policies and adjusting the education mode, the high school education system with Chinese characteristics should be created according to local conditions.

The vigorous and orderly development of education is based on long-term planning and problem solving. In view of the optimization of the allocation of educational resources, foreign policies and implementation can also be referred to as a mirror, and the training mode and experience of the regions with better educational development level in China are the key reference sources in line with China's national conditions. While implementing the education policies of the CPC central committee and the local government, it still needs to learn from each other and help each other in the provinces and the continuous innovation and progress, as well as the positive thinking of educators and scholars in related fields, as well as the understanding, support and supervision of the people. We still have a long way to go in building a system of socialist high schools with Chinese characteristics (Fang, 2014; Li, 2018; Shen, 2019).

References

Fang, Y. K. (2014). The research report on the balanced development of urban and rural compulsory education resources in China—based on field investigation and analysis of 17 districts (cities and counties) in 8 provinces in the east, central and west. *Education Research 14*(11), 1002–5731

Li, W. (2018). Qinghai provincial department of education, Qinghai development and reform commission, Qinghai provincial department of finance, Qinghai provincial department of human resources and social security. *Qinghai Education, 8*(7), 0529–3502

Shen, W. Z. (2019). Reflection on the connotation and construction of educational equity in the new era. *Teaching and Management, 19*(36), 1004–5872

Chapter 5
An Analysis of the Enrollment Policy of College Entrance Examination

This chapter involves an analysis of the enrollment policy of college entrance examination. Specifically, the question on what the admission policy of the general college examination in China is have been explored to understand the rationale of enrollment policy. Both the questions and suggestions on the enrollment policy of general college examination have also been offered. In addition, the suggestions on enrollment reform are also been examined.

5.1 What Is the Admission Policy of the General College Examination in China?

5.1.1 The Reform of Enrollment Policy

After the "cultural revolution", the country's population was cut off. Compared with the developed countries in the same period, China's science and technology and education lag behind by 20 years. On reflection, the party recognizes the importance of respecting knowledge and talent and opposes the erroneous idea of disrespecting intellectuals. In 1972, the university resumed enrollment, not to recruit this year's senior high school graduates, recruit "have two to three years of practical experience of the outstanding agricultural and industrial soldiers, generally should be junior high school education", voluntary application, the masses recommended, the leadership approval, school review. To the requirement of culture level is in junior high school graduate above can, but must pass two years above labor to train, abolish recruit student's examination, worker farmer soldier university student appears from this. However, there are many loopholes in the way of recruiting students from agricultural, industrial and military colleges, which not only make a large number of outstanding young people stop or interrupt their study, but also make the phenomenon of "through the back door" popular, the social impact is extremely bad. On October 12, 1977, the State Council approved the Ministry of Education in accordance with Deng Xiaoping's instructions on the work of college enrollment in 1977, the resumption of the college entrance examination, and in the winter held so far the only national winter college entrance examination.

From the beginning of the fifth five-year plan in 1953 to the adoption of the decision on economic system reform at the third plenary session of the 12th central committee of the communist party of China in 1984, the planned economy occupied a dominant position in China. Tuition fees by the country, after graduation also want to obey the country to allocate absolutely. After the resumption of the college entrance examination, colleges and universities used the method of admission in 1952, according to the state planning commission issued by the ministry of education enrollment plan, in strict accordance with the admission from high to low scores, unified score line enrollment. In the enrollment plan, the national higher education enrollment quota by the ministry of education according to the number of cadres trained by the state, the category of uniform provisions. In 1983, the Ministry of Education formally put forward the concept of "targeted recruitment and targeted allocation", stipulating that in some colleges and universities subordinate to the central department or the commission of science, technology and industry for national defense, targeted recruitment in rural areas, farms, pastures, mining areas, oil fields and other difficult industries shall be implemented in a certain proportion. In 1984, the country began to recruit students, recommended by the middle school, institutions of higher learning assessment agreed, exempted from the college entrance examination, directly into the university students. The target students generally include outstanding students at the provincial level, fresh high school graduates who have won prizes in the provincial and national finals of the national Olympic Games for middle school students and students from some foreign language schools (Li & Li, 2019; Xing, 2018; Xue & Li, 2020; Zhuang, 2010).

In the same year, with the deepening of reform and opening up, the rapid economic development, the township enterprises need a lot of talent, the Ministry of Education, Ministry of Finance and development planning commission on June 24, the measures for the trial of commissioned to train students of institutions of higher learning, the provinces, municipalities directly under the central government, autonomous regions, the central, the Ministries and commissions of the State Council, the whole people, collectively owned enterprises and self-employed, can entrust training colleges and universities, college students and graduate students. In 1985, the ministry of education stipulated that colleges and universities could recruit a small number of self-financed students from the candidates who participated in the unified college entrance examination. In this way, college enrollment formed two tracks: national planned enrollment and self-financed students. In 1994, the college entrance examination admission fees and track system pilot, the college entrance examination admission "track" reform was launched. In 1996, colleges and universities tried to "merge" the enrollment, cancel the enrollment of self-financed students, correspondingly, higher education fees increased, from now on, "self-financed students" become history, college tuition fees increased substantially. That is, before 1990 university student tuition, living expenses to tuition and miscellaneous fees full free (excluding self-cost students), after the reform of the charging system, the implementation of the system of charging part of the culture fee to students, the original two kinds of charging standards under the form of two kinds of enrollment plan "merge" into one. Moreover, after the "merger", most graduates' employment will be carried out under the guidance of national policies and within a certain scope of the system of self-employment. In 1999, the ministry of education issued the action plan for the revitalization of education in the 21st century, which started the expansion of college enrollment. In the following five or six years, college enrollment expanded by nearly three times, and "popular education" replaced "elite education". In 2001, the ministry of education announced the abolition of the "unmarried candidates, the age is generally not over 25 years old" limit, anyone can not be restricted by age, marriage conditions to take the college entrance examination. The general college enrolling work of 01 years realizes net enrolling completely for the first time. In 2003, the ministry of education decided to move the Gaokao forward from July to June each year to avoid high temperatures and flooding. In the same year, the ministry of education allowed Hong Kong universities to recruit students on their own in the mainland. Twenty-two universities, including Peking University and Tsinghua university, were given 5% right to recruit students independently (Li & Li, 2019; Xing, 2018; Xue & Li, 2020; Zhuang, 2010).

5.1.2 The Changes in College Entrance Examination Subjects and Modes

In 1978, after the resumption of the national unified entrance examination, colleges and universities were still divided into two categories: politics, Chinese, mathematics, history, geography and foreign languages. Medical classes of workers and peasants to take an examination of politics, Chinese, mathematics, physics, chemistry, foreign language, foreign language set up English, Russian, French, German, Spanish, Arabic, a total of seven languages (no longer set Arabic) since 1981, as the local recovery biology teaching in middle school teaching, reasonable medical exams of workers and peasants in 1981 subjects have been added for biology, after years of adjustment and supplement of the university entrance exam subjects setting local stability. In 1987, the state education commission issued the "provisional regulations on the enrollment of ordinary institutions of higher learning", the examination subjects are set as: literature and history (including foreign languages), politics, semantics, mathematics, history, geography, foreign languages: science, agriculture and medicine, politics, Chinese, mathematics, physics, chemistry, biology, foreign languages. The above two kinds of foreign language test is divided into English, Russian, Japanese, French, German, Spanish six languages, by the candidate's choice. Candidates registered for the department (subject) of a foreign language institution shall be interviewed in addition to the written test. In the aspect of examination method, in view of the general implementation of the general high school graduation examination, the college entrance examination also carries out the reform of subject setting, accordingly, reducing the burden has been the focus of the college entrance examination reform.

1. **"3 + 1" college entrance examination mode**. In 1985, Shanghai first carried out the pilot reform of the college entrance examination. The three subjects of the college entrance examination were Chinese, mathematics and foreign language.

2. **Group examination of subjects.** In 1991 and 1992, Hunan, Yunnan and Hainan made new attempts. The subjects of the college entrance examination are divided into Chinese, politics, history, foreign language, mathematics, Chinese, physics, foreign language, mathematics, chemistry, biology, foreign language, mathematics, Chinese, geography, foreign language. The reform, which is based on the national examination, is known as the "three south plan".

3. **"3 + 2" college entrance examination mode.** In 1992, on the basis of the "three south program" experiment, the state education commission put forward a revised version of the "three south program"—the "3 + 2" college entrance examination reform program, that is, the three subjects of language and number as the common test subjects (mathematics cent, paper), arts plus politics, history, science plus physics, chemistry, each subject full score original score of 150 points. To 1995, the country except Hong Kong, Macao and Taiwan. The reform of "3 + 2" college entrance examination on the basis of the examination was fully implemented. Due to the provinces into and termination "3 + 2" in the form of the test time is different, according to the university entrance exam pilot experience, in order to reduce examination subjects, candidates for the narrow scope, the college entrance examination from 7 families, 5 families, in addition to language, mathematics, foreign languages, arts and politics, history, science, and physical chemistry, liberal arts reduced the geography, reduced the biological science department, the college entrance examination teaching content relatively simple geographical, biological subject to solve in the high school examination, and form two groups of new course setting.

   Malpractice: the physics that did not include liberal arts college entrance examination, chemistry, biology, liberal arts student does not learn almost, the geography that did not include science college entrance examination, history, politics suffers science student to be ignored, because the science and art do not take an examination of geography, biology, geography and biology became pure decoration in high school teaching.

4. **3 + X college entrance examination mode**. In 1999, Guangdong province began to adopt the "3 + X" college entrance examination model. "3 + X" in the most characteristic is "X" and "comprehensive" subject setting, highlighted the examinee basic knowledge and basic ability of the examination, fully considered the student personality play and comprehensive knowledge structure needs, regardless of science and art. Students choose according to their interests,

hobbies, special skill "X" discipline, increase listening English, comprehensive test of knowledge involving 9 subject in the junior middle school and my personal experience, proposition and emphasis on examining students' understanding of knowledge and skills, ability to innovate, each students according to their interests and ability, learns to choose a course at most. The setting of "comprehensive" subject not only reflects the requirement of students' comprehensive knowledge structure, but also prevents the occurrence of students' premature bias and early class division (Li & Li, 2019; Xing, 2018; Xue & Li, 2020; Zhuang, 2010).

In the early 1980s, the college entrance examination is a temporary concentration of a number of teachers by experience, because there is no unified proposition standard, the question difficult and easy. In the examination course of the same year, some subjects average scores more than 80 points, some subjects average scores only more than 30 points. The examination level lacks unified regulation, the whole college entrance examination work lacks coherence, the stability. In 1985, the pilot program of standardized tests introduced from the United States began, and the pilot program of English and mathematics was carried out in Guangdong province. After the experiment of Guangdong province from 1985 to 1988, and gradually summed up the experience after the trial, in 1989, the state education commission decided to carry out the standardized examinations in the whole country. On June 27, 1989, the state education commission issued the plan for the national unified examination and standardization of college enrollment. The college entrance examination will be marked by machine. The standardized test pushes forward the scientization of the college entrance examination with a big step in the technical means, normalizes the college entrance examination topic, and marks the paper by machine, which greatly reduces the workload of the college entrance examination and has a milestone significance in the technical means reform of the college entrance examination.

5. **A standard scoring system was introduced in 1993**. Due to the different difficulty of proposition of each subject, the original scores of each subject cannot be directly compared, resulting in the difficulty of interpretation of scores, the original scores of each subject are not added up reasonably, and the original score system cannot reveal the position of the score of the examinee in the score of the examinee group. The standard score system is a set of system about score report, score explanation and score use. In 1993, the national education commission examination center, after many discussions and tests, stipulated that the standard score system was composed of provincial norm scale score, equivalent scale score and grade scale score, and completed its process from practice to implementation. Disadvantages: the standard score system will introduce modern scientific methods into the college entrance examination enrollment, although there is scientific reason, but it is very inconvenient to operate, now many provinces have to give up this practice, implement the original score system.

The political aspect. From the law of educational policy decision, the political system decides the educational policy decision mechanism, the educational policy decision mechanism decides the educational policy, and the educational policy decides the educational development. As an important part of education policy, the enrollment policy cannot be made or modified without the influence of the law of education policy. Therefore, we can interpret the enrollment policy from the influence factors of education policy on the political level. The results of the policymaking and decision-making of educational policies always reflect the interests of different groups, classes and individuals in different periods. China is a socialist country, is the country of the working class as the masters of the country, so it is not difficult for us to find in the earliest university admission resumption adopted the recruitment of "agricultural soldiers" recruitment methods. Before the third plenary session of the 11th central committee of the communist party of China (CPC), the planned economy was dominant in China and everything had to be carried out under the plan. With the continuous progress of the understanding of China's national conditions, the domestic transition from the absolute planned economy to the commodity economy, the enrollment policy also from the national unified division of the score line, the transition to the "national planned enrollment" and "self-financed students" "double track" system enrollment. From this, we can see the influence of national interests on the politics of enrollment policy in different periods. How to make the decision of education policy reflect the interests of the majority to the greatest extent, it is necessary to have an open, transparent and democratic policy decision mechanism to ensure the fairness and benefit of education policy. This is called the democratization of educational policymaking and decision-making. It is well understood that in China, every reform of education policy can be implemented only after the resolution of the people's congress or the standing committee of the people's congress, and the people's congress at all levels represents the interests and wishes of the local and even the whole country (Li & Li, 2019; Xing, 2018; Xue & Li, 2020; Zhuang, 2010).

In order to make the decision-making process of education policy a rational process, it is necessary to establish a mechanism of policy decision-making and make the decision-making process of education policy always in a system and state that can be supervised and open through the implementation of certain procedures. This is the problem of institutionalization and procedure of educational policy decision. With the development of The Times, the national levels and various management decision system gradually standardized and systematized. In the early days after the founding of the People's Republic of China, it was pointed out in the constitution that the National People's Congress of the People's Republic of China (hereinafter referred to as the National People's Congress and the National People's Congress) is the highest organ of state power, and its standing body is the standing committee of the National People's Congress. The National People's Congress and its standing committee exercise the legislative power of the state. Therefore, the change of education policy or enrollment policy should be approved by the National People's Congress or the education department directly under the state. The political system is the fundamental of the educational policy decision-making mechanism, which is the expression of the educational interests of the political subject through the political system. In the political system will not occur under the condition of big changes, education policy decision-making mechanism is not likely to appear large change, because of political subjects did not change, the political main body education interests appeal has not changed, so we can see that although the education policy or admissions policies has been to try and change, but keep the consistency and stability of the national conditions and under the premise of no significant changes in political system, education policy, or admissions policies will not fundamentally change, will only make adaptive adjustment along with the time development. The fundamental purpose of education is to maintain the governance and social stability. Therefore, from a political perspective, the political system determines the education policy or the enrollment policy, and the interests of the ruling group affect the change and development direction of the education policy or the enrollment policy in different periods.

The economic aspects. As an important part of the education system, the college entrance examination and enrollment system play an important role in guiding and influencing the effective play of the social function of education. The economy plays a big role. On the whole, the college entrance examination and the economy play a mutual role. On the one hand, the economic growth itself requires the education sector to send a large number of workers with certain technical and cultural levels, and the college entrance examination is the most important way to select talents. On the other hand, the development of education is always in accordance with the national strength of the same country, the more developed the economy.

In recent years, there are obvious differences in the scores of the college entrance examination between provinces and cities, and the difficulty degree of the college entrance examination is not the same among provinces and cities. Of course, this also leads to one of the most important concerns of the college entrance examination— fairness. We know that there is no absolute fairness, we can only pursue relative fairness. The college entrance examination system varies from place to place for the sake of the relative fairness of the whole society (Li & Li, 2019; Xing, 2018; Xue & Li, 2020; Zhuang, 2010).

From the perspective of economy alone, it is known to all that China is the largest developing country in the world, and it is necessary to cultivate some points of economic growth so as to promote the economic development of the whole country. Moreover, the vast geographical area of China makes the economic development level of each region have great differences, which also leads to the education conditions and education level of each region have great differences. In large cities like Beijing, the living standard and educational conditions are far from being comparable to the backward regions in the central and western regions. Because the starting point of competition is different due to economic reasons, it is necessary to tilt the admission score line like the backward regions in the central and western regions to make up for this gap, which is also a reflection of the relative fairness of the college entrance examination.

The national economic development needs the overall development, to make the central city's economy and society develop rapidly, but also to promote the development of backward areas. Assume that if each region of the college entrance examination system are the same, center the city university enrollment quota must be mostly in the center of city, backward area students it is difficult to enter into the college, and most people want to go to big cities struggle, makes the already rare candidates don't want to return to local, in the long run, can appear the strong stronger, the phenomenon of the weak weaker, make each region's economic level gap is more and more big, the country's economic development will be deformed. In order to avoid the occurrence of such a situation, the college entrance examination system of each region should be adjusted accordingly, with differences, giving more possibilities to the examinees in the backward regions, which also brings more possibilities to the development of the backward regions.

The purpose of education is also to make the country strong and the society stable, and the college entrance examination, as an important point in the field of education, should have enough attention. From the perspective of economy, it means that economic development provides basic guarantee for education and college entrance examination, and high-quality talents are selected to meet the market demand through college entrance examination, which also promotes balanced development of social economy and education.

The general college entrance examination enrollment policy is the national level according to the specific social education rules, its purpose is to select outstanding talents for the national construction. Since the resumption of the college entrance examination in 1977, China's college entrance examination enrollment policy has undergone many major adjustments. For example, the policy of merger and reform, the policy of enrollment expansion, the policy of independent enrollment, as well as the recently launched "strong foundation plan", all have very deep social soil, which is to summarize the experience of college enrollment in depth, and combine with the specific practice situation to put forward various education policies suitable for China's social conditions. The revision and reform of this step by step college enrollment policy is of great significance to the establishment of the college entrance examination enrollment system with Chinese characteristics. Since the reform and opening up in China, the relationship between college enrollment policy and society is inseparable.

As a member of several policies in our country, the formulation and implementation of college entrance examination and enrollment policy cannot be separated from the elements of general policy, such as subject and object, clear purpose, close relation with value, and specific social environment. By comparing and analyzing these factors, we can find that the college entrance examination policy is very social. From the perspective of the policy making environment, policy is the product of specific time and space, so there is no policy that is always applicable, and no policy that is applicable to all places and regions. This is the case with the college entrance examination policy. Horizontally, the college entrance examination policy of different provinces is generally consistent, but there are also many regional differences. Vertically, since the reform and opening up in different periods of college entrance examination policy has also undergone many changes. Although there are differences in time and space in the environment of making smart policies, the conflicts of values throughout them are diachronic and relatively consistent. The high recruitment policy is a complex issue involving the relationship between higher education and society, between universities and the government, and the reform of the internal operating mechanism of higher education. The policy itself has the "endogenous" conflict, but also bears the political, economic and cultural value demands under certain social and historical conditions, thus resulting in a series of "exogenous" value conflicts. In 1999, China's college enrollment expansion policy has started the popularization process of China's higher education. Whether "endogenous" or "exogenous" value conflict is the reflection of different levels of social conditions. Therefore, it can be seen that the factors brought by the examination and enrollment policy of general colleges determine its objective connection with the society in terms of its source and content. It can be said that the examination and enrollment policy of general colleges and universities in China is "selected" based on various social factors.

The intersection of educational policy and sociology has been well recognized by many scholars, and a cross field of pedagogy and sociology—educational sociology came into being. In terms of theoretical and methodological orientation, educational sociology not only studies the relationship between the objects involved in the activity of education, but also involves the issues of race, ethnicity and educational equality. In terms of the development and expansion of education, the educational sociology compares and summarizes the educational models from the historical perspective. In the study of school organization, educational sociology USES Coleman's method to explore the problems related to social system and norms. In terms of the research on the output of education, the sociology of education starts from the relationship between education, market and social division of labor, and involves the influence of school education on personal life. In terms of the policy connotation of educational sociology research, educational sociology focuses on the theme of the appropriateness and inappropriateness of sociological research and educational policy. Sociology of education affirms the impact of social science research on the process of education policy making and considers this to be fundamental. The research results of educational sociology provide a sufficient social basis for the formulation of college entrance examination policy.

Based on the above mentioned horizontal and vertical policy making environment, in this part, this paper will mainly take this as a clue to the reform and opening up of China's college entrance examination and enrollment policy is analyzed. On the synchronic level, this paper will focus on the policy of deepening the comprehensive reform of college entrance examination and enrollment system in Hebei, Jiangsu and Guangdong provinces in 2019, and explore the social motivation behind it. On the diachronic level, this paper divides the reform and development of the college entrance examination system into four stages, with the reform of merging the tracks, the policy of expanding enrollment, the policy of independent enrollment, the reform of the new college entrance examination and the recently issued strong foundation plan as the main time nodes. Here, this paper will only on the track reform, the new college entrance examination reform contains social factors for specific research.

The policy interpretation of the reform plan of college entrance examination and enrollment system issued by the people's government of Hebei province follows the spirit of the third plenary session of the 18th CPC central committee, especially the decision of the CPC central committee on several major issues concerning comprehensively deepening the reform (hereinafter referred to as the decision). Based on in September 2014 of the State Council issued "on deepening the reform of examination recruitment system of the implementation opinions" (hereinafter referred to as the "implementation opinion"), in Hebei province actively learn from the first and the second batch of the university entrance exam comprehensive reform of the successful experience of the pilot provinces (municipalities), and considering the province college entrance examination pattern, the original level of basic education development, higher education and the layout of disciplines, develop with the local characteristics of the university entrance exam comprehensive reform (Li & Li, 2019; Xing, 2018; Xue & Li, 2020; Zhuang, 2010).

Hebei province has been designated by the ministry of education as one of the third batch of provinces to promote the comprehensive reform of college entrance examination. The implementation plan of Hebei province divides the contents of the reform into four aspects: one is to deepen the reform of unified college entrance examination, which mainly includes examination subjects, examination arrangements, composition of college entrance examination results, requirements for elective examination subjects, and improvement of enrollment methods. Second, to adjust and improve the general high school academic level test, adhere to the basic, highlighting selectivity, mainly including examination subjects, examination content, examination organization, examination objects, examination arrangements, performance presentation; Third, to establish and standardize the general high school students comprehensive quality evaluation system, to establish a scientific comprehensive evaluation system, to promote the comprehensive and personalized development of students; Fourth, we will promote the recruitment of students for classified examinations in higher vocational education.

Guangdong province's plan to deepen the comprehensive reform of the college entrance examination and enrollment system in 2019 is also aimed at the implementation and improvement of the new college entrance examination policy. The purpose of the reform is basically the same as that of the last two provinces—"starting from the first year of high school students entering in the fall of 2018, the examination and enrollment mode of classified examination, comprehensive evaluation and diversified admission will be basically formed by 2021." In addition to improving the academic level examination system for ordinary high schools, the new college entrance examination policy issued by Guangdong province also emphasizes the importance of improving the comprehensive quality evaluation system for ordinary high school students, which is also reflected in the reform of the college entrance examination system for ordinary colleges and universities. Such as in the "examination subject", in addition to English, Russian, Japanese, French, German, Spanish as a foreign language can also be included in the choice of the examination subject category, which is undoubtedly to students in many aspects of quality development to create conditions and space; In terms of "exam contents", Guangdong's new Gaokao policy also places special emphasis on students' "independent thinking" and "ability to analyze and solve problems", apparently due to the consideration of comprehensive quality education. The flexible time arrangement and subject selection of the examination reflect the reflection and breakthrough of the social status quo of "one examination for life" in the new high recruitment policy of Guangdong province. As far as possible to provide students with all-round high-quality education, which reflects the effective feedback of this policy to the social education malpractice of "reading too much and reading too little" (Li & Li, 2019; Xing, 2018; Xue & Li, 2020; Zhuang, 2010).

To sum up, although in Hebei province, Jiangsu province, Guangdong province in the process of deepening the reform of examination in common colleges and universities enrollment system integrated in the issued policy does not completely consistent, but the new college entrance examination scheme by comparing the three take the implementation of the measures, it can be seen in common among them, the three provinces are deeply considered before the traditional entrance policy implemented in society and gaps, and take the positive and effective measures on the reaction and make up. Although the new college entrance examination plan is only a transitional step in the reform of college entrance examination enrollment policy in China, its response to the social status quo is of great significance and reference value.

The social environment of the reform is very complicated, which highlights the conflict and competition among various values. This complex social environment is mainly reflected in the economic aspect, that is, the contradiction and conflict between the planned economy and the market economy. The lack of autonomy leads to the suppression of individual interests and development and the sacrifice of students' individual autonomy. Thus, the national education policy of "unified package and unified division" has obviously no longer adapted to the development of society. With the reform of the economic system, the policies in the field of education, especially the policies of college entrance examination and enrollment, have changed. In 1984, the trial method of entrusting ordinary colleges and universities to train students was promulgated, and ordinary colleges and universities began to recruit self-financed students and commissioned students. 1985 "decision on reform of the education system of the central committee of the communist party of China pointed out that" to reform the system of university enrollment plan, the ordinary university also combines national task plan and regulatory plan enrollment planning system, which appeared in the same school in grades between students of the same profession, educational level and the economic cost has the very big disparity, formed the enrollment system of the "double track". Under such special social conditions, in 1994, the state education commission issued the pilot opinions on further reforming the enrollment and employment system for graduates in ordinary institutions of higher learning and established the university fee system and the system of awards and grants, commonly known as the "merger" reform (Li & Li, 2019; Xing, 2018; Xue & Li, 2020; Zhuang, 2010).

5.1.3   Reform of the New College Entrance Examination

In September 2014, the implementation opinions of the state council on deepening the reform of the examination and enrollment system were officially released, which marked the beginning of a new round of college entrance examination reform. The recruitment mode of "classified examination, comprehensive evaluation and diversified admission" has been gradually formed in the continuous advancement of the reform. Admittedly, the new college entrance examination reform has brought many challenges and anxiety to the pilot areas, and even led to some chaotic educational phenomena. The most important positive impact of the new college entrance examination policy on the society is the "re-emphasis on the value of 'people'", which is also the social original intention of the policy reform.

Since the resumption of the national college entrance examination in 1977, the reform and debugging of education policies have been continuous, and their core purpose is to adapt to the social development in different historical periods. However, any policy has its limitations of The Times, and many education policies have gradually deviated from their original intention in the implementation process. Although the high recruit policy has always emphasized the importance of "people", but after many years, the glory of this value is no longer the original. New college entrance examination reform at the joint point arises at the historic moment, it is designed to promote the formation of classification test, comprehensive evaluation and multiple admission examination recruitment mode, perfect promote fair, scientific selection, system mechanism of effective supervision, build bridging communication of all kinds of education at all levels, approved a variety of learning outcomes "overpass" lifelong learning.

The content of the new college entrance examination reform has been discussed in the "synchronic level" part above, and it will not be repeated in this part. According to the risk society theory of sociology, the new college entrance examination reform will face multiple risks in the process of implementation: the "pendulum phenomenon" between quality-oriented education and exam-oriented education; (2) lack of characteristics in running high schools; alienation of high school students' independent development. These risks are hidden in the new Gaokao policy, which will be exposed gradually with the deepening of the reform. But on the other hand, the introduction and implementation of any policy is risky, it is impossible to completely avoid the risk. According to the risk society theory, "the concept of risk is directly related to the concept of reflective modernization. Risk can be defined as the way in which the dangers and insecurities of modernity itself are systematically addressed." It can be seen that the risks exposed in the implementation of the policy are actually a reflection on the society. Facing and dealing with the risks in the reform correctly is conducive to the deepening of the reform and the progress of the society. In a word, the current college entrance examination policy in China is a relatively reasonable and objective policy from both the diachronic level and the synchronic level, from the theoretical point of view and from the practical point of view. The policy has deep historical roots but is also in the process of continuous reform. It can be said that this policy comes from the society and must be applied to the society.

College entrance examination culture is the core of the development of college entrance examination system. Therefore, the construction of college entrance examination culture is also related to the cultivation of talents and the overall development of the country, which also indirectly affects the development of political economy and society. Below, I will analyze the reasons for the emergence of China's college entrance examination policy from several perspectives:

Culture refers to the people from the Angle of social history, the perspective analysis and summarizes the real problems involved in the cognitive domain, the object of study the university entrance exam as a culture, reading history books, the college entrance examination system in China has a long history, the history of ancient Chinese national examination is similar to that of the college entrance examination is the most the imperial examination, the examination in the system of social operation system point of view is called the imperial examination system. The imperial examination system began in the sui dynasty and ended in the late Qing dynasty. The selection and appointment of officials lasted for more than one thousand years, which created a unique cultural tradition of examination in China.

Cultural identity. The imperial examination system, by extension, has replaced the imperial examination as one of the most effective representatives of social justice. The common people in China all have a special plot to the unified examination, the content of the examination is objective, the examination system is fair, so the examination results cannot be ignored. Because of this, Gaokao, as the largest unified exam in contemporary China, was accepted by the public, selected by history, and passed down to today. Cultural identity. Therefore, the study of "China" college entrance examination system from the perspective of cultural perspective, where China is given a specific meaning.

Cultural gene of history. The long history of the imperial examination has shaped China's unique examination culture. The establishment of the college entrance examination system is not an accident in a certain historical period, but an inevitable choice in the development history of the examination. The imperial examination system, which lasted for more than 1,300 years, is a typical representative in the history of Chinese examinations. The centralized rule laid the cultural gene for the unified examination, which is also the underlying reason for the smooth promotion of the college entrance examination system.

From the space point of view, China is one of the birthplace of the world's four major ancient civilization, is one of the largest developing countries of east Asia and the socialist countries, areas, 56 ethnic groups in the big family of the Chinese nation, has five thousand years of Chinese excellent traditional culture, national culture by Chinese people from learning and inheriting, formed the socialist culture with Chinese characteristics. Among the many theoretical achievements on the reform of the college entrance examination system in China, the author thinks that the research on the value orientation is extremely important. As an objective existence and a kind of culture, college entrance examination is created for human beings, so its content must have certain value orientation.

Cultural conflict perspective. The internality and essence of college entrance examination culture determine the different characteristics of its cultural conflict. Cultural conflict is determined by the nature of culture, and its process and the presentation of its results is a relatively long process, which is different from triggering a war or a regime change, etc. It is simple and clear. It mainly refers to the fact that in the process of communication and interaction between two or more cultures, due to the existence of confrontation and collision, the two or more cultures feel pressure and conflict. The cultural conflict is like the intersection between water flows, which seems to be just a superficial imagination, but actually develops continuously with the conflict. The culture with high potential energy will flow into the culture with low potential energy, and the culture with high potential energy will also be influenced by the culture with low potential energy. This kind of spontaneous transformation between cultures comes into being indirectly, which promotes the continuous cultural conflicts and the continuous integration and production of new cultures of different nature, which reflects the indirectness and continuity of cultural conflicts. There are many cultural subjects participating in the college entrance examination, with different levels and different values and concepts, so the cultural conflicts are bound to be indirect and continuous (Li & Li, 2019; Xing, 2018; Xue & Li, 2020; Zhuang, 2010).

The whole culture consists of the main body of the communication, the audience and the media of the communication, the cultural information and the value demand. As far as a certain culture is concerned, its content has been very rich. In the process of interweaving multiple cultures, cultures interact and collide with each other. Through different cultural forms (material, spiritual and institutional) and different cultural contents (spirit, habit and behavior), it penetrates into all fields of human life. Usually, the cultural conflict will show a state of intricacies and disorganization, with nonlinear characteristics. Like a spider weaving a web, it is not the work of a day, but when the web is finished, the scope of higher education will be expanded, and when on the stage of higher education, it will be integrated with the culture of other countries.

In the process of globalization, culture is a big stage. The contradictions of homogeneity and heterogeneity between China's college entrance examination culture and other countries' college entrance examination culture, as well as the cultural conflicts within China's college entrance examination culture, promote the reform and development of better quality of China's college entrance examination culture.

In our country and other countries of the university entrance exam culture are quite different, take South Korea college entrance examination culture, South Korea for the college entrance examination is divided into admissions and college entrance examination at any time, at any time refers to the students at ordinary times in the school's academic attitude and external events will give a result, is to a broader field of vision to look at is suitable for the system to which university students, and in the university entrance exam out after students can choose three universities, in the second year after January and February to attend universities independent of second-round exam questions, which is similar to the Chinese professional art school, students and school system is multiple choice, Such as a student admitted by two schools at the same time, so he can choose to which university, while the Chinese college entrance examination is divided into several classes, including the national exam, independent recruitment of students, the high level group, walks, accepted way using the Internet, according to the examinee volunteers provided, the university can be divided into several batches merit, on these points, China and South Korea for the college entrance examination culture differences (Li & Li, 2019; Xing, 2018; Xue & Li, 2020; Zhuang, 2010).

Take the mathematics of college entrance examination as an example. The mathematics college entrance examination in China has always emphasized the basic knowledge, basic skills and operational ability, logical thinking ability, and spatial imagination ability. It pays attention to the systematic transmission of knowledge and the training of abstract thinking. But the static question lacks the relation with the real life, cannot well reflect the mathematics value and the mathematics teaching goal. South Korea's mathematics examination introduced the reality factor more, in the emphasis on the knowledge imparting while emphasizing the students experience the mathematics activity, understanding the reality mathematics. Especially the mathematics examination question of Korea, with examining the student's image thinking and understanding ability to give priority to more.

In 1999, the proposition idea of "ability" was put forward for the first time. In this paper, students' ability to apply knowledge in specific situations is tested by designing novel situations, which changes the previous situation that "artificial" word problems are not applied. With ability to set the meaning of the proposition, in the selection of materials, the field of vision is broader, not rigidly bound by the discipline of knowledge, more focus on the general thinking of mathematical science, focus on the general value, practical significance of the problem or use of the background. Questions in the design is inclined to the understanding and application of knowledge, especially comprehensive and flexible application, involving the content including methods, ideas and capabilities and so on.

For colleges and universities, entrance examination is the best choice for colleges and universities to recruit qualified and qualified students. Especially, the unified entrance examination can not only expand the candidates' enrollment scope, improve the enrollment rate of freshmen, but also help to simplify the recruitment operation of colleges and universities, reduce the labor and material costs of the recruitment work, and the entrance examination becomes the diachronic choice of colleges and universities. For examinees, the deep yearning for the university has very profound economic and psychological factors as the foundation, based on the traditional social values, the society advocates knowledge, respects the talent and only sees the diploma of the trend, to promote many families to train their children to become college students as the highest goal. The deposition of family aspiration, social fashion, public opinion and social habit and psychology interweaves into a huge strong tension field. The students living in the field are inevitably affected by all kinds of tension and resultant force. The inevitability of things makes some students accidentally achieve the purpose of entering the university, in addition, more students will be in the heart of the success of the envy, and then form their inner stress. Thus, individuals continue to create social capital for themselves, and strive to adapt to major technological and economic changes, through the admission examination to achieve basic interests.

Culturally, the Chinese nation has a long and enduring history. We have a fine tradition to be proud of and cherish. In our view, the process of objectifying, not meaningless, it makes us in the long educational history in the picture shows the meaning of culture field of vision, and found that at least three problems or features: one is that in the context of Chinese culture, ancient couplet of school system and keep the system have a relationship, the ancient couplet of school system and keep the system have a relationship, education system and the selection system isomorphism, modern performance for China's education reform impetus of exogenous type—from top to bottom; Second, for a long time, the semantics of "reform" and "revolution" have been confused with each other. It is worth noting that in the more than 30 years after the end of the "cultural revolution", the whole society started to distinguish between "reform" and "revolution". This confusion often leads to confusion in direction, to reversals, to strategic wobbles, to missteps. Third, Chinese education has a profound cultural tradition and the educational culture is integrated, but the rational cultural vision is relatively weak. In contemporary times, it is dispelled by the discourse hegemony of politics and then economy and the pan-ideology formed by the alliance between them.

Although the status of the college entrance examination is very high, the reform of the college entrance examination system has achieved certain results, more and more reflects the characteristics of the socialist society with Chinese characteristics and is accepted by the masses. However, there is no denying that in the process of the reform and implementation of the college entrance examination system, there are some confusions and problems. For example, due to the influence of the stubborn remnants of feudal culture, many countries adhere to the "only fraction theory" and other invariable educational ideas and concepts, in addition, the one-child family is now in the majority, the parents of the excessive desire for their children to become successful, hope that women become successful, many times will backfire, forcing students to pursue knowledge blindly. But neglect to ability and comprehensive quality education, let many students in the face of the reform of the college entrance examination system, become the "affected"; In turn, it leads to more serious rebellious psychology in adolescence, and more and more deviant behaviors of students, which will directly affect the reform results and the overall direction of the college entrance examination in China. Of course, the reform is to continuously identify problems and solve them. All the results brought by the reform of the college entrance examination system are in urgent need of our review and study. In particular, the problems and confusions generated during the reform will be gradually improved and improved with the continuous development of the society (Li & Li, 2019; Xing, 2018; Xue & Li, 2020; Zhuang, 2010).

5.2 Questions and Suggestions on the Enrollment Policy of General College Examination

5.2.1 The Status Quo of the Enrollment of General College Examination

To study the status quo of college entrance examination from the aspect of the gross enrollment rate of higher education, we should first understand the meaning of the gross enrollment rate of higher education. According to the statistical index system of China's education monitoring and evaluation, the gross enrollment rate of higher education (%) = the total enrollment scale of higher education/the population of the 18–22 age group * 100%.

The gross enrollment rate of higher education not only shows the proportion of the enrollment in higher education, but also shows the threshold of higher education in China. According to the definition of the gross enrollment rate of higher education, this value can reflect the proportion of the number of people receiving higher education in the corresponding age group in the overall target, and it is a kind of refract data of the educational level per capita. According to its numerical changes, the stage of higher education in the society can be judged statistically, and the change of the difficulty of enrollment in the general college examination can be obtained apparently. Data from the 1910s show that the gross enrollment rate of higher education in China has been rising steadily year by year since 2011, with an average annual increase of 2–3%.

Although the gross enrollment rate of higher education in 2019 has not been accurately announced, as early as February 26, 2019, fan hailin, deputy director of the higher education department of the ministry of education, said that "China is about to enter the popularization stage from the popularization stage of higher education". On May 8, 2019, wang jiping, director of the department of vocational education and adult education of the ministry of education, further introduced that "this year, higher vocational education will expand its enrollment by 1 million people, making it a" stepping foot for the popularization of higher education, directly promoting the popularization of higher education in China. Therefore, we can know that the gross enrollment rate of China's higher education will be over 50% in 2019, and we can conclude that the gross enrollment rate of China's higher education will still be on a steady rise until 2019.

And higher education gross enrollment rate reached 50%, means that since this year, not only in the working-age population, average every two people that have existed in one admission to accept higher education, which means that per capita higher degree, and means that the rise of China's higher education resource utilization rate, a drop in the quality of higher education, the lower threshold of higher education and employment threshold to rise.

First of all, the increase in the gross enrollment rate of higher education means that if we want to maintain better education quality, the number of full-time teachers should be correspondingly increased, or the ratio of students to teachers will face a higher number, the use of educational resources is increased, the level of education is inevitable to decline.

Secondly, the increase in the gross enrollment rate of higher education also makes people think about the allocation of resources in ordinary colleges and universities, such as the small campus space, the overcrowding of the university canteen, the difficulty of grabbing classes, the shortage of classrooms, and the insufficient allocation of university research funds, etc., all of which are worth considering whether the university can accommodate such a large number of students.

In addition, the increase of gross enrollment rate in higher education also requires the upgrading of management platform and the improvement of the quality of managers. Many university learning systems have problems such as the system crash in the race for class hours, the delay in the update of sports platform system, and the continuous failure of the health punch system initiated by the school in the case of pneumonia, which all reflect the imbalance between the management platform technology and the number of students today. However, in National Day activities, the school is not responsible for the students' return trip, the resources promised to students are difficult to be distributed, and the students are perfunctoriness of offline records instead of online registration, which all reflect the imbalance between the quality of many managers and the number of students.

In addition, the increase of the gross enrollment rate in higher education has made the superior management of the direct department of students pay more attention to the level of students' exam scores and fail to take into account the level of other qualities of students. The suicide of female students in Peking University in 2019 shows the low psychological quality of some students and the lack of moral quality of some students. In the era of universalization of higher education, people should put forward higher requirements on the knowledge control and application of higher education, control the growth of the gross enrollment rate of higher education, and then control the quality of higher education. In particular, the enrollment expansion of higher vocational colleges in 2019 reminds people to pay more attention to the quality of higher education.

5.2.2   Allocation of Enrollment Places in Each Region

A school in each region of the allocation of enrollment places in addition to the allocation of enrollment places in previous years similar, but also with the number of general high school graduates in each region, each region of high school education resources, territorial enrollment, the school itself location, school culture, national special policies and so on.

According to the data of the enrollment quota of universities in various regions (excluding Hong Kong, Macao and Taiwan) in 2018, Henan province accounted for 7.87% of the total enrollment quota in China, making it the province with the largest enrollment quota in the country. Correspondingly, it can be found that the number of ordinary high school graduates in Henan province is also the maximum of the number of ordinary high school graduates in various regions (excluding Hong Kong, Macao and Taiwan).

Some people often put forward that "students in Beijing area are more likely to be admitted to qingbei" to Beijing examinees questioned, but also some people to give their children a better chance to enter the university, family moved to Beijing. For example, according to the data published on the official website of Peking University in 2016, in the fields of electronic information (electronics, microelectronics, computer, intelligent science and communication engineering), Peking University's enrollment in Beijing was 22, while that in Henan province was 3. This appearance has aroused a lot of people's yearning for a Beijing hukou, but having a Beijing hukou is not a cure-all, and the preference for Beijing in the allocation of enrollment places of various schools is more due to the superiority of Beijing students (Li & Li, 2019; Xing, 2018; Xue & Li, 2020; Zhuang, 2010).

College entrance examination is the ability to test and get more opportunities, more capable and enrollment quota allocation to a certain extent, reflected the region to participate in college entrance examination of students' ability, the quality of students, the college entrance examination content is not much, individual learning ability of students and influence degree of the dominant in the minority, and moderate levels of students in various places are the most majority, for these students, the pros and cons of high school education resources in a larger extent, directly affect the level of students, so the ability of students in the region and to a certain extent reflects the strengths and weaknesses of the region's high school education resources.

Beijing, Tianjin, Shanghai, the three provinces with the most enrollment quota, are also worthy of the name of education resources. Taking these three provinces as examples, these three provinces have more education contents, higher education requirements, rich educational resources, and strong comprehensive strength of students. Moreover, they conduct the college entrance examination with their independent content. These three provinces have the highest number of places for students with only average grades and are likely to be the best in other provinces.

School culture is a school of the sum of material culture, spiritual culture, system culture, in a sense, after college, school culture will seep into the students work habits, self-restraint, its decision to the one of the students graduated from school, into the society of professional quality and the direction of career choice, and therefore, in order to better fit my future career, when students select, is bound to consider the difference between school culture and regional culture.

Take Harbin Institute of Technology as an example. Harbin Institute of Technology is a typical strong university in science and engineering. Its spiritual culture has strong scientific color. In view of its own school culture and the characteristics of Beijing, Shanghai, Tianjin and other cities, hit has certain characteristics in the allocation of enrollment places in 2019. In the enrollment plan published on the official website of Harbin Institute of Technology in 2019, the number of science and technology students assigned to Beijing, Tianjin and Shanghai is 37, 44 and 20, respectively. The total number of science and technology students assigned to Inner Mongolia is 97, which is significantly different from that of other comprehensive universities. And looked into the reasons, Beijing, Tianjin, Shanghai is more developed, the formation of regional culture in the people's preference for services, and Harbin Institute of Technology itself for classes in science and engineering school, where students consider their future career development, choice of Harbin Institute of Technology is less, naturally, Harbin Institute of Technology itself less open enrollment quota industry in these areas. Compared in terms of the three cities, remote place area, in Inner Mongolia itself does not like Beijing, Tianjin, Shanghai economic development, its economic culture and the grassland culture in the demand for industrial and cultural fit with Harbin Institute of Technology itself, so the student enrollment than many of the Inner Mongolia assigned to that year of high school graduates more than the number of regions (Li & Li, 2019; Xing, 2018; Xue & Li, 2020; Zhuang, 2010).

The general college entrance examination is referred to as the college entrance examination, which is a selective examination taken by qualified high school graduates or students with the same educational level in China. General colleges and universities according to the examinee scores, according to the admission plan in advance, in the provinces to select eligible candidates. In 1952, the People's Republic of China established a unified enrollment system for regular institutions of higher learning. The college entrance examination could better show the fairness, which also met the need of the country to select talents quickly. In 1977, Deng Xiaoping became vice premier of the state, in charge of culture and education, presided over the resumption of the college entrance examination. The resumption of the Gaokao has changed the lives of millions of people, saved Chinese education, and saved the whole of China. Since the reform and opening up 42 years ago, the economy has developed rapidly. As a basic national policy of the country, college entrance examination and enrollment has been constantly improved to promote the development of the contemporary society. However, in the process of development, as such a basic national policy of selecting talents for the country, there are also many problems. The main problems are summarized as follows: The core contents of high school teaching and talent training in our country are "knowledge and ability", "process and method" and "emotion attitude and value". The direct cause of this phenomenon is the current college entrance examination enrollment system. Therefore, the scientific problem of "one examination decides lifetime" has become an unavoidable and urgent problem in the college entrance examination and enrollment system. Admittedly, there is no denying that the existence of the "one examination-for-life" system has its rationality, which can reduce the work of talent selection.

The scientific problem of "fractional theory only". In the current college entrance examination and enrollment system in China, the scientific nature of "fractional theory only" has always been a hot issue in all walks of life. On the one hand, the existence of "only score theory" defines a unified standard for talent selection, reduces the difficulty of talent selection, and reduces the cost of talent selection. On the other hand, it is a problem that needs to be clarified whether the "only score theory" selects the "examination talents" or the real all-round development talents. At present, the scientific insufficiency of "fractional theory only" is social consensus, and the problems caused by it are as follows:

First, the "only fraction theory" affects the development of quality education. In the college entrance examination and enrollment system, scores directly determine whether students can go to university and what kind of university they can go to. Therefore, higher scores become the focus of school teaching and the only goal of students' study. In some schools, under the influence of the theory of "only scores", all activities unrelated to the improvement of scores are suspended or weakened, and students' all-round development and quality education can only stay on the slogan, it is difficult to really implement.

Second, "only the score theory" is easy to lead to the occurrence of exam fraud, and thus lead to unfair. Under the "score-only" system, students only need a high score in the college entrance examination to go to a better university, and the relevant departments do not pay attention to the students' learning process in high school. This allows some criminals to cheat in the college entrance examination by various means, allowing some students who do not meet the requirements of knowledge level to get high scores, thus "crowding out" other students in the college entrance examination. The existence of "only score theory" makes the unfair college entrance examination under such fraud more and more serious and restricts the selection of excellent talents in the college entrance examination.

At present, the college entrance examination and enrollment in China is implemented in the way of combining the national unified examination with the independent proposition of each province and city, which makes the students' examination content in different regions vary greatly. To some extent, this difference also reflects the lack of fairness in the college entrance examination system. For example, the national unified examination papers are divided into one, two and three volumes, which are tested in different provinces and cities. And Beijing, Tianjin is the form of independent proposition. Such big provinces as Hebei and Henan have a large population base, and the examination paper is one volume of the college entrance examination, which is more difficult. The independent test paper of Beijing and Tianjin is less difficult than that of the whole country, but the educational resources of Beijing and Tianjin are obviously better than those of Hebei and Henan. It is undeniable that the educational resources of primary and secondary schools in Beijing and Tianjin are among the best in the country, and the comprehensive quality of students is relatively comprehensive. However, as far as the college entrance examination is concerned, there is a mismatch between the examination difficulty content and educational resources, that is, there is an unfair phenomenon in the region.

Of admissions policy at present our country each district regional differences, shown as: student enrollment to tilt the region education developed areas, thereby increasing the other relative backward area to enjoy more the difficulty of the high quality education resources, from the data showed that Beijing university, Tsinghua university, Fudan university around the country in the enrollment scale, the acceptance rate of the city with three major universities is far higher than the rest of the country, and Beijing, Shanghai, due to various factors such as politics, economy, culture synthesis, education resources are the most concentrated, the most advanced.

This makes the unfairness of the regional enrollment policy plan of the college entrance examination is further amplified.

The college entrance examination additional score policy plays a very important role in maintaining the fairness of college entrance examination education and trying to guarantee the fairness of each student's entrance opportunity in higher education. But on the other hand, the economic development of China's vast territory and each region is not balanced, thus in the development of education degree and uneven distribution of education resources, also is not the same, especially in the underdeveloped areas of examinee, the examinee in comparison with the rest of the candidates, at a serious disadvantage in the college entrance examination, in order to ensure their education entrance opportunity fairness is particularly important. The college entrance examination additional score policy mainly refers to the behavior rules that the ministry of education and the administrative departments of education of various provinces and cities give certain preferential and considerate college entrance examination scores to the students according to their ethnic groups, ideological and political performances, awards in competitions and contributions to the society. There are three kinds of ways to take care of them: priority admission, point reduction admission and additional points admission. The additional score of the college entrance examination policy is to take care of some disadvantaged groups, but in the implementation, process will inevitably appear biased, so there is an unfair phenomenon (Li & Li, 2019; Xing, 2018; Xue & Li, 2020; Zhuang, 2010).

At present, there are 14 extra points for the college entrance examination stipulated by the national ministry of education, and 192 preferential policies in various places. Among the 196,000 examinees in a city in 2016, the number of examinees who obtained various additional points reached as high as 70,000, accounting for more than 35% of the total number of examinees. Among the examinees, the number of students who obtained additional points was very large. Such a large number of preferential policies changed the nature of fair competition in the college entrance examination. For example, with the help of parents or social profit-making organizations, some students can make some non-original creations to get bonus points. In order to take advantage of the current low-score policy, some parents have taken part in the "Gaokao immigration", transferring their children to ethnic minority areas or changing their household registration in a short period of time. Although according to relevant national policies and regulations, the additional score policy for special students will be canceled after 2020, there are certain loopholes in such policies as additional score policy for registered permanent residence, additional score policy for ethnic groups, and various "invention" additional score policy for independent enrollment. On the management and operation level, due to the lack of supervision and opacity, the bonus points policy has become a "near-water platform" for a few people to make profits. There are many students with special skills in literature and art and sports who have false qualifications. "fake ethnic minority students", "fake overseas Chinese students" and "fake second-level athletes" emerge in an endless number of places.

More and more experts and scholars have criticized the current college entrance examination system. Under many pressures, the provincial education departments continue to reform the college entrance examination and enrollment system, among which the subject selection and examination system is a top priority. In the traditional college entrance examination mode, the examinees are divided into liberal arts and science majors, among which Chinese, mathematics and English are compulsory subjects, science majors physics, chemistry and biology, and liberal arts majors history, geography and politics. The division of science and arts is too obvious, which is not conducive to the cultivation and improvement of students' overall quality. However, some provinces have adopted the optional examination system. Chinese, Math and English are still compulsory subjects, but three subjects are selected from history, geography, politics, physics, chemistry and biology to take part in the examination. There is no change in the number of exams, but in this system, it is very easy to lead to the formation of students' egoistic behavior, that is, in the process of learning is not to face the difficulties, but to figure out which subjects are easy to learn, easy to test. This system may also have a negative impact on examinees' values.

China's current college entrance examination and enrollment system is unable to meet the needs of innovative talent cultivation. With the gradual advance of China's education reform and the continuous development of the economy and society, quality-oriented education has become a more important standard to cultivate contemporary talents. However, there are still some contradictions between the college entrance examination and enrollment system and the demand for innovative talents cultivation.

A.   The current college entrance examination and enrollment system is the embodiment of exam-oriented education in China, which lacks the cultivation of innovative talents. At present, China's college entrance examination and enrollment system is mainly based on the examination of book knowledge. This makes school education centered on improving students' scores, while inhibiting the cultivation of innovative abilities that have nothing to do with improving scores. The whole society requires students to be obedient and get high marks, which makes it difficult to form a development environment that supports students' innovation. Under the current college entrance examination system, the society is based on whether students are admitted to universities or not, and the main criterion of moral education is whether students are obedient or not. Therefore, the whole society is opposed to students' individual ideas and innovative practice. This inhibits the development of students' innovative thinking and practical ability, which is not conducive to their innovative and comprehensive development.

To sum up, the current college entrance examination system is not scientific enough, not fair enough and not compatible enough. As a national policy of basic education in China, college entrance examination and enrollment have to some extent-maintained fairness and provided a channel for talent selection.

5.3 Suggestions on Enrollment Reform

The national college entrance examination, or Gaokao for short, is a selective examination taken by qualified high school graduates or students of the same educational level in China (excluding Hong Kong special administrative region, Macao special administrative region and Taiwan province). The college entrance examination has changed the fate of millions of people. In the eyes of most people, the college entrance examination is an opportunity to change their fate. General institutions of higher learning according to the examinee's score, in accordance with the confirmed enrollment plan, moral, intellectual, physical, the United States, labor, comprehensive and balanced development, the best admission. The college entrance examination has a long history in our country. It is a kind of selection examination for talents who are suitable for our country's national conditions. Such a large selection test will certainly have many problems, such as the above mentioned "one test for life", "score-only", regional inequality and other problems, are we need to solve.

One examination determines life. Although an exam, college entrance examination is very difficult but we can be in for some subjects to take several exams and get the highest score in this form, to the system of "one youngster" ignore those parts of the students "performance", cause the excellent talents for the college entrance examination defeat and ultimately unable to continue their education problem to change; For the students themselves, the college entrance examination is by no means a single choice. It is not the choice between you and the university, but a two-way choice. Now we take the parallel voluntary measures are to change this situation, to give students more choices, but also let the university students have more understanding and choice.

The "fractional theory only". As for the problem of college entrance examination enrollment, we should pay more attention to the study of knowledge rather than just scores. Therefore, on the basis of the original college entrance examination, we should put forward certain requirements for the five aspects of moral, intellectual, physical, aesthetic and labor, and certain tests and assessments of knowledge and accomplishment. In addition, we can also have a certain selection system.

For "only the score theory" this problem, at present our country university recruit students to carry out is on the net recruit students, by the high score to the low score union volunteer carries on the admission, to recruit students the fair justice gave the strong guarantee, deeply broad masses of recognition. But if you think about it, you can see the problem. In the process of college enrollment selection, test scores should not be the only criterion for college admission, so, we should take a multi-dimensional evaluation, the best admission. In the college enrollment evaluation, in addition to considering the university's unified entrance examination results, interview results, oral examination results, Chinese colleges and universities should also refer to:

A variety of comprehensive evaluation results, such as the characteristics of the middle school, reputation and the recommendation letter from the principal or the classroom, students' extracurricular activity records, subject research, special expertise, competition results, gizmos, etc., can be the basis of the evaluation. This can also be applied to the "one exam for life" problem, not only for the exam itself, in addition to the exam itself there are many evaluation criteria. Comprehensive quality evaluation report or record bag for reference of student growth. This is in addition to the score of other assessment can be referred to things, this is the overall development of the students' quality shape width and performance level of the evaluation, I think this can be used as college admission candidates must material.

Senior high school education is an important basic education stage in the process of talent cultivation. It is a high-level basic education that further improves the national quality and faces the public on the basis of nine-year compulsory education. High school education should lay the foundation for students' lifelong development. Therefore, the goal of high school education is not only to enter the school, for institutions of higher learning to send qualified freshmen is only one of the important tasks of high school education, the cultivation of comprehensive quality of people is the core task of high school education, we should stand in the height of conducive to the students' lifelong development design college entrance examination. Therefore, on this basis, we should make the reform of the admission policy can be in the selection of examination content not excessively biased to pure subject education, more should have a high-quality high school graduates as the standard.

Correctly handle the relationship between knowledge examination and ability examination. There has always been a dispute between knowledge examination and ability examination in general college entrance examination. In the limited examination time, the limited examination form, the comprehensive examination examinee's knowledge and ability is very difficult. The test that emphasizes ability blindly, often weakened the examination of basic knowledge, make ability examination lose support; Blindly emphasize to the knowledge of the system examination, and easy to lead to the examinee rote memorization and engage in sea tactics. Therefore, the design of the college entrance examination, whether in form or content should be considered as a whole, not to miss bias.

The college entrance examination is unfair. The fairness of the college entrance examination and enrollment system is insufficient, mainly manifested in the following aspects:

In fact, summed up, in fact, it is no other than the above several. At present, the college entrance examination admission is on the implementation of national exam with a combination of various provinces and cities autonomous propositions, so that students from around the test content is larger difference, the state examination is divided into the national 123 volumes, some provinces is its own way, as well as the regional policy of enrollment, education developed area will student enrollment tilt to the region, and for backward area, cannot enjoy more high-quality education resources. There is also the bonus point policy, such as the bonus point for ethnic minorities. Some parents immigrate to places where they can get bonus points in order to improve their children's score, or their children whose household registration is their own become a fake ethnic minority, which is unfair to others.

Unification test to this, we should adhere to the standardization and unity throughout the country to organize the implementation, the parts of the areas in need of unified based diversified forms of test selection, unfairness of enrollment policy, we should be strict management of the relatively developed areas, the local colleges and universities places want to open more, again, for some less reasonable policy, we should put it out rather than stay.

Because of the unfairness, we should correctly handle the relationship between science, fairness and benefit of admission examination. Educational equity is a fundamental issue throughout China's educational reform. The e reform of entrance examination is no exception, fairness is the soul of the college entrance examination, the college entrance examination policy should reflect as far as possible for all the personnel to participate in the examination to provide a fair opportunity, a fair environment, a fair standard. On the one hand, the college entrance examination policy should have a merit-based admission index system, which should be a comprehensive assessment of examinees' morality, intelligence and physique, rather than a system where scores determine everything. But the system must be fair to candidates of any background, which is the key to the science and fairness of Gaokao policy. On the other hand, under the premise of ensuring science and fairness, the benefits of the entrance examination should be considered. As the college entrance examination is a large-scale and periodic selection examination, any reform must consider the benefit problem, the pursuit of absolute fairness, the benefit will be restricted, and the sacrifice of fairness to blindly pursue high benefit is unacceptable to the society.

Although there are gaps in the economic development of different regions in our country, we should also insist on standardized unified tests. First, this unified college entrance examination standardization first, proposition science, management norms, test validity, reliability is high; Second, the unified college entrance examination is based on fairness and objectivity as the criteria for talent selection, ensuring that individuals receive education equally with their talents. Unified examination is the basic or main form of talent selection in China. Through years of practice, its fairness and efficiency have been widely recognized by the society. However, the unified examination also has many limitations in the comprehensive quality assessment and personality evaluation of students, so it is necessary to establish a diversified entrance examination system based on the unified examination to move from "unified" to diversified.

1. Increase the number of exams, adjust the setting of majors, and build a multi-dimensional "overpass bridge" between different majors in each school, so as to return the autonomy of students to when they want to go to college and what they want to learn.

2. Explore the reform of hierarchical examination admission. Different schools have different levels and goals, so their examination selection mode should be different, and the examination admission method should adapt to the multi-levels and multi-types of schools.

3. Expand the autonomy of college enrollment. For example, the implementation of joint enrollment, that is, the same school according to the school's own development direction and professional characteristics through joint enrollment. In addition, still can use the method of recommend interview, be opposite namely "all ability" but the examinee that has special ability in certain discipline or the

examinee that wins an award in national or even international contest, pass the method that interview and investigation photograph unifies by the university, independent decision enrolls students. Secondary schools should use a unified new college entrance examination evaluation system and reflect the evaluation system in the examination (Li & Li, 2019; Xing, 2018; Xue & Li, 2020; Zhuang, 2010).

References

Li, J., & Li, J. (2019). Educational policy development in China in the 21st century: A multi-flows approach. *Beijing International Review of Education, 1*(1), 196–220.

Xing, M. D. (2018). Practical strategies and practical significance of college entrance examination and enrollment system reform. *Contemporary Education Practice and Teaching Research, 18*(06), 55–56.

Xue, E., & Li, J. (2020). Top-down education policy on the inclusion of ethnic minority population in China: A perspective of policy analysis. *Educational Philosophy and Theory, 52*(3), 227–239.

Zhuang, X. P. (2010). Practice and reflection on deepening the reform of college entrance examination and enrollment system. *Education Measurement and Evaluation* (theoretical edition), *10*(2), 45–49.

Chapter 6
An Analysis of the Diversified Development of High School Education in China

This chapter concentrates on an analysis of the diversified development of high school education in China. In particular, this study aims to understand What is the policy change of diversification in Chinese high schools and why this policy. In addition, the Issues and suggestions on diversification development policies of senior high schools, the problems in the diversification of high schools, and suggestions on the diversified development of high schools have been provided to examine the landscape of the diversified development of higher school education in contemporary China.

6.1 What Is the Policy Change of Diversification in Chinese High Schools?

In the whole school education system, high school education is in a very special and important position, with irreplaceable educational role and value. It is not only the "special territory" that cannot be ignored in the national talent strategy system, but also the "transition period" that cannot be ignored for individual life happiness and career success. It is not only the top of basic education, but also the beginning of vocational preparatory education; The academic development of a person is not only a rapid progress of school age, but also a person's personality and character is becoming mature age. In a word, no matter from the perspective of individual healthy growth and life happiness, or from the perspective of improving national competitiveness, high school education is an educational proposition that cannot be ignored. From the perspective of school system reform, China's high school education can be roughly divided into three periods: from the beginning of the founding of new China to the end of the "cultural revolution", high school education is only a single ordinary high school education; After the reform and opening up, especially after the promulgation and implementation of the decision of the CPC central committee on the reform of the education system in 1985, under the background of adjusting the structure of secondary education and vigorously developing vocational and technical

J. Li and E. Xue, *Education Policy in Chinese High Schools*, Exploring Education Policy in a Globalized World: Concepts, Contexts, and Practices, https://doi.org/10.1007/978-981-16-2358-5_6

education, the original high school education was gradually divided into ordinary high schools and vocational high schools. In 1995, the national general high school education work conference divided the general high school into "preparatory education, comprehensive high school, focus on vocational preparatory education high school and characteristic high school" and other four modes of running schools. Since then, the general high school education took the road of classified development as the prelude, and the diversified development of the general high school started the "ice-breaking journey" (Li, 2020; Li & Eryong, 2020; Li et al., 2019, 2020; Xue & Li, 2019, 2020a, 2020b). At present, the ordinary high school education in educational system, educational pattern and training pattern has gradually formed the pattern of diversification, but still not reach ideal level, level and quality of the relevant supporting measures are far from perfect, each layer of the operating mechanism of all kinds of school also has many defects, even there is no lack of "appropriate", further straighten out, standard, improve and improve.

6.1.1   The Exploration of Educational Diversity

In 1993, the state council of the CPC central committee pointed out in the program for China's educational reform and development: the running system and running mode of ordinary high schools should be diversified. Since then, the state has put forward diversified development ideas for ordinary high schools, requiring them to develop in a diversified way, and gradually realize diversification in terms of system and mode. Later, in 1995, the state education commission held a national work conference on ordinary high school education, the meeting stressed that to continue to ordinary high school education mode reform, changes in the history of the legacy of a single model aiming at entrance of the development, to the entrance as a part of the training objectives of ordinary high school, are considered in this part of the high school can be further lay the foundation for the students, new students qualified for colleges and universities; While most of the other high schools should develop towards comprehensive development. Students can choose appropriate courses in the school and achieve diversion through the mechanism of course selection. Such comprehensive high schools have two functions, namely, enrollment and employment. In addition, there are employment-oriented high schools, as well as characteristic high schools, whose development direction is to adapt to the needs of society and develop the needs of students' personality development, for example, it can be foreign languages, sports, arts and high schools (classes) with special emphasis on a certain subject.

6.1.2   The Prospect of Educational Diversification

In 1994, *the Opinions of the State Council on the Implementation of the Program of China's Educational Reform and Development* put forward that by the year 2000, each county should establish one or two key secondary schools for the whole county. We will focus on the construction of about 1,000 experimental and demonstration high schools nationwide. The guidelines stressed that the outline of China's education reform and development is a blueprint for education reform and development in the 1990s and early next century, and a programmatic document for building a socialist education system with Chinese characteristics. Earnestly implementing the program is an important duty of party committees and governments at all levels and the central task of educational administrative departments at all levels and schools of all types.

When referring to the date and tasks of China's educational development in the year 2000, the implementation opinions pointed out that, according to the strategic deployment of China's socialist modernization drive, the outline determined the overall date for the development of China's educational cause: by the end of this century, the national level of education has significantly improved; The pre-service and post-service education of urban and rural workers has developed greatly; The possession of various kinds of specialized talents basically meets the needs of modernization construction: forming the basic framework of the socialist education system with Chinese characteristics and facing the twenty-first century. By the year 2000, nine-year compulsory education will be basically universal throughout the country. According to the principle of zoning, classified guidance and step-by-step implementation, the development goals and speed of different regions of the country may vary. All provinces, autonomous regions and municipalities directly under the central government shall formulate and implement the phased plan for the popularization of nine-year compulsory education in counties and townships, organize its implementation, and shall be responsible for inspection and acceptance on the basis of county (city, district) self-inspection in accordance with the measures for the evaluation and acceptance of the popularization of nine-year compulsory education issued by the state education commission.

According to the implementation guidelines, on the basis of the popularization of nine-year compulsory education, senior high school education (including regular senior high school and senior high school vocational education) should be actively popularized in large urban areas and coastal areas with a relatively high degree of economic development. Ordinary high school can according to the need of each place and the right amount of development is possible: carry out plan ground after primary school, after junior high school, after senior high school 3 class shunt. We will make great efforts to develop vocational education, and gradually form a series of education programs in which primary, secondary, and higher vocational education and general education develop together, connect with each other, and have a reasonable proportion. The higher education should take the road of connotation development, make the scale more appropriate, the structure more reasonable, the quality and the benefit improve obviously; We will vigorously develop adult education with emphasis on literacy, job training and continuing education. By the year 2000, illiteracy among the young and the middle-aged will have been basically eliminated, and the non-illiteracy rate among the young and the middle-aged will be about 95%. The state council decided to establish a national inter-ministerial coordinating body for literacy work to provide overall guidance for literacy work; We will attach importance to and develop education for ethnic minorities. The central and local governments should adopt special preferential policies towards the education of ethnic minorities in the areas of education funds, teacher training and world bank funds. We will actively develop radio and television education and audio-visual education in schools, promote the use of modern teaching methods, and basically complete a nationwide network of audio-visual education by the year 2000. We will further strengthen international educational exchanges and cooperation, open education wider to the outside world, establish the state administration committee for overseas students, and legalize the recruitment, selection and management of foreign students in China and abroad. The development of education should focus on improving its quality and efficiency. To study and formulate standards for the basic conditions and quality of schools of all levels and types, and to establish and improve the system of educational monitoring, evaluation and supervision; To strengthen the overall planning of education development and adjust the structure and distribution of education; We should actively promote the association and cooperation between institutions of higher learning and secondary vocational schools (Li, 2020; Li & Eryong, 2020; Li et al., 2019, 2020; Xue & Li, 2019, 2020a, 2020b).

6.1.3 The Steady Progress in Educational Diversification

In 1995, the national general high school education work conference divided the general high school into "preparatory education, comprehensive high school, focus on vocational preparatory education high school and characteristic high school" and other four modes of running schools.

The curriculum reform in this period has the following distinct characteristics:

(1) "quality-oriented education" is emerging. 1990 years later, the former state education commission in adjust the opinion of the current ordinary high school teaching plan in ordinary high school education task oriented in "the nine years of compulsory education on the basis of further improving the students' ideological and moral qualities, scientific and cultural quality, psychological quality, body will make students personality get healthy development, to cultivate socialist builders and successors to lay the good foundation", start high school education emphasis on "quality" requirements. In 1993, the program clearly stated that "primary and secondary schools should shift from 'exam-oriented education' to the track of comprehensively improving the quality of the nation", requiring them to "comprehensively improve the ideological and moral, cultural and scientific, labor skills and physical and psychological qualities of students" on the basis of "facing all students". In order to achieve this goal and task, "the outline" proposed, further change of educational thinking, reform of teaching content and teaching methods, to overcome the phenomenon that school education, to varying degrees, is divorced from the needs of economic construction and social development. In accordance with the new achievements in the development of modern science, technology and culture and the actual needs of the socialist modernization drive, we should update

the teaching content and adjust the curriculum structure. Strengthen the cultivation and training of basic knowledge, basic theories and basic skills, attach importance to the cultivation of students' ability to analyze and solve problems, and pay attention to the discovery and training of students with special skills. The curriculum plan of full-time senior middle school (experiment) issued in 1996 reiterated the quality requirements and further transformed it into the training goal of ordinary high school (Li, 2020; Li & Eryong, 2020; Li et al., 2019, 2020; Xue & Li, 2019, 2020a, 2020b).

(2) Reform and adjust the curriculum structure to adapt to the running mode of ordinary high schools. The outline puts forward the requirement of "diversification of running systems and modes of running schools in ordinary senior high schools", and the opinions on the implementation of the outline further emphasize the planned implementation of post-senior high school diversion, and the mutual connection and cooperation with vocational education. In 1995, the former state education commission in the "several opinions" reaffirmed "basic education" properties of ordinary high school, multidimensional illustrates the ordinary high school education task, not only further strengthen the function of education to serve the society, also highlights to the attention of the students' quality and personality development, further indicate the ordinary high school can make "entering education" "employment preparation education" to "both entering education and employment preparation education" "focus on foreign languages, sports, art, and strengthen the characteristics of a school" four patterns. On this basis, the request "from the nature of ordinary high school training goal, task, and, according to the school-running mode diversification requirements, curriculum reform actively, strengthen the construction of teaching material, changing the course system of the entrance to a single target, strengthen the pertinence, diversity, gradually formed by the subject courses (including public required course and a variety of elective courses) and action classes, of course can adapt to the development of society, economy, science and technology course system". In 1996, the former state education commission issued by the "full-time ordinary senior middle school curriculum program (trial)", "the several opinions" embodied the spirit of rendering, further identified as required, the limits of the courses elective and arbitrary elective three, and in accordance with the employment preparation education, emphasize particularly on entrance preparatory education of liberal arts and sciences curriculum Suggestions are given. The plan seeks to "provide all students with a basic degree in the form of compulsory courses" and "give students more freedom through a large number of elective courses and extracurricular activities". In 1994, the basic education department of the former state education commission also developed and issued the outline of vocational guidance for ordinary middle schools (trial), requiring senior high school students to carry out vocational planning guidance, to enhance students' vocational awareness and the ability to adapt to the future career. The curriculum plan for full-time ordinary senior middle school issued in 2002 no longer particularly emphasizes the task orientation of "two focuses" of ordinary high schools and the reform of running mode of high schools, but also simplifies the adjustment of three types of compulsory courses, limited elective courses and optional courses into compulsory courses and optional courses.

(3) Adapt to the training of "four freshmen" requires continuous strengthening of moral education. For a boycott of bourgeois liberalization and all the erosion of decadent ideas of the exploiting classes, determined to build socialism with Chinese characteristics in the belief that "promote students to establish a scientific world outlook and outlook on life" serving the people, and put forward the guidelines "with Marxism-Leninism and MAO Zedong thought and the theory of building socialism with Chinese characteristics education students, the firm correct political direction in the first place, have ideal, morality, culture and discipline new socialist, the school moral education is the basic task of ideological and moral education", and on this basis, The guidelines for the implementation of the program further emphasize education in the legal system, the traditional virtues of the Chinese nation and the revolutionary tradition. "Full-time ordinary senior high school curriculum plan (experiment)" in all subjects are classified as "compulsory" and "limited elective" two kinds of courses, adhere to the "ideological and political" course for three years all compulsory. In view of the fact that "history education itself is the best way to carry out the education of national conditions and patriotism", the total class hours of history were increased, from 136 class hours for all students to 105 class hours for all students and 258 class hours for liberal arts students. At the same time, the content of Chinese modern and contemporary history has been strengthened in the history discipline, and the patriotic education and national conditions education have been strengthened in combination with the historical facts of the patriotic and kind-hearted people who saved the country and made great efforts to become strong in modern times. In addition, continue to strengthen labor technology courses and social practice activities, social practice activities every school year for two weeks of class hours, it is required to organize students to carry out social surveys, participate in industrial and agricultural production labor and military training activities. The curriculum plan of full-time senior high school issued in 2002 further explored the educational connotation of social practice activities, and defined it as "national defense education, production and labor education for students, and the cultivation of organizational discipline, collective concept and hard-working spirit". "Community service" is specially added to guide students to participate in various public welfare activities, "to carry out the awareness of social responsibility, the spirit of helping others to serve the construction and development of the community".

(4) Promote the reform of learning methods and add research learning courses. To cultivate students' innovation spirit and practice ability, the transformation of the mode of students' learning and teachers' teaching methods, the Ministry of Education in the full-time ordinary high school curriculum program (experimental revised), adding "inquiry learning", and the original curriculum of "labor and technology education" and "social practice", and the new "community service" are collectively referred to as "comprehensive practice", at the same time in comprehensive summary refining Shanghai curriculum reform experience, on the basis of study and establish the "ordinary high school" inquiry learning "implementation guidelines (trial)" (taught) [2001] 6. "Inquiry learning" advocated "on the basis of students' autonomy, exploratory learning, from the student life and social life in the choose and determine the research topic, mainly in the form of individual or group cooperation", to "direct

experience obtained through hands-on practice, foster scientific spirit and scientific attitude, master the basic scientific methods, improve the comprehensive ability to use knowledge to solve practical problems". The implementation of research learning activities, on the one hand, has greatly stimulated the enthusiasm and creativity of ordinary high schools, and once became the highlight of the curriculum reform of schools around the world. Inquiry learning activities for the students, on the other hand, has opened up out of the classroom, out of school curriculum, guide the student warmly concerned about the actual social fields, based on the relevant knowledge of discipline curriculum actively carry out research activities, not only promoted the students to change the way of learning, cultivate the innovative spirit and practice ability, and promote the students' sense of social responsibility.

(5) Establish the "three-level curriculum management system" in line with the reform of the basic education system. Made clear that the guidelines "on the relationship between the central and local, to further establish the central and provincial (autonomous regions and municipalities directly under the central government) classification management and classification is responsible for the education management system", the state is responsible for the basic length of schooling, curriculum and curriculum standards promulgated, everywhere has the right to determine the region of the system, selection of teaching plans, teaching materials and compiling the teaching material, examination and province and endows local and school curriculum autonomy. The full-time ordinary high school curriculum program (trial) "for the first time put forward the" ordinary high school courses prescribed by the central, local and school level 3 management, allowing the provincial education administrative department according to the spirit of the curriculum, according to the actual situation of "province to implement curriculum planning, the paper puts forward and action classes on any elective subject curriculum implementation plan", the school can be in the central and local education administrative departments, under the provisions of "the compulsory subjects and the limit of optional subjects to make specific arrangements, setting up reasonable school course selection and activity". More breakthrough significance is, 2002 promulgated "the full-time ordinary high school curriculum plan" provisions of the "local and school elective course" deviate and week, means that the local and school have the rights of independent development course, at the same time, further defined national curriculum management responsibility lies in training objectives, curriculum setting and scheduling, and promulgated (Li, 2020, Li & Eryong, 2020; Li et al., 2019, 2020; Xue & Li, 2019, 2020a, 2020b).

6.2 Why This Policy?

6.2.1 The Political Aspect

The 14th National Congress of the Communist Party of China under the guidance of the theory of building socialism with Chinese characteristics, to determine the main task of the reform and construction in China in the ninetys, which clearly put forward "must put education on the strategic position of priority development, efforts to improve the ideological and moral and ethical, scientific and cultural levels, this is the implementation plan of the modernization in China". The following is a political analysis of the reasons for the policy change of high school education diversification.

The Third Plenary Session of the Eleventh Central Committee of the Communist Party of China (CPC) pointed out that, the educational reform has been carried out gradually, and vocational and technical education has developed to a considerable extent.

In September 1982, the 12th national congress of the communist party of China proposed to take education as an important guarantee for quadrupling the economic development in the past 20 years and raise the cause of education to one of the party's three strategic priorities. In 1992, the 14th national congress of the communist party of China was held and the basic framework of establishing a socialist market economy system was put forward. However, China's education in general is still relatively backward, cannot adapt to the needs of speed up the reform and opening up and modernization drive, since the university entrance exam system restore, for countries to cultivate a large number of basic talents of average high school, but along with the progress of the era, the society changed the way of choose and employ persons, education system and operational mechanism is not adapt to the need of deepening the political system reform, the school need to further strengthen and improve ideological and political work; In order to better solve these problems, the program for China's education reform and development in 1993 put forward for the first time the requirement that "the running system and running mode of ordinary high schools should be diversified". The diversification of ordinary high schools is the need of the development of The Times. It initially establishes a new education system that is compatible with the reform of the socialist political system and the scientific and technological system, and also lays a foundation for the establishment of a socialist education system with Chinese characteristics. In 1994, in order to strengthen the basic normal education, the diversity and selectivity, promote the reform of ordinary high school, better training excellent talent of socialist construction, the state issued by the State Council on the implementation of the (Chinese education reform and development compendium) opinions put forward, by 2000 each county to county focus oriented to organize one or two middle school. In order to promote the horizontal development of high school education and cultivate more knowledge-oriented talents and scientific and technological talents for higher education, China will focus on building about 1,000 experimental and demonstration high schools. At the same time, in order to meet the requirements of different potential of students' development, cultivating various talents for national development and modernization, in 1995, in order to further the formation of the reasonable structure of high school education, to implement vocational training mode innovation, national work conference on ordinary high school education will be divided into ordinary high school of entering education, comprehensive high school, focusing on the employment preparation education characteristics of high school and senior high school" and so on four kind of school-running pattern, provide students with diverse learning options, for training various talents, forming the reasonable structure of high school education has laid the foundation. In order to fully implement the party's education policy, we will conscientiously implement "the central committee of the communist party of China, the state council on deepening education reform and comprehensively promote quality education decision" (found [1999] 9), 2001 of the state council on the decision of the elementary education reform and development", put forward to excavate potential existing schools and encourage conditional region implements the separation of complete high school, junior high school, expand the scale of high school. Encourage social forces to take various forms to develop high school education. We will maintain a reasonable proportion of regular high schools and secondary vocational schools and promote their coordinated development. Encourage the development of communication between general education and vocational education in senior high schools. We will support the development of high school education in rural areas in the central and western regions where nine-year compulsory education is compulsory. In order to realize the goal of building a well-off society in an all-round way and implement the spirit of the party's 16th national congress, the state council approved and transferred the action plan of education revitalization from 2003 to 2007 issued by the ministry of education in 2004. To increase support for the development of the rural high school, and guide the demonstrative high school construction, speed up the construction of basic BoRuoJiao, expand the supply of high quality education resources ability, efforts to implement the party's historical task put forward by the 16th national congress, building the modern education system of socialism with Chinese characteristics, in order to establish a learning society in the people will learn or even pursue life-long education will lay the foundation for the modernization construction to provide greater contribution to the knowledge and intellectual support.

According to the party congress about the priority to the development of education, we aim to establish the human resources power strategy to improve the national quality, promote the scientific development of education career, accelerate the process of socialist modernization. *The National Medium and Long-term Education Reform and Development Plan Outline (2010-2020)* (hereinafter referred to as the outline) determine the direction of the new policy, including the improvement of the compulsory education of public service delivery, perfect the preferential policies to encourage fair competition. We shall support private schools in innovating their systems, mechanisms, and modes of education to improve their quality, develop their characteristics, and run a number of high-quality private schools well. The outline clearly states: "high school education is a crucial period for the formation and independent development of students' personalities, which is of special significance to the improvement of national quality and the cultivation of innovative talents. We will focus on cultivating students' abilities of independent study, self-improvement, self-reliance and adaptation to society, and overcome the tendency of exam-oriented education" (Li, 2020; Li & Eryong, 2020; Li et al., 2019, 2020; Xue & Li, 2019, 2020a, 2020b).

From the perspective of the whole education system, high school education plays an important role, which is not only the advanced stage of basic education, but also the preparatory stage of higher education. Ordinary high school bear the transition effect, which forms a connecting link between the preceding and the qualified students for higher schools, and for the construction of modern society to cultivate qualified labor reserve force, therefore, in order to balance the relationship between education and employment, cultivating advanced talents with professional talents for the construction of modern society, gradually improve and improvement of the diversification of average high school policy has very profound significance. The setting of the dual tasks of the promotion function and the employment function of the ordinary high school is a very distinct setting of the tasks and goals of the ordinary high school from the perspective of "social standard". In the name of "the state council" and "the central committee of the communist party of China", these major policies on education established the overall goals and plans for the development of education and pointed out the direction for the implementation of specific measures. These typical policies and documents reflect the changing needs of national policies in different periods. The setting of "dual" tasks should be more based on the needs of the society, so as to cultivate suitable talents in line with the construction of China's modern society (Li, 2020; Li & Eryong, 2020; Li et al., 2019, 2020; Xue & Li, 2019, 2020a, 2020b).

6.2.2   The Economic Aspects

Since the restoration of the college entrance examination system, the education in senior high school has continuously cultivated talents for the development of China's economy. Since the reform and opening up in 1978, great changes have taken place in China's economy and society. With the continuous development and progress of the society, the traditional and single education model has been unable to adapt to the needs of China from a country with large human resources to a country with strong human resources and strong science and technology. The following will analyze the reasons for the diversification of ordinary high schools from the perspective of economy.

First of all, education for the promotion of the economic effect is various, from the macro point of view, education to promote the development of national economy is reflected in: education can not only the needs of training for the economic production professionals, promote the productivity, and for scientific discoveries to cultivate advanced high-tech talents, promote the innovation of science and technology, improve the economic production of scientific research innovation ability, lead to greater productivity improvement. At the same time, education can also train a series of excellent management talents, effectively disseminate and develop the scientific knowledge, manufacturing process and production experience accumulated in economic production, and develop the productivity of scientific ideology. High school education not only undertakes nine-year compulsory education, but also trains talents for higher education and employment, accounting for a very important proportion of education's role in promoting economic development. Therefore, the formulation of reasonable high school education policy is of great significance to the economic development, which is also the economic reason why since the reform and opening up, China has gradually improved and improved the legal system related to high school education, and actively improved and developed the education policy that suits the current national conditions and development needs. The demand of economic development and the actual situation are one of the motivations and reference conditions for the policy change of high school education diversification (Li, 2020; Li & Eryong, 2020; Li et al., 2019, 2020; Xue & Li, 2019, 2020a, 2020b).

Since the reform and opening up, great changes have taken place in China's economy and society, and the quantity and structure of the demand for talents have also changed. Since the restoration of the college entrance examination system, high school education has cultivated a large number of talents for the economic construction and achieved certain results and development. In December 1978, the third plenary session of the 11th CPC central committee shifted the focus of the party's work to economic development, providing important policy support and creating a good social environment for educational reform and development. Since the reform and opening up, the single mode of high school education is no longer in line with the needs of the development of productive forces. In 1992, the party's 14th is put forward in the establishment of a socialist market economic system "in" goal, the Chinese society which took to the establishment of a socialist market economy with Chinese characteristics new development path, at this point, establish a compatible with market economy system essential education management system, the reform of education system be vividly portrayed. As an important part of the education process, the diversification of running systems and modes of running schools in ordinary high schools is well in line with the demand of talents for economic development (Li, 2020; Li & Eryong, 2020; Li et al., 2019, 2020; Xue & Li, 2019, 2020a, 2020b).

Among them, the secondary vocational education has the necessity and the economic significance, it is the modern education important component, is the industrialization and the production socialization, the modernization important pillar. As an important part of high school education, it undertakes the important task of training hundreds of millions of high-quality workers and is an important basis for China's economic and social development. Nine-year compulsory education in our country's basic conditions, if not speed up the development of secondary vocational education, is bound to influence to achieve the goals of high school education development in our country, restricting our take a new road to industrialization, solving the problem of "agriculture, rural areas and farmers" and the construction of urbanization process, and can not adapt to the comprehensive construction well-off society's need for high-quality workforce. Maintaining a reasonable proportion of ordinary high schools and secondary vocational schools can promote the coordinated development of the economy. Therefore, the program of educational reform and development in China in 1993 mentioned that vocational and technical education should be developed to meet the needs of local economic development. In areas where nine-year compulsory education is basically universal, the focus should be on the development of post-secondary vocational and technical education. In areas where nine-year compulsory education is not yet universal, vocational and technical training should be provided to primary school graduates who are unable to enter junior high schools. All localities should actively develop diversified post-secondary education and provide vocational and technical training to ordinary high school graduates who have not yet entered institutions of higher learning. Ordinary middle schools should also set up vocational and technical education courses in different circumstances to train a large number of skilled talents and high-quality workers for economic construction.

The development of rural education also has a great boost to the construction of rural economy. Promoting the development of rural education is conducive to expanding employment, reducing surplus labor force and cultivating talents for the development of rural economy. The strategy of vitalizing rural areas in China depends on talents, and the cultivation of talents depends on education. For rural areas, high schools have the functions of disseminating knowledge and teaching skills and provide talent support for rural construction. Therefore, rural education plays an irreplaceable role in rural revitalization. From the perspective of "promoting the integration of urban and rural compulsory education", promoting social equity through education equity, or from the perspective of running rural education well to facilitate the smooth implementation of the rural revitalization strategy, its importance is self-evident. In 2004, the state council approved and transferred the action plan of education revitalization from 2003 to 2007 issued by the ministry of education, stressing again that "we should increase support for the development of rural high schools, guide the construction of demonstration high schools, speed up the construction of weak schools and expand the supply capacity of high school education resources" (Li, 2020; Li & Eryong, 2020; Li et al., 2019, 2020; Xue & Li, 2019, 2020a, 2020b).

The development of foreign language schools is also worth thinking about. Since the reform and opening up, the import and export trade increased, and the exchange between China and other countries increased, which led to the establishment of a number of foreign language high schools. As China becomes the world's second largest economy, the country needs to win more say in the competition for the world economic order. And with the countries in the economic and social success, the unique advantages of foreign language high school already, a response time of education thinking is becoming all the high school education development concept—training with global literacy, wealthy Chinese spirit, is committed to a new era of the great rejuvenation of the Chinese nation and this puts forward new requirements for the development of the high school education. To sum up, in the process of diversified development and reform of high schools, professional talents should be trained for the task of economic construction according to the current economic demand of our country. The content of the reform should be more based on the needs of the economy and society, so as to train professional talents and innovative talents for the construction of China's modern society and promote better economic development.

6.2.3   The Social Level

1. Social background of diversification policy in high school education. From the perspective of the world, the secondary education in the modern sense has a history of more than 400 years. In the first half of the nineteenth century, with the wave of the industrial revolution, vocational and technical education took the lead in Germany and the United States, which led to the diversified reform of high school education. In the history of China, the traditional Confucianism advocated official learning, the status of scholars was higher than that of craftsmen, and the status of cultural education was higher than that of vocational education, which mainly depended on the inheritance of teachers and apprentices, and there was no large-scale secondary vocational education. Until the end of the Qing dynasty, with the establishment of modern national industry, China's vocational education began to develop systematically and institutionalized. Since the founding of the People's Republic of China, after the "cultural revolution", after the resumption of the revival of the college entrance examination, until the early 1980s, China's high school education only ordinary high school education model. After the reform and opening up, with the promulgation and implementation of the decision of the central committee of the communist party of China on the reform of the education system in 1985, high schools were divided into ordinary high schools and vocational high schools. In 1995, the national general high school education work conference divided high schools into four modes: preparatory education, comprehensive high school, high school with emphasis on pre-employment education and characteristic high school, which laid the foundation for the diversified development policy of China's modern high school education.

The diversification of high school education is also reflected in the diversification of training direction and evaluation system of ordinary high schools. Since 1993, the central committee of the communist party of China under the State Council in the "Chinese education reform and development compendium" ordinary high school put forward the reform target, ordinary high school education in our country from the original pure entrance oriented "exam-oriented education", gradually transformed into a comprehensive "quality education", on improving the quality of the national curriculum structure is divided into compulsory courses and elective courses. In addition, small-scale, experimental specialty education, such as "youth classes" for high-achieving students, is also offered in some high schools.

2. The significance of diversity in high school education to society. The diversified development of high school education is of rich and positive significance to our contemporary society. Since ancient times, China has advocated the educational concept of "teaching students according to their aptitude and no class for them". Among them, "teaching students according to their aptitude" requires us to have educational resources matching the educational needs of the society, while "teaching students according to their aptitude" requires us to carry out education in many aspects and at many levels. From the perspective of the overall needs of the society, the diversification of high school education can better adapt to the employment needs of the contemporary society. In addition, high school education diversity also promotes all levels of society (Li, 2020; Li & Eryong, 2020; Li et al., 2019, 2020; Xue & Li, 2019, 2020a, 2020b).

6.2.4   The Cultural Aspects

At the beginning of reform and opening up, the development of high school education itself is not perfect. In this period, the high school enrollment rate itself is relatively low, high school education is mainly for the promotion of services, coupled with the public understanding of high school education is less, therefore, there is no diversified development of high school education conditions. During this period, the educational policy mainly tended to develop high school education and increase the high school enrollment rate, striving to make high school education no longer exclusive to a few people. Gradually, the high school education is accepted by more and more people, the high school education is more and more popular, the high school education itself is also constantly developing, constantly being improved.

With the development of high school education and the process of reform and opening up, China has more and more exchanges with other countries, and vocational education has gradually come into people's vision. In fact, as early as the end of the Qing dynasty, in China, the establishment of a special vocational education school, in the period of the republic of China, many people also advocated: to pay attention to vocational education, we must vigorously develop vocational education, vocational education into the school education.

However, until now, the development of vocational education in China is full of setbacks. First of all, the time for vocational education to enter school education is still short. The universalization of senior high school education itself is not a long time, the vocational education development time is shorter, therefore, since the reform and opening up until today, the school education in the vocational education has not developed to a mature stage, the vocational education is not quite as common as ordinary high school education, there is no ordinary high school education has a relatively perfect system.

Secondly, due to the influence of various traditional ideas, people discriminate against vocational education to some extent. In ancient times, vocational education was separated from school education. The purpose of school education was to train people so that the educated could become officials and get rich. The idea of "learning to excel is an official" is deeply rooted in people's minds. Moreover, in ancient times, the social status of officials is also higher than other professions, this idea has also been handed down, and deeply rooted in the hearts of people. Today, there are still a majority of people believe that the purpose of education is to improve the social status of the educated. The vocational education, which aims to cultivate people's skills and make them better at a certain profession, is despised by many people. "Why get an education when you're going to end up in a 'low status' position? Why should

I choose this kind of education, when it is necessary to take a 'low position'?" That's how most people feel these days (Li, 2020; Li & Eryong, 2020; Li et al., 2019, 2020; Xue & Li, 2019, 2020a, 2020b).

Furthermore, the quality of vocational education in school education itself is not satisfactory under the comprehensive influence of the above-mentioned factors. First of all, compared with ordinary schools, the teachers and teaching equipment of vocational education schools are not good, and the overall development level of vocational education schools is not dominant. And, as a result of the influence of the above people's traditional ideas, the majority of people cannot accept vocational education, they would rather go to the worst of ordinary high school, also do not want to enter a vocational technical school, therefore, most in vocational education school students in the examination scores than ordinary high school students admit fractional line, while the standard of academic achievement is not all, but to a certain extent, academic scores, also can reflect the category into vocational education school students in learning ability, and learning attitude to weaker than the other students, students in vocational education school "presenteeism" phenomenon also will be more serious, To some extent, this has made the public's impression on vocational schools worse. In addition, in the process of developing vocational education, there will be a lot of wrong understanding of vocational education. The public usually thinks that vocational education is to cultivate the vocational skills of the educated. However, the vocational education in school education should not only focus on the training of vocational education, but also on the cultivation of the comprehensive quality of the educated.

In general, the vocational education school is influenced by various aspects, including the influence of the above mentioned main culture, the development is not well, but, with the development of the society, the development of education, social demand for different types of talents is more and more big, there are more and more career had suffered discrimination, now face by the public. Therefore, naturally, the current development of vocational education cannot meet the needs of the society. Therefore, in recent years, more and more policies have started to encourage the development of vocational education. But more policy guidance is needed to ensure that people receive vocational education as fully as they do in ordinary high schools (Li, 2020; Li & Eryong, 2020; Li et al., 2019, 2020; Xue & Li, 2019, 2020a, 2020b).

In the diversified development of high school education, there are not only vocational and technical schools which are different from ordinary high schools, but also comprehensive schools which integrate vocational education with ordinary high schools. In addition to setting the education content of ordinary high schools, these schools need to adjust the education mode appropriately and add some vocational education content. In this way, students studying in comprehensive schools can receive both preparatory education and vocational education. After the student's study in the school, according to the different performance of students, students can choose a more suitable education mode.

From the perspective of culture, comprehensive schools are more suitable for promoting the diversified development of high school education in China than ordinary vocational and technical schools. Comprehensive school itself is a kind of diversified attempt. Comprehensive school is not only different from ordinary high school, but also different from vocational and technical school. Comprehensive school makes the model more flexible. In the learning process of comprehensive schools, students can explore and guide themselves to discover their own internal potential, so that students can choose a more suitable for their own path. This also breaks with the common idea of "good academic performance in ordinary high schools, poor academic performance in vocational and technical schools", and makes it easier to teach students according to their aptitude. The emergence of comprehensive schools is undoubtedly an exploration of a new mode, which injects vitality into the diversification of high school education and further promotes the cultivation of various types of talents.

In addition, the comprehensive schools can help promote more access to vocational education. Comprehensive schools are usually developed from ordinary high schools that have the capacity to develop new modes of running schools. Students do not discriminate against the school when they enter the school for the first time. The school still provides a path to the higher education, but at the same time, it also provides relevant vocational education. In the process of learning in school, some students who are obviously not suitable for further study can be exposed to vocational education, while some students who have greater potential in related career direction also have the opportunity to further vocational education. Though, this does not fundamentally change the vocational education directly impression in people's minds, but also can let part of suitable personnel receive the professional education, and once accepted the vocational education have found receive vocational education is a good choice, and more and more people have empathy, vocational education will change in people's impression of alarm clock. Comprehensive schools can actually be used as a breakthrough to break people's prejudice against vocational education, so that people naturally experience vocational education and gradually recognize vocational education.

Comprehensive schools are also conducive to improving the overall quality of vocational education in schools. Since comprehensive schools are usually developed from competent ordinary high schools, vocational education in comprehensive schools can also be guaranteed. And comprehensive school not as vocational and technical schools, ignoring the cultivation of the students' comprehensive quality, comprehensive school model of development is diverse, he in different directions meet the students' future development needs, at the same time can be more easily to receive vocational education students and students receiving education for entrance of the same overall quality education. And attend the employment of students, the future and the future intention enters a higher school students in the same school, also can urge the school, teachers' teaching work earnestly, to all the students alike, in turn, the status of vocational education in the people's will also increase gradually, gradually close to the ordinary high school education, which is beneficial to eliminate social discrimination against vocational education, to break a vicious cycle of vocational and technical school (Li, 2020; Li & Eryong, 2020; Li et al., 2019, 2020; Xue & Li, 2019, 2020a, 2020b).

In order to respond to the needs of society and the supply side, people who need to learn a vocational skill in order to seek a career; Demand-side: demand from departments that need to employ relevant technical personnel. In recent years, the government has also introduced many policies to promote the diversified development of high schools, the development of vocational education and the construction of comprehensive schools, such as: Cultivate cognitive ability, guide students to have independent thinking, logical reasoning, information processing, learning, language expression and writing literacy, develop the awareness and ability of life-long learning. We need to develop the ability of cooperation, guide students to learn to self-management, learn to cooperate with others, learn to live a collective life, learn to deal with the relationship between individuals and society, abide by and fulfill the moral code and code of conduct. Cultivate the ability of innovation, stimulate students' curiosity, imagination and innovative thinking, develop innovative personality, and encourage students to have the courage to explore, make bold attempts and create new ideas. Cultivate professional ability, guide students to adapt to the needs of society, establish a professional spirit of dedication and excellence, practice the unity of knowledge, and actively practice and solve practical problems.

We need to promote the diversification of ordinary high schools. We diversify the school-running system and expand high-quality resources and promote the diversification of training modes to meet the development needs of students with different potentials. We explore ways to find and train innovative talents. Encourage ordinary high schools to develop their own characteristics. We aim to encourage qualified ordinary high schools to increase the teaching content of vocational education according to their needs. Explore the development model of comprehensive high school. The 13th five-year plan for the development of China's education sector emphasizes the exploration of multiple models such as comprehensive high schools and featured high schools to provide more choices for students. To speed up the development of comprehensive high schools is to deal with the relationship between general education and vocational education in high schools, break the oversize of ordinary high schools, break through the "one thousand schools", and alleviate the problems of vicious competition. It is of great theoretical and practical significance to reform the supply of high school education services, provide more choices for high school students and improve their comprehensive quality. Vocational and technical schools, comprehensive schools are still not the mainstream, the relevant system is still not perfect. Current policies should further promote the development of vocational education and encourage the construction of comprehensive schools. At the same time, in order to solve the influence of traditional ideas, we should strive to vocational education school to do a good job in comprehensive school, improve teaching quality. We try to enhance the school satisfaction to win public praise for the vocational education in the schools.

6.3   Issues and Suggestions on Diversification Development Policies of Senior High Schools

1. Related policies on the diversification development of high schools. The Decision of the CPC Central Committee on Several Major Issues Concerning Upholding and Improving the Socialist System with Chinese characteristics and Promoting the Modernization of the Country's Governance System and Governance Capacity was issued to be adopted at the fourth plenary session of the 19th central committee of the communist party of China (CPC). It states that we need to uphold and improve the system of ensuring the people's well-being by balancing urban and rural areas to meet the people's growing needs for a better life. The construction of the education system that serves the whole people's lifelong learning is the key to the people's livelihood and has great strategic significance. This requires us to focus on the present, take a long-term view, and actively build an education system that serves the people's lifelong learning, so as to ensure that the people enjoy the opportunity of lifelong learning. To build an education system that serves the whole people in lifelong learning, we must give higher priority to education. We must adhere to the principle that education serves the people and socialism, ensure that everyone has access to education, and ensure that the fruits of education development are Shared by all people in a more equitable way.

To build an education system that serves lifelong learning for all, we need to work together to win the battle against poverty through education. Education plays an irreplaceable role in winning the battle against poverty. We need to fulfill the main responsibility of local governments, increase financial support, give full play to the strengths of talents in the education system, and build a multi-party, coordinated education to lift people out of poverty. We need to develop preschool education, consolidate and raise the level of nine-year compulsory education, strengthen the ranks of rural teachers, and increase support for special groups, so as to lay a solid foundation for poverty alleviation in education. We try to speed up the development of secondary vocational education, carry out extensive public welfare vocational skills training, and improve our ability to lift people out of poverty through education. We will actively develop regular senior high school education, continue to implement the preferential policies for higher education enrollment, improve the system of subsidization services for students seeking employment, and expand channels for education to lift people out of poverty.

We aim to build an education system that serves the whole nation in lifelong learning and promote the development of education at all levels at a high level. We should make an overall plan for education at all stages, improve the mechanism for the coordinated development of vocational and technical education, higher education and continuing education, pool the efforts of education at all stages, and give full play to the synergy of "1 + 1 > 2" in personnel training. We adhere to the principle of universal benefits in preschool education, establish a more comprehensive preschool education management system, a kindergarten operating system and an investment system, vigorously develop public kindergartens, accelerate the development of inclusive private kindergartens, and improve the quality of care and education. We will promote the integrated development of compulsory education in urban and rural areas and strengthen the weak implementation of compulsory education.

The Ministry of Education has been standardizing the implementation of "3 + 2" five-year higher vocational education at the starting point of junior high schools and promoting the in-depth connection of specialties and courses in middle and higher vocational colleges. In 2010, the Ministry of Education issued *the Notice on the Catalogue of Secondary Vocational School.* In 2014, 230 professional teaching standards of secondary vocational schools were published in two batches, specifying the training objectives, curriculum structure, curriculum setting and requirements, teaching implementation and teaching evaluation of each major, optimizing the secondary vocational curriculum setting, and further improving the quality of technical skills training. *The opinions on the Work of Setting up Colleges and Universities During the 13th Five-Year Plan Period* also clearly include application-oriented education as an important type of higher education in the work of setting up colleges and universities.

At present, the vast majority of provinces have carried out transformation and reform, and more than 300 application-oriented universities have been selected for pilot programs. A number of pilot colleges and universities actively explored the reform of cooperation between schools and enterprises, the cooperation between schools and enterprises, the construction of teachers, the reform of talent training programs and curriculum system, and the school governance structure. During the 13th five-year plan period, the national development and reform commission and the ministry of education launched and implemented the project to modernize education and promote the construction of application-oriented colleges and universities, supported 100 application-oriented colleges and universities across the country, and strengthened the construction of environments, platforms and bases for internships, experiments and training.

We need to optimize the talent structure and training mode based on demand. Many colleges and universities have optimized and integrated the related majors serving the same industrial chain, creating a number of application-oriented specialty clusters with prominent advantages and distinctive characteristics that are urgently needed in some places. To promote the transformation of colleges and universities to deepen the reform of talent training programs and curriculum system, and constantly explore the integration of industry and education, collaborative education of talent training mode. *The Opinions of the State Council on Deepening the Reform of the Examination and Enrollment System* (issued by the state council [2014] no.35) clearly states that by 2020, a modern education examination and enrollment system with Chinese characteristics should be basically established, and a lifelong learning "flyover bridge" should be built that connects and communicates with all levels of education and recognizes various learning outcomes. *The 13th Five-year Plan for the Development of National Education (issued by the state council [2014] no. 4)* clearly requires "promoting the classified examination of higher vocational colleges and highlighting the evaluation method of 'cultural quality + vocational skills'". Secondary vocational school graduates apply for higher vocational colleges, to participate in the cultural basis and vocational skills combined with the test. In 2015, there were 1.71 million students enrolled in the classified examinations, accounting for 50% of the total enrollment plan. Compared with 2015, the number of students enrolled in the classified examination of higher vocational colleges in 2016 increased by 150,000, accounting for more than half of the total number of students enrolled in higher vocational colleges, which has become the main channel.

We try to get through the higher vocational, application-oriented undergraduate to professional postgraduate channels. Through the higher vocational, application-oriented undergraduate to professional degree graduate channels. We need to standardize the channels of secondary vocational promotion undergraduate. In June 2015, the Ministry of Education issued *Opinions on the Recruitment of Students for the Classified Examinations of higher Vocational Education in 2015 (no. 6 [2015] of the department of education)*, which required that secondary vocational education and undergraduate education should be standardized. A small number of majors that meet the social needs, are suitable for the study of secondary vocational graduates, have high technical requirements, strong practical operation and long training cycle, and are selected to be piloted in the catalogue of undergraduate majors of general institutions of higher learning (2012) (no.9 [2012] of higher education). We need to steadily promote the horizontal integration of vocational education and general education. In 2016, opinions of the ministry of education on promoting credit recognition and conversion in higher education (education reform [2016] no. 3) made it clear that the Open University of China, based on its "credit bank", organized some vocational colleges and universities to carry out credit recognition and conversion. We need to meet the needs of the economic and social development of diversified high-quality talent, diversified choice for students to establish "overpass" and multipath, moderately improve the specialty of higher vocational colleges and universities to recruit the proportion of secondary vocational school graduates, the proportion of recruits graduates of vocational colleges undergraduate institutions of higher learning, accelerate the development of the modern vocational education system. According to China education news, "the proportion of senior high school students in the general employment ratio should still adhere to the principle of general parity and cannot be shaken."

By the end of 2016, China had 24,700 high schools (including regular high schools, adult high schools and secondary vocational schools) with 39.701 million students. Among them, there are 13,400 regular high schools with 23.665 million students. There are 10,900 secondary vocational schools (including general technical secondary schools, adult technical secondary schools, vocational high schools and technical schools) with 15.990 million students. The gross enrollment rate for senior high schools nationwide was 87.5%, an increase of 2.5 percentage points over 2012. The graduation rate from junior high school was 93.7%, up 5.3 percentage points from 2012. The graduation rate of ordinary high schools was 94.5%, 7.5 percentage points higher than that of 2012, and the vast majority of ordinary high school graduates went on to study in institutions of higher learning. The employment rate of secondary vocational graduates has remained above 95% for many years, and that of their counterparts above 70% (Li, 2020; Li & Eryong, 2020; Li et al., 2020; Xue & Li, 2019; 2020a, 2020b). In March 2017, the ministry of education, the national development and reform commission, the ministry of finance, the ministry of human resources and social security and other four departments jointly published the key plan for the popularization of high school education (2017–2020), which set out five specific goals. "The key is to ensure basic necessities, strengthen weak links and promote equity. The focus is on four areas, three groups of people and three prominent problems."

In 2018, the gross enrollment rate of senior high schools nationwide reached 88.8%, an increase of 0.5 percentage points over the previous year, and closer to the target of "reaching 90%" set in the outline. The number of full-time teachers in regular high schools and secondary vocational education was 1.813 million and 834,000, respectively, and the number of students was 23.754 million and 15.553 million, respectively. The national average public budget for education for students in ordinary senior high schools and secondary vocational schools was 15,000 yuan and 14,200 yuan, respectively, an increase of 8.6 and 7% over the previous year. The average public expenditure per student in the general public budget was RMB 360,000 yuan and RMB 520,000 yuan, respectively, up by 7.4% and 6.1% over the previous year. Secondary vocational education [64] enrolls 5.57 million students, 15.552 million students and 4.873 million graduates. Regular high schools have 7.927 million students, 23.754 million students and 7.792 million graduates. There are 24,300 high school education schools in China, 298 fewer than the previous year, down 1.21%. Enrollment reached 13.4976 million, down by 320,300, or 2.37%; There were 39.3467 million students on campus, 363,200 fewer than that of the previous year, a decrease of 0.91 percent. The gross enrollment rate of senior high school is 88.8%, 0.5 percentage points higher than that of the previous year.

6.4 The Problems in the Diversification of High Schools

1. Differences between local and non-local household registration in high school enrollment. At present, China's urbanization has entered a period of rapid growth. China has the largest number of cities in the world, and the urban population accounts for 60% of the total population. In the current situation, the urban and rural population mobility on the one hand as an important driver to accelerate the process of urbanization; At the same time, it also brings problems such as urban crowding, uncoordinated urban-rural development and one-way flow of resources. With the development of social economy, a lot of young adults in rural life in order to improve the family living conditions, migrant workers, a husband and wife into the family is not in a few cities, in order to avoid the migrant children become left-behind children, also in order to improve their level of education, many parents choose to children with him, go to the city to accept more good education. As large Numbers of urban migrants and migrant workers work in other cities, the problem of their children receiving high school education and taking the college entrance examination is becoming more and more urgent.

2. **Differences in the choice of high school enrollment between urban household registration and non-urban household registration.** According to the national education development plan, the number and enrollment scale of high schools are generally proportional to the local population base and the number of school-age students, so the distribution of high schools in space is more balanced. As a result of still adopt "delimit" recruit students recruit students means, the graduate of city census register and non-city census register is in when enter oneself for an examination of high school existence is disparate choice. For students with urban household registration, in the city high school in their choices, and in the urban areas, some of the less populous county often only two high school (in a county, an ordinary high school), a vocational schools, it seems, has urban household registration and the urban household registration students both enjoyed high school enter oneself for an examination resources difference is obvious (Li, 2020; Li & Eryong, 2020; Li et al., 2020; Xue & Li, 2019, 2020a, 2020b).

The emergence of exam-oriented education in China begins with the college entrance examination, which is a basic educational examination system with distinct Chinese characteristics. It is not only a hub connecting high schools and universities, but also an important bridge between universities and society. In China, which has a long cultural tradition of 5,000 years and a history of more than 1,000 years of imperial examinations, the tradition of attaching importance to educational diplomas has gradually formed in the process of long-term historical development. In such a social environment, the college entrance examination is of great significance to individuals, schools, communities and countries. As an ordinary high school, in order to improve the popularity, it is bound to improve the enrollment rate from this aspect, and the most common means to improve the enrollment rate is to adhere to the exam-oriented education. In the teaching method, the lack of emotional enlightenment, lack of creative vitality, focus on infusion education, emphasis on imparting knowledge.

In the heat of the college entrance examination under the influence, there are often of average high school course content beyond the situation of curriculum, course is difficult, often in colleges, class time also increased dramatically, in three schools in order to improve graduation rates lesson six days a week and a half, the weekend is often used to carry out all kinds of simulation test. From the content of the textbook, the difficulty may be reduced, but the difficulty of the college entrance examination is not reduced, so it is still difficult to change the exam-oriented education mode within a certain period of time. The new high school curriculum plan is difficult in this environment. The new high school curriculum plan focuses on students' innovative thinking, research ability and practical ability. The original high school teachers need to learn the new teaching methods and contents in advance, and the children need to be exposed to the new teaching methods and contents. On top of the original teaching burden, add new pressure.

In recent years, encouraged by the national preferential policies and influenced by the difficulty in finding jobs for college students, the secondary vocational schools in China have developed greatly in scale after a long period of recession, which has provided a large number of practical talents for the society. The quality of secondary vocational education, reflect in the aspect of students on the one hand, due to the development of vocational education scale still did not meet the national requirements, the students of secondary vocational education plan is adequate, in many parts of the secondary vocational school as long as you pay the money can come to school, students in secondary vocational school to learn, because some students examination defeat came to the school, the thinking of change an environment to continue learning, can be due to the influence of the so-called "presenteeism" ethos, they lost. In order to increase the number of students, no matter how students, secondary vocational schools are not rejected, resulting in the entire secondary vocational school education quality is not high. On the other hand, the connection between curriculum and employment practice is not high, many secondary vocational schools teaching methods and means are still relatively backward, the original equipment and equipment obsolete lack of update, the number of equipment is insufficient, curriculum training requirements and the actual distance. The existing curriculum also lacks flexibility, which cannot meet the diversified needs and personalized development of students and lacks the cultivation of students' practical ability. There are also quite a few problems in the curriculum setting of secondary vocational schools. At present, the curriculum form is generally theory before practice, which results in the obvious disconnection between practice and theoretical knowledge. Students in the absence of perceptual knowledge, the theoretical knowledge is difficult to understand, not interested in, feel boring, makes the classroom teaching is not ideal: students grasp better even in terms of theoretical knowledge, will happen in the training class object does not accord with the name, the course content design lags behind the market demand, in dark course theory, the lack of practicability and sophistication, not professional. Under the condition that theoretical courses and practical courses are separated from each other, even if students master these theoretical knowledges in some ways, the mastery is only in the book level, and cannot be connected with the real work situation (Li, 2020; Li & Eryong, 2020; Li et al., 2019, 2020; Xue & Li, 2019, 2020a, 2020b).

The "idealized" comprehensive reform of comprehensive high schools. After the reform and opening up, China's high school education to form the two rails of general education, vocational education pattern, in 1990, after the comprehensive high school also appear again, in the early 90s had extensive pilot, and around 2000 by the national policy, in order to form, and comprehensive high school three rail parallel structure of high school education, realize the diversification of structure of high school education. But in practice, comprehensive high school still cannot go out of the shadow of the exam-oriented culture, comprehensive reform of the original intention is also gradually far away.

Comprehensive high school is a new mode of education in which general education and vocational education permeate and merge with each other. In terms of training objectives, high quality graduates with basic knowledge of senior high school culture and professional knowledge and skills of secondary vocational education, as well as the ability to continue learning and employment; In the course goal, we should promote the all-round development of students' morality, intelligence, physique and beauty, and embody the requirements of students' development. In terms of curriculum structure, it is required to set up comprehensive senior high school courses as a whole, and reasonably set up general senior high school cultural courses and professional and technical courses, so as to integrate the education of basic knowledge of general senior high school culture and the education of professional knowledge and skills in secondary vocational education.

In the actual implementation process, the comprehensive high school also follows the practice of ordinary high school in terms of the educational goal and mode, which leads to a dead end of taking an examination. The graduation rate is still the biggest sign of comprehensive high school, which changes people's understanding of comprehensive high school and affects the normal development of comprehensive high school. In terms of concept, not only the general public have a unclear understanding of comprehensive high school, but also the teachers of comprehensive high school have a lack of understanding of the essence of comprehensive high school, which is to give students a variety of choices and full freedom. In the actual process, there exist the application of ordinary high school curriculum, one-sided pursuit of graduation rate, and the return to the old way of exam-oriented education. In practice, there is still too much emphasis on academic learning, lack of understanding of students' diversified and personalized needs, and lack of cultivation of students' ability.

6.5 Suggestions on the Diversified Development of High Schools

In the face of the existing problems of psychological education for students, we need to break down one by one and improve one by one. In terms of the quality of will, we need to focus on cultivating students' several qualities: "self-consciousness, decisiveness, tenacity and self-control"; In terms of self-consciousness, students should be educated to have a clear understanding of themselves, neither blindly arrogant, nor inferiority, look at themselves objectively, cultivate confidence; In terms of emotional cultivation, in the market economy, students should be encouraged to form an enthusiastic, unrestrained and resolute "open character", and their ability to think independently should be trained, so as to get rid of psychological contradictions and discomfort caused by improper emotions. Interpersonal communication, during the period of college education, should first promote students form the correct treat others respect, mutual respect is the precondition of good communication, sincere encouragement and praise, to the person rather than hypocritical praise, to make a comment on error, not sarcasm and ridicule, correct understanding of cooperation and competition, so as to achieve the purpose of common progress. Professional awareness, should educate students, no matter what they do, as long as serious study of professional knowledge, their energy and love into it, and devote themselves to study, try their best to complete the work, with their own actions to win social respect, rather than relying on empty talk and the so-called "hot major". If can do the above content, the students' psychological quality is sure to be greatly improved, in the higher vocational education and ordinary education in colleges and universities after fusion, participants will maintain a relatively good condition to face the changes and challenges, rather than blindly to escape and fear, and only in this way, diversification of high school to achieve its purpose.

In the process of teaching, students should be inspired to learn by classification and batch. As the foundation and goal are not the same, there are still places where they can learn from each other in the process of learning. Therefore, from the perspective of students, differences in teaching should be accepted. From the perspective of teachers, differences and similarities should be considered in the teaching process, and students should be encouraged to develop knowledge beyond the required courses, so as to lay a more solid foundation for their later life. From the management level, policies should be issued to encourage mutual learning, thus promoting the diversification of colleges and universities. Since the training modes are different, we can adopt the dual teaching mode, which can be divided into two types of classes with different proportions of students, which can effectively promote the integration of diversity in colleges and universities.

1. Reduce restrictions brought by household registration. Under the influence of urban-rural relationship from dualization to integration, the restriction of identity and household registration in ordinary high school enrollment and college entrance examination is gradually improving. Under the condition of relatively sufficient resources of pugao, it can meet the desire of some excellent students from other provinces and cities to read pugao. It is impossible to break the barrier of household registration, reduce the enrollment restrictions brought by household registration, relax the high school enrollment restrictions for the non-registered population in this province and city, and gradually relax the conditions of receiving high school education for the children of non-registered population. On September 1, 2012, the general office of the state council issued a document, requiring all regions to release specific measures for the college entrance examination before December 31, 2012. On July 30, 2014, the state council held a press conference to introduce the opinions on further promoting the reform of the household registration system (hereinafter referred to as the opinions). According to the guidelines, we will improve the pre-registration policy for cities with an urban population of more than five million and establish and improve the points-based registration system.

References

Li, J. (2020). Compulsory educational policies in rural China since 1978: A macro perspective. *Beijing International Review of Education, 2*(1), 159–164.
Li, J., & Eryong, X. (2020). Unveiling the 'logic' of modern university in China: Historical, social and value perspectives. *Educational Philosophy and Theory, 52*(9), 1–13.

Li, J., Shi, Z., & Xue, E. (2020). The problems, needs and strategies of rural teacher development at deep poverty areas in China: Rural schooling stakeholder perspectives. *International Journal of Educational Research, 99,* 101496.

Li, J., Yongzhi, Z., Eryong, X., & Zhou, N. (2019). Faculty ethics in China: From a historical perspective. *Educational Philosophy and Theory, 52*(2), 126–136.

Xue, E., & Li, J. (2019). Exploring the macro education policy design on vocational education system for new generation of migrant workers in China. *Educational Philosophy and Theory, 52*(10), 1–12.

Xue, E., & Li, J. (2020a). What is the ultimate education task in China? Exploring "strengthen moral education for cultivating people" ("Li De Shu Ren"). *Educational Philosophy and Theory, 53*(2), 1–12. https://doi.org/10.1080/00131857.2020.1754539.

Xue, E., & Li, J. (2020b). Top-down education policy on the inclusion of ethnic minority population in China: A perspective of policy analysis. *Educational Philosophy and Theory, 52*(3), 227–239.

Lightning Source UK Ltd.
Milton Keynes UK
UKHW020630310522
403779UK00005B/370